BRADSHAW ON: THE FAMILY

A Revolutionary Way of Self-Discovery

John Bradshaw

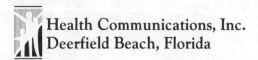

Health Communications, Inc.
Deerfield Beach, Florida

John Bradshaw
Houston, Texas

Library of Congress Cataloging-in-Publication Data

Bradshaw, John E., 1933-
    Bradshaw on the family.

    1. Family — United States — Psychological aspects.
2. Self-actualization (Psychology)   3. Family — United
States — Religious life. I. Title.
    HQ536.B72   1987   306.8'5   87-21233
ISBN 0-932194-54-0

©1988 John Bradshaw

ISBN 0-932194-54-0

Cover design by Reta Kaufman

Published by Health Communications, Inc.
            Enterprise Center
            3201 Southwest 15th Street
            Deerfield Beach, FL 33442

Dedication

To my wife Nancy who is my best friend and the most gentle person I have ever known. Together we've shared a sometimes difficult and always exciting journey of family-making.

To my son John, my stepchildren Brad and Brenda — whose love, wisdom and forebearance have completely ensconced my craziness. They have taught me more about living than they will ever know!

The Videotape and Audiotape series for

BRADSHAW ON: The Family

as well as other series are available for purchase from

John Bradshaw
5003 Mandell
Houston, Texas 77006
(713) 529-9437

John Bradshaw gives workshops and lectures throughout the country in the areas of management, addiction, recovery and spirituality.

Contents

Foreword

Carol Burnett

Emmy-winning actress and comedienne
of television, film and theater.

This book is an expansion of John's PBS TV series by the same name. When John originally conceived that series, he asked me if he could use some excerpts from the Eunice skits which were part of my weekly show. John and I both see Eunice as a tragicomic symbol of all adult children from dysfunctional families. We agreed that Eunice allows us to look honestly at the consequences of family shame, but in a way that lightens our pain.

I was flattered and gave my permission. However, syndication technicalities and time deadlines prevented John from using the Eunice episodes. I certainly hope that as Eunice continues on syndication, she will offer relief from the hurt and humiliation that result from family dysfunction. Who knows, I might even revive her!

For me, the material in this book on families as rule-bound systems was a real eye-opener. If I understand it correctly, it means that we must always look at emotional illness as a social crisis. Everyone in the family is involved. I like that. It puts responsibility on everyone but eliminates blame.

I share John's energetic commitment to family life and I believe that many families will be helped by this book. John's understanding of family dynamics offers hope for us all. After reading this book, I feel I know myself better. It inspires me to be more loving and intimate with my family. And it inspires me to work harder for the unity of the whole human family!

Carol Burnett
November, 1987

Preface

The material presented here is an amplification of a recent television series entitled *Bradshaw On: The Family*. These programs were recorded ad lib before a live audience during which I used no manuscript or teleprompters. Consequently the material often lacked detail. In that medium this lack was acceptable as my goal was to present material not only for content but also for emotional impact on the listener.

This book is for those who want to pursue the material in more depth. It is also for anyone from a dysfunctional family, whether they viewed the series or not, and for anyone in our society who is not aware of the potential for addiction embodied in our rules for raising children.

The chapters follow the general outline of the television series. I've extended the material on Families as Systems and made a separate chapter out of it. I've also changed the specific titles of the last three programs.

In this series I offered a new understanding of emotional health and illness, as well as an understanding of the way this health and illness is multigenerationally transmitted. This book offers you a way to recover your lost childhood self, as well as a platform to begin the journey of discovering your true self.

Much has been written about the family as a system. Most of the writing has been directed toward counselors, therapists and clinicians, the professional practitioners in the field. To my knowledge, little has been directed to the layman, the non-expert. But the layman also needs a bridge of understanding to these innovative powerful concepts. The most important aspect of this understanding is how each of us lost our true self in the family system shuffle and how our family systems embody and create the addicted society we live in.

While only 35-years-old, the concept of understanding families as systems is a new and effective approach to the understanding not only of oneself but of major social problems as well.

Ronald Laing, the great existentialist psychotherapist, has suggested that the theory of family systems is in as much dramatic contrast to past theories as the work of Sigmund Freud was to the practice of imprisoning disturbed people in asylums. This may be an exaggerated claim, but, I'm convinced that unless I know and understand the family system from which I came, I can't understand my true self and the society I live in.

What has been said about cultural history is true of individuals: If we do not know our familial history, we are most likely to repeat it.

In what follows, I shall draw freely from the work of many pioneers in the field of family systems theory. Men such as Milton Erickson, Murray Bowen, Nathan Ackerman, Gregory Bateson, Jay Haley, Carl Whitaker immediately come to mind as fathers of this movement; and the great mother of the movement, Virginia Satir, has had a tremendous impact on my own work. I also acknowledge my indebtedness to Alice Miller, Renee Fredrickson, Gershen Kaufman, Robert Firestone, Sharon Wegscheider-Cruse and Bob Subby.

Special thanks go to Terry Kellogg, who appeared on programs seven and eight of the television series. Terry's insights have been an important help in clarifying some aspects of my own position. In all cases unless I quote these sources directly, I take responsibility for my interpretations of the thoughts and ideas of others. Like it or not, each of us has a unique mental map from which we chart reality. Each and every thought we have is directed by this map. Followers are always traitors to some degree. So I assume total responsibility for the material which follows.

As a theologian I have concern for the spiritual issues involved in our knowing and loving ourselves. These issues, grounded in the family, have a major impact on society. I have underscored this concern by my choice of the subtitle: A Revolutionary Way of Self-Discovery.

My belief is that spirituality is about wholeness. The source of the wounds which destroy our wholeness can be uncovered by exploring our family systems. My thesis is that there is a crisis in society today that is reflected in our families, a crisis in which we are cut off from our true selves. As others have said before me, we live behind masks and act out performances based on scripts we never wrote.

The hope of remedy is that we can identify the roots of the crisis in the families our society creates and the society created by our families. The family is the source of the wars within ourselves, and to a large degree, the wars with others. These wars within I call addictions.

Addiction and war are evils. They embody lying and killing. They seem to have a power that transcends individual choice. One of my great teachers, Gregory Baum, has defined the demonic as "a structure of evil which transcends the malice of men and women". In Baum's sense this book confronts the demonic in human experience and offers some choices as to a way out.

A Parable

The Tragedy of Tragedies
The Story of Hugh

Once upon a time a Royal person was born. *His name was Hugh. Although I'll refer to Hugh as 'he', no one actually knew what his sex really was and it didn't really matter. Hugh was unlike anyone who had ever lived before or who would ever live again. Hugh was precious, unrepeatable incomparable, a trillion-dollar diamond in the rough.

For the first 15 months of life, Hugh only knew himself from the reflections he saw in the eyes of his caretakers. Hugh was terribly unfortunate. His caretakers, although not blind, had glasses over their eyes. Each set of glasses already had an *image* on it. So that each caretaker only saw Hugh according to the image on his glasses. Thus, even though Hugh's caretakers were physically present, not one of them *ever actually saw him.* By the time Hugh was grown, he was a mosaic of other people's images of him, none of which was who he really was. No one had really ever seen him, so no one had ever mirrored back to him what he really looked like. Consequently, Hugh thought he was the mosaic of images. He really did not know who he was.

Sometimes in the dark of the night when he was all alone, Hugh knew that something of profound importance was missing. He experienced this as a gnawing sense of emptiness — a deep void.

Hugh tried to fill the emptiness and void with many things: power, worldly fame, money, possessions, chemical highs, food, sex, excitement, entertainment, relationships, children, work — even exercise. But no matter what he *did,* he never felt the gnawing emptiness go away. In the quiet of the night when all the distractions were gone, he heard a still quiet voice that said: "Don't forget; please don't forget me!" But alas! Hugh did forget and went to his death never knowing who he was!

---

*For grammatical consistency and clarity, the pronouns "he", "his" and "him" have been used throughout instead of "she or he", "his or her" and "her and him". No sexual bias or insensitivity is meant.

1

Overview: The Crisis

*"Our very psychology has been shaken to its foundation . . .
to grasp the meaning of the world today we use a language
created to express the world of yesterday. The life of the past
seems to us nearer our true nature, but only for the reason
that it is nearer our language."*

Antoine de Saint Exupery

The last 35 years have ushered in a new awareness about the impact
of families on personality formation. While it's always been known that
our families influence us, we're now discovering that the influence is
beyond what we had imagined. We now understand that families are
dynamic social systems, having structural laws, components and rules.

The most important family rules are those that determine what it
means to be a human being. These rules embrace the most fundamental
beliefs about raising children. What parents believe about human life and
human fulfillment govern their ways of raising children.

Parenting forms children's core belief about themselves. Nothing could
be more important. Children are any culture's greatest natural resource.
The future of the world depends on our children's conceptions of
themselves. All their choices depend on their view of themselves.

But there is a crisis in the family today. It has to do with our parenting rules and the multigenerational process by which families perpetuate these rules.

Sickness of the Soul: Shame

My thesis is that these rules are abusive and shaming. They destroy children's inner identity. They result in shame. According to Gershen Kaufman in his book, *SHAME*, shame is . . .

> ". . . a sickness of the soul. It is the most poignant experience of the self by the self, whether felt in humiliation or cowardice, or in a sense of failure to cope successfully with challenge. Shame is a wound felt from the inside, dividing us both from ourselves and from one another."

According to Kaufman, shame is the source of most of the disturbing inner states which deny full human life. Depression, alienation, self-doubt, isolating loneliness, paranoid and schizoid phenomena, compulsive disorders, splitting of the self, perfectionism, a deep sense of inferiority, inadequacy or failure, the so-called borderline conditions and disorders of narcissism, all result from shame. Shame is a kind of soul murder. Once shame is internalized, it is characterized by a kind of psychic numbness, which becomes the foundation for a kind of death in life. Forged in the matrix of our source relationships, shame conditions every other relationship in our lives. Shame is a total non-self acceptance.

Shame and Guilt

Shame is a being wound and differs greatly from the feeling of guilt. Guilt says I've *done* something wrong; shame says there *is* something wrong with me. Guilt says I've *made* a mistake; shame says I *am* a mistake. Guilt says what I *did* was not good; shame says I *am* no good. The difference makes a profound difference.

Our parenting rules have not been seriously updated in 150 years. The high divorce rate, teenage disorders, massive drug abuse, epidemic incest, eating disorders and physical battering are evidence that something is radically wrong. My belief is that the old rules no longer work. Our consciousness has changed as has our view of the world.

Shame Through Abandonment

Our parenting rules primarily shame children through abandonment. Parents abandon children in the following ways:

1. By actually physically leaving them.
2. By not modeling their own emotions for their children.
3. By not being there to affirm their children's expressions of emotion.
4. By not providing for their children's developmental dependency needs.
5. By physically, sexually, emotionally and spiritually abusing them.
6. By using children to take care of their own unmet dependency needs.
7. By using children to take care of their marriages.
8. By hiding and denying their shame secrets to the outside world so that the children have to protect these covert issues in order to keep the family balance.
9. By not giving them their time, attention and direction.
10. By acting shameless.

Children's needs are insatiable in the sense that they need their parents continuously throughout childhood. No five-year-old ever packed his bags and called a family meeting to thank his parents for their support and guidance as he leaves to make his way in the world. It takes 15 years before nature will awaken these urges to leave home and parents. Children need their parents to be there for them.

In abandonment the order of nature is reversed. Children have to take care of their parents. There is no one to take care of them. The preciousness and uniqueness which every human child possesses is destroyed through abandonmnent. The child is alone and alienated. Abandonment creates a shame-based inner core.

Emergence of the False Self

Since one's inner self is flawed by shame, the experience of self is painful. To compensate, one develops a *false self* in order to survive.

The false self forms a defensive mask which distracts from the pain and the inner loneliness of the true self. After years of acting, performing and pretending — one loses contact with who one really is. One's true self is numbed out.

The crisis is far worse than anyone knows because the adults who parent their children were also abandoned and are separated from their own true inner selves. The adults who parent are covering up their shame-based inner selves. So the crisis is not just about how we raise our children; it's about a hundred million people who look like adults, talk and dress like adults, but are actually adult children. These adult children run our schools, our churches and our government. They also create our families. This book is about the crisis in the family today — *the crisis of adult children raising children who will become adult children.*

The Family Rules

The rules about raising children are the most sacred of all rules. They are authenticated by religious teaching and reinforced in our school systems. To even seriously question them is considered sacrilegious. This is why the crisis is far worse than most people realize.

The house is on fire, but like the story of the emperor with no clothes, we are not supposed to look. We are to share a collective denial and a *cultural no-talk rule.* This 'no-talk' rule is rooted in the rules which govern parenting. Children are to speak when spoken to; children are to be seen and not heard; children are to obey all adults (any adult) without question. To question is an act of disobedience. And so the rules are carried by the obedient child in all the adults who are raising families. The hidden child in every adult continues to obey so that the rules are carried multigenerationally, and 'the sins of the fathers are visited on the children to the third and fourth generation'.

The crisis is far worse than we realize because *one of the rules comprising the sacred rules is that we can't question any of the rules.* We are not supposed to talk about the rules. This would dishonor our parents.

We have no alternative. We must break the Rule and question these rules for unless we talk about them, there is no way out. We must evaluate them in the light of our new found knowledge of families as systems.

We must examine these rules in order to come to terms with our compulsiveness. Shame with its accompanying loneliness and psychic numbness fuels our compulsive/addictive lifestyle. Shame is like a hole in the cup of our soul. Since the child in the adult has insatiable needs, the cup cannot be filled. As grown-ups we can't go back *as children* and sit in Mom's lap or have Dad take us fishing. And no matter how hard we try to turn our children, lovers and spouses into Mom and Dad, it never works. We cannot be children again. No matter how many times we fill the cup — the hole remains.

Shame fuels compulsivity and compulsivity is the black plague of our time. We are driven. We want more money, more sex, more food, more booze, more drugs, more adrenalin rush, more entertainment, more possessions, more ecstasy. Like an unending pregnancy, we never reach fruition.

Our dis-eases are about the things of everyday life. Our troubles are focused on what we eat, what we drink, how we work, how we sleep, how we are intimate, how we have orgasm, how we play, how we worship. We stay so busy and distracted that we never feel how lonely, hurt, mad and sad we really are. The hole in our soul marks the ruins of what Auden calls 'our ranches of isolation and our busy griefs'. Our compulsivities tell us of a lost city — a place deep inside of us where a child hides in the ruins.

Compulsive/Addictive Behavior

Compulsive/addictive behavior has been defined as "a pathological relationship to any mood-altering experience that has life-damaging consequences". Such a definition helps us move from our stereotyped pictures of the dives and back alleys of drug and alcohol addiction to the respectable corporate and religious lives of work and religious addicts. It also helps us to see the effect of the broken relationship with our original caretakers which produced shame. Because our original dependency bridge with our survival figures has been broken, we are set up for problems with dependency and with relationships. In the abandonment relationships which shame us, our compulsivities are set up.

Our families are the places where we have our source relationships. Families are where we first learn about ourselves in the mirroring eyes of our parents, where we see ourselves for the first time. In families we learn about emotional intimacy. We learn what feelings are and how to express them. Our parents model what feelings are acceptable and family authorized and what feelings are prohibited.

In our families we adapt to the needs of our family system. We take on roles necessitated by the dynamics of the system. Such roles demand that we learn certain feelings and that we give up certain feelings.

When we are abused in families, we learn to defend ourselves with ego defenses. We repress our feelings; we deny what's going on; we displace our rage onto our possessions or our friends; we create illusions of love and connectedness; we idealize and minimize; we dissociate so that we no longer feel anything at all; we numb out.

Our addictions and compulsivities are our mood alterers. They are what we develop when we numb out. They are our ways of being alive and our ways of managing our feelings. This is most apparent in experiences that are euphoric, like using alcohol, drugs, sex, carrot cake, adrenalin rush or the feelings of ecstasy and righteousness. It is not as obvious in activities which are used to distract from emotions, such as working, buying, gambling, watching television and thinking obsessively. These are mood-altering nonetheless.

Addiction has become our national lifestyle (or rather death style). It is a death style based on the relinquishment of the self as a worthwhile being to a self who must achieve and perform or use something outside of self in order to be lovable and happy. Addictions are pain-killing substitutes for legitimate suffering. To legitimately suffer we have to feel as bad as we feel.

The lives of over 60 million people are seriously affected by the pain-killing use of alcohol alone. This says nothing of the car murders and domestic violence related to alcohol. Alcohol is the leading killer in this country.

Next comes heart disease and cancer. Major contributors to heart disease are obesity, stress and smoking. Smoking is itself an addiction, as is obesity. Cancer, it has been discovered, has a correlation to emotional repressions.

Americans are killing themselves with food through overeating, starving, vomiting and improper diet. Eating disorders are addictions based on the denial of emotion, especially anger. A commentary on this condition is the fact that around 60% of women and 50% of men in this country have eating disorders.

The fastest-growing problem in our country is sexual addiction. Some estimates say that the number of sex addicts is equal to the number of chemical addicts. Grave social consequences have arisen from this problem. While all sex addicts are not child molesters, most child molesters are sex addicts. A *Life* magazine article estimated that 34 million adult women have been sexually abused.

Another major factor in family dysfunction is the addiction to power and violence. Battered children and battered wives expose the horror of physically abusing families.

Violence itself is an addiction. An essential component in any abusing relationship is the addiction to being *victimized.* Traumatic bonding, a form of learned helplessness, is a true addiction which enslaves and soul-murders.

I stated earlier that the old rules no longer work. What are these old rules?

Poisonous Pedagogy

Alice Miller in her book, *For Your Own Good,* has grouped these parenting rules under the title "poisonous pedagogy". The subtitle of the book is, "Hidden Cruelty in Child-Rearing and the Roots of Violence". She argues that the poisonous pedagogy is a form of violence which violates the rights of children. Such violation is then re-enacted when these children become parents.

The "poisonous pedagogy" concept exalts obedience as its highest value. Following obedience are orderliness, cleanliness and the *control of emotions and desires.* Children are considered "good" when they think and behave the way they are taught to think and behave. Children are virtuous when they are meek, agreeable, considerate and unselfish. The more a child is "seen and not heard" and "speaks only when spoken to" the better that child is. Miller summarizes the poisonous pedagogy as follows:

1. Adults are the masters of the dependent child.
2. Adults determine in a godlike fashion what is right and wrong.
3. The child is held responsible for the anger of adults.
4. Parents must always be shielded.
5. The child's life-affirming feelings pose a threat to the autocratic parent.
6. The child's will must be "broken" as soon as possible.
7. All this must happen at a very early age so the child "won't notice" and will not be able to expose the adults. *(p. 59)*

If followed, these family system rules result in the absolute control of one group of people (parents) over another group of people (children). Yet in our present society, only in extreme cases of physical or sexual abuse can anyone intervene on a child's behalf.

Abandonment, with its severe emotional abuse, neglect and enmeshment is a form of violence. Abandonment, in the sense I have defined it, has devastating effects on a child's belief about himself. And yet no agency or law exists to monitor such abuse. In fact, many of our religious institutions offer authoritarian support for these beliefs. Our schools reinforce them. Our legal system enforces them.

Another aspect of "poisonous pedagogy" is to impart to the child from the beginning, false information and beliefs that are not only unproven, but in some cases, demonstrably false. These are beliefs passed on from generation to generation ("sins of the fathers"). Again, I refer to Alice Miller who cites examples of such beliefs:

1. A feeling of duty produces love.
2. Hatred can be done away with by forbidding it.
3. Parents deserve respect because they are parents. (*Note: Any 15-year-old can be a parent without any training. We give telephone operators more training than parents.*) (Italics mine.)
4. Children are undeserving of respect simply because they are children.
5. Obedience makes a child strong.
6. A high degree of self-esteem is harmful.
7. A low-degree of self-esteem makes a person altruistic.
8. Tenderness (doting) is harmful.
9. Responding to a child's needs is wrong.
10. Severity and coldness toward a child gives him a good preparation for life.
11. A pretense of gratitude is better than honest ingratitude.
12. The way you behave is more important than the way you really are.
13. Neither parents nor God would survive being offended.
14. The body is something dirty and disgusting.
15. Strong feelings are harmful.
16. Parents are creatures free of drives and guilt.
17. Parents are always right. (p. 60)

Probably no modern parents embody all of the above. In fact, some have accepted and imposed the opposite extreme of these beliefs with results just as abusive. But most of these beliefs are carried unconsciously and are activated in times of stress and crisis. *The fact is, parents don't even have a choice about such beliefs until they have worked through and clarified their relationships with their own parents.* I referred to this earlier as the problem of adult children. Let me explain further.

Children's Belief Patterns

The great paradox in child-parent relationships is that *children's belief about parents comes from the parents.* Parents teach their children the meaning of the world around them. For the first ten years of life, the parents are the most inportant part of the child's world. If a child is taught to honor his parents no matter what they do, why would a child argue with this?

The helpless human infant is the most dependent of all living creatures. And for the first eight years of life, according to the cognitive psychologists, such as Jean Piaget, children think magically, non-logically and egocentrically. If you ask a four-year-old, who has a brother, if he has a brother, he will answer "yes". But if you then ask him if his brother has a brother, he will usually either be confused or answer "no".

Another example is to stand across from a pre-five-year-old child who knows his right hand from his left. Hold your hands out and across from him. Ask him which is your right hand and your left hand. As his right hand will be opposite your left hand, he will say that your left hand is your right hand. His mind is immature and has not yet attained the ability to completely differentiate or separate himself from objects around him. The child projects his own view of the world on everything. His viewpoint is the only viewpoint. Winnie-the-Pooh has exactly the same feelings the child does. Little matter that Winnie is a toy bear. This egocentricity contains a survival value for the child.

Survival value has to do with self-preservation. The magical part of the child's thinking *deifies the parents.* They are gods, all-powerful, almighty and all-protecting. No harm can come to the child as long as he has parents.

This magical idealization serves to protect the child from the terrors of the night, which are about abandonment and to the child, death. The protective deification of the parents, this magical idealization, also creates a potential for a shame-binding predicament for the child.

For example, if the parents are abusive and hurt the child through physical, sexual, emotional or mental pain, *the child will assume the blame, make himself bad, in order to keep the all-powerful protection against the terrors of the night.* For a child at this stage to realize the inadequacies of parents would produce unbearable anxiety.

In essence, children are equipped with an innate ability to defend their conscious awareness against threats and intolerable situations. Freud called this ability an *ego defense.* He identified ego defenses as denial, repression, disassociation and idealization, to mention a few. The defenses are archaic and *function automatically and unconsciously once formed.* It is this unconscious quality of these defenses which potentially makes them so damaging.

Robert Firestone's recent book *The Fantasy Bond* elaborates on Freud's work. According to the author, the fantasy bond is the core defense in all human psychological systems, ranging from those of psychotics to fully-functioning individuals. The fantasy bond is the illusion of connectedness we create with our major caretaker whenever our emotional needs are not adequately met. The fantasy bond is like a mirage in the desert that enables one to survive.

Since no mother, father or other parenting person is perfect, all humans develop this fantasy bond to some degree. In fact, growing up and leaving home involves the overcoming of this illusion of connection and protection. Growing up means accepting our fundamental aloneness. It means that we face the terrors of the night and grapple with the reality of death on our own. Most of all, it means giving up our parents in their illusory and idealized form.

The more emotionally deprived a person has been, the stronger his fantasy bond. And paradoxical as it sounds, *the more a person has been abandoned, the more he tends to cling to and idealize his family and his parents.* Idealizing parents means to idealize the way they raised you.

Not only is the fantasy bond set up in the core of the person's selfhood, but several additional layers are added in his psychological defense system. Table 1.1 is an adaptation of Robert Firestone's work.

Table 1.1. Primary Defense System

(1)	(2)	(3)
Original Spell: Delusion and Denial Fantasy Bond Idealization of Family and Parents	Abandonment: Shamed Self 'Bad Me' Feel Flawed Primary Ego Defenses — Denial, Repression, Dissociation, Displacement	False Self: Rigid Roles and Scripts Loss of Self in Family System Roles Proscribe and Deny Feelings
(4)	(5)	(6)
Introjected Parent is Projected onto Others (Strangers): Ones Not of My Family Strategies of Defense Against Shame: Control, Perfectionism, Rage, Criticalness	Internalization of Shame: All Emotions, Needs and Wants are Shame-Bound Internal Shame Spirals Function Autonomously Cause Withdrawal and Withholding of Self	Self-indulging Habits and Pain Killers: Compulsive/ Addictive Behaviors

Development of the False Self

No child, because of his helplessness, dependency and terror, wants to accept the belief that his parents are inadequate, sick, crazy or otherwise imperfect. Nature protects the child by providing an egocentric, magical and non-logical mode of cognition. To be safe and survive, a child *must idealize his parents and make himself bad.* He then projects his own split and forbidden self onto others. These split-off parts are actually his parents rejected parts. Others are the strangers who are not of one's clan. He then introjects the parent's voices. This means that the child continues to hear internally the shame dialogue he originally had with the parent(s).

The child parents himself the way he was parented. If the child got shamed for feeling angry, sad or sexual, he will shame himself each time he feels angry, sad or sexual. All of his feelings, needs and drives become shame-bound. The inner self-rupture is so painful, the child must develop a 'false self'. This false self is manifested in a mask or rigid role which is either determined by the culture or by the family system's needs for balance. Over time the child identifies with the false self and becomes totally unconscious of his own true feelings, needs and wants. The shame is internalized. Shame is no longer a feeling, it is an identity. The real self has withdrawn from conscious contact.

Even after the magical period has passed, when around the age of eight the child moves into a more logical way of thinking, nature continues to provide an egocentric idealization of the parents. The youngster begins to think in a concretely logical manner and to assume the point of view of others.

He "gets it" that Santa Claus cannot be in six department stores at the same time. At this stage he begins to cooperate better in games and play. He is less magical (stepping on a crack does not *really break Mom's back*). He begins to really appreciate rules.

Even so, the logical child will remain egocentric and undifferentiated until early puberty. Only then will he have the capacity for full other-centered love and understanding. He will make a hypothesis and then cast it in bronze. If new data emerges to refute this hypothesis, the child will revise the data to fit his hypothesis.

One such hypothesis carried by children (because taught at the magical age) is that adults, parents especially, are benevolent and totally good.

Parents are good and *no amount of evidence to the contrary* will convince them differently. In addition, the emotional and volitional reasons for which the child clings to this belief is that children love their parents and are emotionally bonded to them. Abused children are more powerfully bonded. Abuse creates intense bonding because as a child is abused, their self-worth diminishes and their choices are limited. The more one feels worth-less the more one feels powerless to change. The more one feels powerless — the fewer choices one feels they have. And the more one accepts the rules and introjects the parents voices, *the more one idealizes these rules so as not to separate oneself from one's parents.*

In other words, in order for a child to reflect on parental rules and find them wanting, he would have to *separate and stand on his own two feet.* This, no eight-year-old is going to do, in fact, cannot do.

Once in adolescence, most of the child's energy is directed toward leaving the family, and it often appears as if adolescents are rejecting their parents' rules. In fact, the more fantasy-bonded an adolescent has been, the more bonded he will become to his peer group, which serves as a "new Parent". However, once this identity crisis is over, most adolescents return to the fantasy bond with their families. This becomes especially evident when a person settles down and starts his own family. What was famil(y)iar comes back and feels right and this includes the rules for parenting. The poisonous pedagogy is transmitted multigenerationally as a sacred body of truth.

Sociological Poisonous Pedagogy

From a sociological perspective we can see another reason why the rules of the poisonous pedagogy go unchallenged. Sociologists describe the interplay of individuals and society. In truth, individuals create societies. A bingo party at the church begins to be considered the *annual* bingo party. In five years' time, parishioners will be angry and resentful if the "traditional" annual bingo party is not held. Rules and rituals which originate somewhat arbitrarily become habituated in peoples' consciousness.

The next step is to legitimize the rules and rituals. They then become part of what sociologists call the "consensus reality" — the reality to which all the people consent. Caught up in the terrible dailiness of our lives, decades later we forget that these legitimized rules were really relative and circumstantial. Once legitimized, they become sacred. They are absolute.

Then the following paradox emerges: Individuals create societies out of circumstance and the need for structure. These societies then become legitimized "consensus realities", which in turn create individuals. So it is with our conceptions of the family, marriage and parenting. These beliefs govern the matrix of our lives.

I stated earlier that these parenting rules are out of date. I contend that our consciousness and way of life have radically changed in the last 150 years. The poisonous pedagogy worked 150 years ago for several reasons.

First, life-expectancy was much lower. Families were together a much shorter period of time. Divorce was a rarity. The average marriage was 15 years and there was no adolescent family conflict as we know it. By age 13 most children had lost a parent. By 15 formal schooling was over. Puberty for women occurred at about age 17.

Economically families were bonded by work and survival. Father lived at home. Boy children bonded to their fathers through work-apprentice systems. They watched and admired their fathers as they transformed the earth, built homes and barns and created wonderful goods through manual labor. Today the majority of families have lost their fathers to the new world of work — automation and cybernetics. Fathers have left home (someone estimated that the average executive father spends 37 seconds per day with his newborn).

Most children do not know what their fathers do at work. Mother bonding and the inability to break that bond due to absentee fathering has caused severe marital and intimacy problems. *Women Who Love Too Much*, and *Men Who Hate Women* are the products of this father loss.

Children, especially males, were once the greatest asset to a family. The old Chinese proverb underscores this: "Show me a rich man without any sons, and I'll show you a man who won't be rich very long. Show me a poor man with many sons, and I'll show you a man who won't be poor very long."

Today children are one of our greatest economic liabilities. Supporting children through the completion of college costs a pretty penny. It also necessitates close interaction between parents and children for 25 years.

The rules which governed parenting and personality formation 150 years ago were the result of a scientific, philosophical and theological view of human nature that has changed drastically. One hundred and fifty years ago democracy, social equality and individual freedom were new concepts which were not yet tested by time.

The world was simpler then. Isaac Newton had mapped out the laws of nature. He conceived the world much like the machines which were emerging from the Industrial Revolution. Thinking and reasoning were what progress was all about. Man was a rational animal. Emotions and desires had great power to contaminate and therefore were very suspicious. Emotions needed to be subjected to the scrutiny and control of reason. Men were content to enjoy the security of a fixed order of things. God was in his heaven and all was right with the world as long as men obeyed the laws of nature.

Those laws were also written into the hearts of men (and occasionally in women's hearts). This was the natural law. It was based on unchanging eternal truths.

Mothers and fathers carried God's authority. Their task was to teach their children the laws of God and nature and to be sure they obeyed these laws. Emotions and willfullness had to be repressed. Children were born with an unruly animal nature. Their souls, although made in God's image, had been stained by original sin. Therefore, children needed discipline. Great energy had to be spent in breaking their unruly passions and their unbridled spirit. Spare the rod and you spoil the child. As Alice Miller reports, one 19th-century writer said:

> "blows provide forceful accompaniment to words and intensify their effect. The most direct and natural way of administering them is by that box on the ears, preceded by a strong pulling of the ear . . . It obviously has symbolic significance as does a slap on the mouth, which is a reminder that there is an organ of speech and a warning to put it to better use . . . the tried and true blow to the head and hair-pulling still convey a certain symbolism, too . . ."
>
> *For Your Own Good* (p. 44)

Any reaction to this punishment was deemed obstinate. Obstinate meant having a mind of one's own. Those were the good old days!

The work of Einstein ended this world view. The quantum theory replaced Newton's clockwork deterministic universe and its billiard-ball-like elements. Quantum theory challenged the basic notions of space and time. Everything in the universe became relative to everything else. Heisenberg's principle of uncertainty was soon to follow. He showed that while we can know that infinitesimal parts of matter exist, we cannot *measure* them.

Quantum physics brought a revolution in our way of viewing the universe. "Because of this," Dr. L. Dossey writes in *Space, Time and Medicine,* "we can expect it to wreck astonishing transformations in our views of our psychophysical self."

Others have expressed their authoritarian voices. Neils Bohr writes:

> "The great extension of our experience in recent years has brought
> to light the insufficiency of our simple mechanical conceptions, and
> as a consequence has shaken the foundation on which the
> customary interpretation of observation was based."

Atomic Physics and the Description of Nature

The old world view definitively ended with World War I and 15 million dead.

Mankind had been basking in the illusion of inevitable progress. Rationalism and technological advances had assured everyone that progress was inevitable. Where were reason and enlightenment now?

Stunned, the believers still espoused the faith. The League of Nations, the Weimar Republic were safeguards that this could not happen again.

Less than 20 years later, it did happen again. This time the modern world was shocked beyond any reason. Hitler and his followers were the agents of death for over 50 million people in the space of six years. His regime programmatically exterminated over six million Jews in gas chambers and death camps. The heinousness of these crimes far exceeded anything known to human history, their cruelty and inhumanity lay beyond imagination. What would make a person want to gas millions of people? How could millions of others acclaim and assist him?

How Could Hitler Happen?

Germany had been a citadel of Christianity, the birthplace of the Protestant Reformation. Germany was a philosophical, theological and artistic giant among the nations of the world. How was it possible for all this to happen? *How was Hitler possible?*

Many answers to this question have been offered. None is satisfactory. Nevertheless it is essential that we try to find such an answer. For at the end of the Nazi era came the new development of nuclear weapons with their capacity for the annihilation of the human race.

How could Hitler happen? Certainly part of the answer lies in politics and economics. It has to do with self-interest, greed, the "haves" and "have nots". Part of the answer is sociological, having to do with special interest groups and the laws that govern groups. It has to do with the shared focus and shared denials that group loyalty demands. And part of it is psychological, having to do with families and the rules that govern the family structure.

The family is the place where persons are socialized. The rules governing the prototypical German family were almost a pure caricature of the poisonous pedagogy. Indeed, obedience, rigidity, orderliness, denial of feelings taken to extreme led to the "black miracle of Nazism".

Erik Erikson voiced this powerfully in an article on the legend of Hitler's youth. He writes:

> "It is our task to recognize that the black miracle of Nazism was only the German version, superbly planned and superbly bungled of a universal contemporary potential. The trend persists; Hitler's ghost is counting on it."

The potential for this to happen again resides in the ever-present existence of the poisonous pedagogy. Obedience and corporal punishment are still highly valued as the crown of parental discipline. Our television Evangelists preach this often.

In the twenties it was argued that the Weimar Republic would not succeed because of the totalitarian structure of the German family. The authoritarianism which gave the father such unequal rights over the mother and children did not provide a climate in which democracy could be learned.

Obedience Above All

Added to this was the Lutheran mandates, which formed the religious grounding for authoritarian parental power. The belief of the mandates was that all authority was from God and must be obeyed as a divine command. Catholic doctrine was often interpreted the same way. In its extreme form, this meant that one must obey authority, even if it is judged wrong.

Alice Miller has presented convincing evidence that Hitler was physically and emotionally abused as a child. His father was in every sense, a totalitarian dictator. It is conjectured that his father was half-Jewish and illegitimate and acted out his rage on his children. Hitler was re-enacting his own childhood, using millions of innocent Jews as his scapegoats.

But Hitler could never have done this alone. What seems beyond all human logic is the fact that one madman could corrupt an entire elitist nation like Germany.

Erik Erikson has suggested that Hitler mobilized the dissociated rage of millions of adolescents. He was an adolescent gang leader who came as a brother and offered a matrix which institutionalized their rage. This rage was their unconscious response to their cruel upbringing and was neatly denied in the myth of the "Master Race". The scapegoated Jews represented the victimized part of themselves as they identified with their aggressive totalitarian parent. This national "acting out" was the logical result of an authoritarian family life in which one or two persons, the parents, have all the power and can whip, scold, punish, humiliate, manipulate, abuse or neglect their children, all under the banner of parenting and pedagogy.

In the autocratic German family, mother and children were totally subservient to the father's will, his moods and whims. The children had to accept humiliation and injustice unquestionably and gratefully. Obedience was the primary rule of conduct.

Hitler's family structure was the prototype of a totalitarian regime. His upbringing, although more severe, was not unlike that of the rest of the German nation. It was because of this similar family structure that Hitler could entice the German People.

Alice Miller has said that a single person can gain control over the masses if he learns to use to his own advantage the social system under which they were raised.

At the Nuremberg war trials, murderer after murderer pleaded innocence on the basis of obedience to authority. People such as Adolph Eichmann and Rudolph Hess were trained to obedience so successfully that this training never lost its effectiveness. To the end that they carried out orders *without questioning the content.* They carried them out just as the "poisonous pedagogy" recommended, not out of any sense of their inherent rightness, but simply *because they were orders.*

"This explains," writes Alice Miller, "why Eichmann was able to listen to the most moving testimony of the witnesses at his trial without the slightest display of emotion, yet when he forgot to stand up at the reading of the verdict, he blushed with embarrassment when this was brought to his attention."

Rudolph Hess' strict Catholic upbringing is well known. His very religious father wanted him to be a missionary. Hess writes:

> "I . . . was as deeply religious as was possible for a boy of my age . . . I had been brought up by my parents to be respectful and obedient toward all adults . . . It was constantly impressed on me in forceful terms that I must obey promptly the wishes and commands of my parents, teachers, priests and indeed all adults, including servants, and that nothing must distract me from this duty. *Whatever they said was always right.*"

I believe that Nuremberg was a decisive turning point for the poisonous pedagogy. Obedience, the star in the Christians' crown of glory, the metarule of all modern western family systems, the glory of the Lutheran Mandates had reached its zenith of disclosure in terms of its potential for destruction. Suddenly the childhood idealism of the family structure was exposed as devastatingly destructive and with it the whole substructure of life-denying rules.

Hitler and black Nazism are a cruel caricature of what can happen in modern Western society if we do not stop promoting and proliferating family rules that kill the souls of human beings. Nazism marks the end of an epoch.

The Insidiousness of Total Obedience

Mine is an urgent, even frantic, cry for people to understand how insidious are these rules which form the poisonous pedagogy. Not insidious in themselves, they become insidious as absolutized and totalistic laws of human formation. Obedience and orderliness are essential to any family and social structure. Law as a guide to human safety through its protective structure is essential to human fulfillment. Learning to be agreeable, cooperative, unselfish and meek are useful and valuable.

However, it was obedience without critical judgment and inner freedom which led to black Nazism, Jonestown and Mylai. It was obedience absolutized and cut off from human sensitivity and natural law.

Similarly, cleanliness and orderliness without spontaneity lead to obsessive enslavement. Law and intellectualism without vitality and emotions lead to mechanical coldness and inhuman, heartless control. Considerateness, meekness, unselfishness without inner freedom, inner independence and critical judgment lead to a "doormat", people-pleasing type person, who can be ruled by almost any authority figure.

Soul-murder is the basic problem in the world today; it is the crisis in the family. We programmatically deny children their feelings, especially anger and sexual feelings. Once a person loses contact with his own feelings, he loses contact with his body. We also monitor and control our children's desires and thoughts. To have one's feelings, body, desires and thoughts controlled is to lose one's self. To lose one's self is to have one's soul murdered.

"To live and never know who I really am" is the greatest tragedy of all. It is this tragic sense which releases the rage that dominates our world. The rage is either directed by means of projections against the *strangers*, or it is directed against ourselves as the shame which fuels our addictions, or it is "acted out" in crimes and violence.

My contention is that most families are dysfunctional because our rules for normalcy are dysfunctional. The important issue is to find out what species of flawed relating your family specialized in. Once you know what happened to you, you can do something about it. If Thoreau was right when he said that the mass of mankind lives lives of quiet desperation, then most people do not know what happened to them.

Summary

The key points covered in this chapter can be summed up using the letters from the word **CRISIS:**

C. Compulsive/Addictive Behavior Disorder — The range of compulsive/addictive behavior in modern society is awesome. Three-fourths of the population is seriously affected. The bubonic plague of today is compulsivity. It affects our everyday lifestyle; how and what we eat; how and what we drink; our work; our recreation; our activities; our sexuality; our religious worship. Such behavior is modeled and set up in families.

R. Rules for Child Rearing — The poisonous pedagogy promotes ownership of our children. It preaches non-democratic ways of relating. It especially espouses inequality of power. It promotes the denial of feelings and corporal punishment.

I. Idealization of Parents and Family — One of the rules of the poisonous pedagogy is that the rules cannot be challenged. This means that parents and family cannot be critically evaluated. Children naturally idealize their parents out of survival needs. What emerge are adult children who carry their parents' rules to the next generation. This creates more adult children.

S. Shame — Adult children are adults with a soul-murdered child living inside of them. The true self is ruptured and a false self must be created. Shame is a being wound. It says I am flawed as a person.

I. Ideological Totalism — Nazi Germany — The ultimate expression of the poisonous pedagogy was Nazi Germany. Hitler created the master/slave national state. He used the socialization structures of the German family to create the Nazi Regime. As long as the poisonous pedagogy goes unchallenged, the phenomenon of Hitler is still a potential in the west.

S. Social Systems — We now understand that social systems have laws, components and structural dynamics. Societies create 'consensus realities' which ultimately become unconscious. Families are systems in which the whole is greater than the parts. Such systems have rules which if left unchallenged become closed systems and such closed systems can go on for generations.

2

What Almost No One Knows About Families — The Family As A System

"The image of self and the image of family are reciprocally interdependent."
N. Ackerman
The Psychodynamics of Family Life

In 1957 a researcher named Cristian Midelfort working at Lutheran Hospital in LaCrosse, Wisconsin, published his findings. He had been working with the relationships between his depressed, paranoid, schizophrenic and neurotic clients and their families. He concluded his study with the words: "This study substantiates the idea that all mental illness develops in a family and is present in several members of the family." (*The Family in Psychotherapy*)

Almost simultaneously in 1957, John Howells in Ipswich, England, after working extensively with families concluded:

"In family psychiatry a family is not regarded as a background to . . . help the present patient along. Family psychiatry accepts the family itself as the patient the presenting member being viewed as a sign of family psychopathology."

Family Psychiatry

This type of research reached a zenith in the work of Margaret Singer and Lyman Wynne at the National Institute of Mental Health at Bethesda, Maryland. Wynne and Singer suggested that schizophrenia is not just an entity associated with certain clinical personalities but is caused by the manner in which a person is socialized. Wynne began to see schizophrenia in terms of the family system. He boldly stated that it was a gross oversimplification to see the schizophrenic child as isolated in his sickness. Rather he writes:

"All family members, offspring and parents, are caught up in reciprocal victimizing — and rescuing processes in which they are all tragically enmeshed."

Exploring the Base for Family Therapy

In 1951, Gregory Bateson began work which would engender an interpersonal notion of schizophrenia based on faulty and crazy-making communication. Commanding children to be spontaneous or telling them it is their duty to love their parents came to be known as 'double binding'. To command one to do something that by definition cannot be commanded is crazy-making.

Virginia Satir aided Bateson in the development of a theory of emotional illnesses based on a faulty and paradoxical pattern of interpersonal communication. Satir later elaborated her own theory of family system pathology. Others followed in research and thinking on the relationship between the individual who is considered emotionally diseased and the family from which he came. Murray Bowen and Warren Brodey added a multigenerational focus. Bowen established the role of the grandparents as significant in several cases. In one case he writes:

"The grandparents combined immaturities were acquired by one child who was most attached to the mother. When this child married a spouse with an equal degree of immaturity, it resulted in one child (the patient) with a high degree of immaturity."

A Family Concept of Schizophrenia

Basically Bowen saw the following scenario as the dominant pattern in producing emotional illness. Two people, carrying unresolved conflicts with their parents, get married. As the intimacy voltage rises in the marriage, these conflicts become more intense. The partners try to settle these issues with an emotional divorce, "a marked emotional distance". Very often both agree not to disagree and establish a pseudo-intimacy. The marriage looks good on the outside. There is a facade of happiness. But beneath the surface there is struggle, pain and loneliness.

When a child is born, it is "triangled" into the system. The child becomes the focus of the relationship. The child is locked into the system and finds it virtually impossible to leave the family. This child often becomes emotionally disturbed and is the identified patient who is sent to therapy. Actually the identified patient is only a symptom of the emotionally disturbed marriage. And the patient's so-called emotional illness can be seen and understood only in relation to the emotional system of which he is a part. There is emotional contagion in the whole family. The one who is labeled 'sick' is the symptom-bearer of the whole emotional system itself, which is sick.

Many brilliant and innovative therapists began to put these theories into practice with some extraordinary results. Salvadore Minuchin, Carl Whittaker, Jay Haley and Virginia Satir are notable examples.

Family system thinking is grounded in the fact that we humans are inextricably social. My first beliefs about myself were formed from my mother's feelings and desires about me. My self-definition literally began in the womb.

The Shaping of Our Lives

Data now shows that from the sixth month on, the fetus lives an active emotional life. In his book, *The Secret Life of the Unborn Child,* Dr. Thomas Verny summarizes the current data on the *Life of the Fetus:*

1. The fetus can hear, experience, taste and on a primitive level, even learn and feel *in utero.*
2. What the fetal child feels and perceives begins shaping his attitudes and expectations about himself. These attitudes result from the messages he receives from his mother.

3. What matters is the mother's attitude. Chronic anxiety or wrenching ambivalence about motherhood can leave a deep scar on an unborn child's personality. As also joy, elation and anticipation can contribute significantly to the emotional development of a healthy child.
4. The father's feelings are also significant. How a man feels about his wife and unborn child is one of the most important factors in determining the success of pregnancy.

Thus our lives are shaped from the beginning by our parents. After birth our self-image comes from our primary caregiver's eyes. How I see and feel about myself is exactly what I see in my caregiver's eyes. How my mothering person feels about me in these earliest years is how I will feel about myself. If my parents are shame-based and dysfunctional, they will feel inadequate and needy. In such a state they cannot be there for me. They will need me to be there for them.

Our reality is shaped from the beginning by a *relationship*, we are we, before we are I. Our "I-ness" comes from our "we-ness". Our individuality comes from the social context of our lives. This is the basic foundation for the new thinking of the family.

Vincent Foley in his *Introduction To Family Therapy* uses Tennessee Williams' play, *The Glass Menagerie*, to illustrate the family system's viewpoint. If one separates Laura from her family system (mother, brother), she appears to be a girl living in fantasy and unreality. She could be judged schizophrenic. She is sick and the labeled patient.

However, if we look at Laura from a system's viewpoint, we get a very different picture. We see her interaction with her mother and brother as crucial for keeping the family together. She is no longer the sick, frumpy sister waiting for a "gentleman caller", but a person who is critical to the balance of the family system. The tensions between the son, Tom, and the mother, Amanda, are only tempered and kept in check by Laura. When the voltage of these tensions gets too high, Laura steps in and gets Tom and Amanda to focus on her. This distracts them and lowers the voltage. Thus, Laura performs a crucial and critical role. She keeps the family together.

The family system functions precisely because of Laura's intervention and not in spite of it. One could argue that it is blatantly false to label Laura sick. One could even call her the caretaker and unity-preserver of the family. More precisely, one should say that the Winfield family system itself is sick and Laura is only a symptom of that system. The *shift from the person to the interpersonal is not just another way of viewing pathology, but a totally new and different concept of pathology.*

Families as Systems

The family as a system is a new reality. Only 35 years old, the concept of families as systems helps explain a bewildering array of behaviors. The very notion of mental illness is no longer useful, since it implies some *intra*psychic phenomena. The family systems model shows how each person in a family plays a *part in the whole system.* Family systems help us understand why children in the same family often seem so different. And seeing the family as a system helps us to see how the poisonous pedagogy is carried from generation to generation.

Mental illness is never an isolatable, individualistic phenomenon. The theory of family systems accepts the family itself as the patient, with the presenting member being viewed as a *sign* of family psychopathology. The identified patient then becomes the symptom of the family system's dysfunctiònality. The family itself is a symptom of society at large.

Over and over again, I have seen this family systems reality in my work. In our teen-age drug-abuse program in Los Angeles, some 50 sets of parents (with drug-abusing teenagers) have been through a special clinical enrichment series. As they see themselves in this seminar, they own the dysfunctionality of their marriages. They help us focus the drug behavior of their kids as an "acting out" to take the heat off their parents' marriages. In a certain sense, these kids have kept their families together by being drug addicts. They are the identified patients. But their systemic function is to get the family some help, and indeed, they have succeeded. Each of these families bears the scars of the poisonous pedagogy. Each operated their families on the basis of these rules. Each parent had been brought up in families using these rules.

Systems were first studied in biology. The German biologist Ludwig von Bertalanffy defined systems as "complexes of elements in interaction". He went on to study systems and to deduce a set of principles which apply to all systems. His position is called general system theory.

I shall spend the rest of this chapter summarizing in simple terms how his general system theory applies to families as systems.

Wholeness

The first principle of systems is that of wholeness. The whole is greater than the sum of its parts. This means that the elements added together do not produce the system. The system results from the interaction of the elements. Without the interaction, there is no system.

The system of the family in *The Glass Menagerie* is not the sum of the individual personalities of Amanda, Laura and Tom Winfield, but the vital outgoing interaction between them. Von Bertalanffy uses the term *wholeness* to characterize such interaction.

Relationship

The second characteristic of a system is *relationship*. Any family system is composed of connecting relationships. To study the family as a system, one must see the various connections between the individualized persons and how they interact. Each person in the system relates to every other one in a similar fashion. Each is partly a whole and wholly a part. Each person within the system has his own unique systemic individuality as well as carrying an imprint of the whole family system. I am my family as well as whatever uniqueness I have actualized as a person. I am individual and group simultaneously.

A good way to grasp this property of relationship proportionality is by looking at a new kind of photography that deals with what are called "holograms". A hologram is a three-dimensional picture made from interference patterns of a certain kind of light beam. If a hologram is divided, each half contains the whole picture. If cut in quarters, the whole picture is retained, etc.

Many researchers believe that all organisms are holograms, that the human brain and the universe itself is holographic. The hologram is a good way to grasp the family system. If I am taken away from my family, all the realities of that family exist within me. My deep unconscious has been totally related to all the persons in the system and my reality has been formed by my relationship with each person in the system. The notion of wholeness is a way of expressing the deep organismic unconscious unity of any system and the blood-connected family system especially. The connection of blood which is never undone is more profound than that of friendship.

An example from my own counseling practice may make this clearer. Several years ago a couple came to me because of their son. Both parents were highly achieving professionals. They were extremely intellectual and had almost a disdain for emotions. They would fit most models of work addiction. They were sexually dysfunctional in their marriage. They had not engaged in intercourse in five years. Each, however, had a fairly elaborate secret fantasy sex life. Their marriage was non-intimate and lonely. The only thing that they really enjoyed doing was eating out at good restaurants, which they did at least four times a week. The nine-year-old boy was their only child. He was the reason they came to see me. He was failing in school and at least 100 pounds overweight. He was unchildlike. He was somber, reclusive, had almost no affect and acted like an old man. Over several months I learned that he was compulsively masturbating. He revealed this with great shame. He had a secret ritual for masturbating, which was also a source of shame.

What was clear to me was that he was the symptom bearer of his parents marital dysfunction. He made overt their loneliness, their non-communication, their secret sexual shame and he balanced their intense drive for achievement by underachievement. They liked to eat and he was grossly overweight.

Since he had started counseling, their relationship had improved. He had been taken to several counselors before me. Each had treated him differently. One therapist had put him on anti-depressant drugs. None had treated him as the symptom bearer of his family system's dysfunction. My work was also unsuccessful because the parents refused to cooperate in seeing their marriage as the child's main problem.

Family systems can be either closed systems or highly flexible open systems. In closed systems the connections, structures and relationships are fixed and rigid and the process patterns remain essentially the same. This is useful knowledge when examining the family's problems. Whether the subject is money, sex, children or in-laws, the pattern will be the same.

Family systems, like all systems, relate through a process called feedback. It is the feedback loops that maintain the systems functioning.

For example, in the White family Dad is an alcoholic. He gets drunk and can't go to work the next day. Mom calls in sick for him. The children don't ask questions and pretend to believe that Dad is sick. While they purportedly do all this to save his job and the family's economic security, they in fact are enabling him to remain an alcoholic. He doesn't have to bear the consequences of his irresponsible behavior. He will go through a period of remorse and begin drinking again. Soon the exact same sequence will take place.

In closed system families the feedback loops are negative and work to keep the system frozen and unchanging. This is called dynamic homeostasis. The more one tries to change it, the more it stays the same. Feedback is also maintained in families by *rules* that govern the system. These rules can be overt, such as "children are to be seen and not heard", or covert, such as father's loud and boisterous chauvinism with its covert message that women are to be feared and controlled. These covert rules are often a form of negative feedback. The poisonous pedagogy is carried both overtly and covertly. The poisonous pedagogy produces shame-based people who marry other shame-based people. Each has idealized their parents and their parents' rules. They raise their children the way their parents raised them. The children are shamed in the same way their parents were shamed. The cycle goes on for generations.

New Belief Systems

Positive feedback can break up the frozen status quo of a system. Positive feedback challenges destructive and unexamined rules, both overt and covert. Positive feedback comes in the form of new belief systems which precipitate new ways of acting by making old positions untenable. Challenging the assumptions of the poisonous pedagogy is a way to give positive feedback.

It is not this or that person who needs to be isolated and labeled "sick". It is in looking at the way the whole system operates by initiating movement through the use of feedback which changes how the system works.

On my television series, I attempted to visually represent families with a six-foot stainless steel mobile created by a wonderful artist named Trudy Sween. To illustrate the dynamic homeostatic principle, I would touch the mobile at the beginning of the program and point out later on how it always came to rest in exactly the same position it had started.

I also illustrated the inter-connecting inter-relational principle by showing that when I touched one part of the mobile, every part moved.

An open family system could be illustrated by keeping the mobile in gentle motion all the time.

Family Rules

Family systems fail, *not because of bad people,* but because of bad information loops, bad feedback in the form of bad rules of behavior. The same is true of society. This is important. Our parents are not bad people for transmitting the poisonous pedagogy. The rules are bad.

Families have a wide range of governing rules. There are financial, household, celebrational, social, educational, emotional, vocational, sexual, somal (sickness and health) and parenting rules. Each of these rules has attitudinal, behavioral and communicational aspects.

A household rule may be:

1. Attitudinal: the house should be neat and clean.
2. Behavioral: dishes are cleaned after each use.
3. Communicational: Dad verbally reprimands if dishes are not washed.

Working out a compromise between each one's family of origin rules is a major task in a marriage.

All systems have principles and rules like the ones we have been discussing. Likewise, all systems have components. In a family system the chief components are the mother's relationship to herself and her relationship to the father and the father's relationship to himself and his relationship with the mother. The status of these relationships dominates the system. If the marriage is functional, the children have a chance to be fully functional. If the marriage component is dysfunctional, the family members are stressed and adapt dysfunctionally.

Fulfilling The Family's Needs

Like all social systems a family has basic needs. The family needs: a sense of worth, a sense of physical security or productivity, a sense of intimacy and relatedness, a sense of unified structure, a sense of responsibility, a need for challenge and stimulation, a sense of joy and affirmation and a spiritual grounding. A family also needs a mother and father who are committed in a basically healthy relationship and who are secure enough to parent their children without contamination.

Suppose Mother is a hypochondriac who obsesses on her every ailment, is often bedridden and uses illness to avoid responsibility. Because Mother is unavailable, the marriage has an intimacy vacuum.

The family system needs a marriage. Someone in the system will need to be an equal partner with Dad in order to make a marriage. One of the daughters will get the job. She becomes the Surrogate Spouse. Another child may take over the parenting function while Dad is busy working. This child will become Super-responsible and a Little Parent. Another person in the system may be the one who adds joy to the family by being cute and funny. This person relieves a lot of the tension between Mom and Dad. He is the Mascot.

Another child will take the role of Saint and Hero, becoming a straight "A" student, becoming president of his class and winning honors. This person gives the family a sense of dignity.

Another child may take on Dad's unexpressed anger about Mom by acting out antisocially. He may use drugs, get in trouble at school or start failing his courses. This offers Mom and Dad a distraction. They may actually become more intimate by becoming concerned over this child. This child becomes the family Scapegoat.

In fact, like Laura Wingfield, this child is the symptom bearer of the family's dysfunction. The Scapegoat is often the service bearer for the family. Out of the problems the Scapegoat causes, the whole family is often drawn into treatment.

I've capitalized these roles to show that they are rigid. They result from the needs of the system, not from anyone's individual choice. Nature abhors a vacuum. The children automatically work to provide for the system's overt and covert needs.

Everyone in the family is affected by Mom's and Dad's relationship. As each adapts to the stress in a particular role or roles, each loses his or her own true identity. As a role becomes more and more rigid, the family system closes more and more into a frozen trance-like state. Once this freezing occurs, the family is stuck. And the more each one tries to help by playing his role, the more the family stays the same.

In healthy family systems there are healthy roles. The parental role is mainly to model. Parents model:

How to be a man or woman.
How to be a husband or wife.
How to be a father or mother.
How to be in an intimate relationship.
How to be functional human beings.
How to have good boundaries.

Parents also play the role of nourishing teachers, giving their children time, attention and direction.

Children especially need direction as their role is to be learners. They are curious and filled with wonder. They need to learn how to use their powers to know, love, feel, choose and imagine. They need to learn to use these powers effectively and creatively to get their basic needs.

In healthy family systems the roles are flexible and rotating. The mobile is gently moving. There is healthy role reversal and flexible interchange. Mom may be the scapegoat one month, Dad the next and one of the children the next.

Birth Order Characteristics

One current model of family process work illustrates another aspect of family systems thinking. This model has to do with birth order; is predicated on the needs of any social system, rather than the specific needs of dysfunctional systems. The latter is the basis for Role Theory.*

On the Bach Model every social system has four basic needs:

The need for productivity.

The need for emotional maintenance.

The need for relationship.

The need for unity.

As children are born into a family, these needs will be taken according to their birth order.

First Child

Usually the first child bears the family's conscious and explicit expectations. The first child carries more performance expectations than any other child due to the productivity needs of the system. The first child carries the family's dominant values and themes and will react to and identify most with father (the productivity manager). A first child will make decisions and hold values consistent with or in exact opposition to the father.

---

*What follows is a brief summary of the research done by Dr. Jerome Bach and his colleagues at the Bach Institute and the University of Minnesota.

The behavioral patterns of first children tend to be:

(a) They are other-oriented and socially aware. Firsts will be most conscious of social norms and images.
(b) Firsts thrive on the explicit and obvious. They want detail and tend to go by the letter rather than the spirit.
(c) Because of the expectation and pressure due to parental youth and overcoercion ("first child jitters"), first children often have trouble developing high self-esteem.

Second Child

Second children naturally relate to the emotional maintenance needs of the system. Seconds respond to the covert and unconscious rules in the family system. A second child will normally bond with (react to or identify with) the mother. A second child will make decisions and hold values vis a vis the mother.

The behavioral patterns of second children are dominantly as follows:

(a) They will act out the unconscious expectations and needs of others as well as their own. Seconds will often be an extension of mother's unconscious needs or desires. A male second may become a man just like mother wished she could have married. A female second may become promiscuous because the mother secretly wanted to be.
(b) Second children carry the covert emotional issues in the family and so often have trouble putting together their head and their hearts. What this means is that seconds will often be intuitively aware that something gamey is going on without knowing what or why. They will pick up "hidden agendas" immediately but not be able to express clearly what they feel. Because of this, second children often seem naive and puzzled. Subjectively second children often feel crazy.

Third Child

The third child hooks into the relationship needs of the system. In the family system's process, thirds will identify with the marriage relationship. They will be the best symbol of what is going on in the marriage. In the example I previously gave of the highly achieving professional couple, the son is an *only child*. Only children will often carry all the family process functions. In a healthy functional marriage this can be excellent. And in healthy families only children fare well. In dysfunctional marriages, the only child carries the covert dysfunction. My client, the nine-year-old boy, was an almost perfect readout for what was going on in the parent's marriage. He was overweight; their *only* couple interest was eating. He was sexually secretive; they had sexual secrets. He was lonely and showed little emotion; they were lonely and had almost no feeling in their relationship. He was non-communicative; they had almost no communication in their marriage.

The third child is the best purveyor of the marriage tensions and has a hard time establishing a separate identity.

Third child behavior patterns are generally as follows:

(a) Has relatedness as his main concern.

(b) Appears very uninvolved, but is actually very involved.

(c) Feels very ambivalent and has trouble making choices.

Fourth Child

Takes on the unification needs of the family system. The fourth child will catch and collect the unresolved family tensions. This might be any relational tension in the system. A fourth is like the family radar picking up and identifying with every action and interaction in the family system.

From a behavioral pattern point of view, fourth children feel very responsible yet powerless and helpless to really do anything about what is going on in the family. Fourths will often resort to cutesy mascot-like behavior to distract pain and take care of the family. Fourths will often appear infantile and indulged. They may often be disruptive and scapegoat the family in order to take care of it.

The Bach material is still very much a theory and certainly *should not be* adopted in any rigid fashion. This analysis can be useful in helping one identify certain personality tendencies that are more systematically induced than part of one's natural endowment.

Any children beyond the fourth repeat the sequence. Fifth child operates like a first child, sixth like a second child, etc.

Each family system is part of a larger system called a subculture. This involves nationality and religious preference. Each subculture has its principles, its rules and its components. Subcultures are part of cultures or nations. Each subculture and culture have an impact on the formation of rules and how the rules are enforced.

The Family Trance

Another way to think of a family system is to think of a group of people in a hypnotic trance. Actually trance is a naturally occurring state. Most of us go in and out of trance many times during the course of a day. We daydream, we get absorbed in future fantasies, we relive old memories from "the past", we watch television, read novels or go to movies. All of these affect a state of trance.

In trance a more holistic state of conscious absorption exists. Children are natural trance subjects because of their naivete and trust, as well as the powerful interpersonal bonding with their parents. Once a trance state is affected, all that one learns in that state operates like a post-hypnotic suggestion. If Mom tells you you will never be as smart as your sister, this message will operate until the trance is broken. It is broken by leaving home, growing up and breaking the bond with Mother.

The trance also functions in a circular feedback fashion. Each person is impacted by everyone else's behavior. Like a mobile, you touch one part and all the other parts are affected.

The family trance is created by both parents' individual interactions with the children and by the marriage itself. Father's behavior impacts Mother, who responds or reacts with behavior that impacts Father.

For example, Mom may nag at Dad because he won't talk. When Dad is asked why he won't talk, he says it's because Mom bitches and nags. So Mom bitches and nags because Dad won't talk, and Dad won't talk because Mom bitches and nags. A circular loop is thus created. The children eat, breathe and are formed out of this dyadic trance action. So the whole is the trance that all the parts participate in.

Part of every family trance is the way each person learns about his emotions. The family dictates what feelings you can have and express. The parents model this. I call this the original family SPELL. SPELL stands for our Source People's Emotional Language Legacy. The fantasy bond is also part of our original SPELL. We all start our lives in our family SPELL. We are all in a post-hypnotic trance induced in early infancy.

The role of bonding is especially important in trance process. The children bond with one or both of their parents. This bonding is a powerful form of rapport. Rapport is the name for the process of becoming another person. In rapport we enter the other's model of the world. We take on the other's map of reality. Bonding is the process by which the children are drawn into the trance created by their parents.

In dysfunctional systems this bonding has severe and disastrous consequences. A child who is physically, sexually, emotionally, intellectually or morally abused will form a "traumatic bonding" to such abuse. He will experience the abuse as normal, since he doesn't know anything else or any other way to be in a family. Often he will identify with the persecuting parent. The child does this as a way to feel powerful. Once identified, the child carries the parent's feelings and beliefs.

For example, Jill, one of my clients in Los Angeles had a violent and verbally abusive father. He shamed and humiliated her in front of boyfriends. He constantly accused her of being seductive and prophesied that she would be raped. Jill hated her father and had tremendous repressed anger for him.

When Jill married, she found a Caspar Milquetoast type of man who she criticized, maligned and verbally abused. She copied her offender father's behavior and vented her rage at her father onto her husband. One of her daughters was raped four times!

The same kind of dynamic operates in children who have been victimized by the poisonous pedagogy. They identify with their abusing parents and re-enact the same abuse on their children by vehemently adhering to their parents' way of parenting.

Traumatic bonding and identification with the abuser explains the multigenerational carrying of diseased attitudes. Such identification is an ego defense and allows the child to survive.

The Family Trance Cycle

1. Family systems function through feedback loops which are cybernetic and circular, rather than casual. Therefore, in a family system *everyone is responsible, but no one is to blame.*

   This organismic approach avoids labels, such as "sick" and "mentally ill". It sees dysfunction as an organismic holistic imbalance due to *inadequate rules or belief systems*, which result in frozen feedback loops and circularity. This approach eliminates the need to blame the scapegoat with diagnostic labels. It eliminates the belief that illness is the breakdown of the person's intrapsychic machinery. It is the family that is diseased and not the individual person. The individual does however, behave in a dysfunctional manner.

2. The whole is the behaviorally induced trance. In an open family system, the trance can change because of the flexible choices afforded by the healthy environment created by the marital dyad. In a closed family system, the trance becomes rigid and frozen, so that any member can start the induction by his own particular role behavior. This is why one can leave his family and still be in it. People from dysfunctional families tend to stay in their rigid roles and carry the dysfunctionality into their later life.

3. The family is an incorporation of the subculture and culture of one's upbringing. Subcultures and cultures are created by individuals. They form the social construction of reality which is called the "consensus reality". This "consensus reality" is what all agree to. Families are created according to the rules of the consensus reality. The current consensus reality rules for parenting are the poisonous pedagogy.

4. Systems theory explains how the poisonous pedagogy can be passed on for generations. It is in understanding your own family system that you can rediscover how this poisonous pedagogy sets you up to play a role or act out a script. Connecting with your family history, you can discover what happened to your true self.

Summary

The key points covered in this chapter can be summed up using the letters of the word **FAMILIES.**

F. **Feedback Loops versus Cause/Effect** — The family systems notion sees the family as a dynamic social organism. Such an organism functions by means of interaction and interdependence. Dad won't talk because Mom bitches and nags and Mom bitches and nags because Dad won't talk. Their behavior is cyclical rather than casual.

A. **Autonomy or Wholeness** — The family is a total organism — the whole is greater than the sum of its parts. Everyone in the family is affected by everyone else. Each individual is partly a whole and wholly a part. A whole new social concept of emotional dis-ease emerges from this realization. Individuals are not emotionally dis-eased — whole families are.

M. **Marriage as the Chief Component** — The marriage is the Chief Component in the family. The health of the marriage determines the health of the family.

I. **Individual Roles** — All families have roles. The role of parent is to model the following: how to be a man or woman; mothering and fathering; how to be a person; how to express feelings and desires. The role of children is to be curious and learn. In healthy families the roles are flexible; in dysfunctional families the roles are inflexible.

L. **Laws or Rules** — All families have laws or rules that govern the system. Laws include issues like household maintenance, body care, celebration, social life, financial issues, privacy and boundaries.

I. **Individuation/Togetherness Tension** — The tension in families results from the individuation/togetherness polarity. The need to be unique and self-actualized often clashes with the need to conform for the sake of the system.

E. **Equilibrium** — Families as social systems operate according to the laws of complimentarity. If Dad is angry a lot, Mom is mild and soft-spoken. Like a mobile, the system will always try to come to rest and balance. Families can be open (always in gentle motion) or closed (frozen or rigid).

S. **Systems Needs** — Like individuals, systems have needs. Families, like all social systems, have need for productivity (food, clothing and shelter), emotional maintenance (touching, stroking, warmth); good relationships (love, intimacy); individuality and difference (self-actualization); stimulation (excitement, challenge, fun) and unity (a sense of belonging and togetherness).

3

Profile Of A Functional Family System

"If I am I because I am I
And you are you because you are you,
then I am and you are.
But if I am I because you are you,
and you are you because I am I,
then I am not and you are not."

Rabbi Mendel

Consider this the beginning of your quest for new and fruitful self-awareness. Let your major focus be on your family of origin. Your original family was the unit from which you came. If it was a functional unit, that family was the source of your individuality and strength and emotional buttress. Your family of origin, if functional, gave you a permanent conviction of belonging. Your original family is where you lived out the most passionate and powerful of all your human experiences.

As you examine what a functional healthy family is, you can also focus on the family you are now in or the one you are creating.

There are healthy and fully functioning families. To say that something is functional is to say that everything works. My car, for example, may have rust spots on the trunk, but if it drives well, then it is fully functional. It works.

A functional, healthy family is one in which all the members are fully functional and all the relationships between the members are fully functional. As human beings, all family members have available to them the use of all their human powers. They use these powers to cooperate, individuate and to get their collective and individual needs met. A functional family is the healthy soil out of which individuals can become mature human beings. This involves the following:

a. The family is a survival and growth unit.
b. The family is the soil which provides the emotional needs of the various members. These needs include a balance between autonomy and dependency and social and sexual training.
c. A healthy family provides the growth and development of each member including the parents.
d. The family is the place where the attainment of self-esteem takes place.
e. The family is a major unit in socialization and is crucial for a society if it is to endure.

If the family is the soil for mature peoplemaking, what does it mean to be a mature person? What are the essential components of maturity?

What Is Maturity?

A mature person is one who has differentiated himself from all others and established clearly marked ego boundaries. A mature person has a good identity. Such a person is able to relate to his family system in meaningful ways without being fused or joined to them. This means that one is emotionally free and can choose to move near without anger or absorption and move away without guilt.

For example, one of the grown-up children in a family may decide to go on a Christmas holiday trip with their own family or network of friends. In a functional family, this would probably occasion some sadness in the other family members that the family member would not be home for Christmas. But the parents and other family members would be glad that their fellow family member is happy and has a network of friends.

In a dysfunctional family the other members would be angry. The parents would more than likely be manipulating with guilt and the person staying away for the holidays would surely feel guilty. Let's say they felt so guilty that they cancelled their plans and came home for the Christmas celebration. They would be resentful and angry while they were there. This latter scenario is common in dysfunctional families.

The process of differentiation of self is essential to us all. The difference between individuation and belonging is one's place on a continuum. We are all somewhere on the continuum and all in need of becoming more differentiated. Our individuality is equivalent to our identity. Having a good identity means having a good sense of worth and having a significant other or others who affirm that sense of worth. We cannot have an identity all alone. We need at least one significant other who verifies our sense of worth. Our identity is the difference about us that makes a difference. It must always be grounded in a social context — in a relationship.

Identity unites our self-actualizing needs with our need for belonging. Good identity is always rooted in belonging. In fact, the individuation drive and the need to conform and belong are always in polar tension. We cannot have one without the other.

For individuation and differentiation to take place the family must be stable and secure enough so that one can get one's needs met. A healthy family environment provides the opportunity for all members to get their needs met. Figure 3.1 outlines the range of human powers and needs.

Each person needs self-worth, self-love, self-acceptance and the freedom to be the unique and unrepeatable one that they are. Each person needs to be touched and mirrored.

Each person needs a structure which is safe enough to risk growth and individuation. Such a structure will change according to the stages of one's development. Each person needs affection and recognition. Each person needs their feelings affirmed. Each person needs challenge and stimulation to move through each stage of development. Finally, each person needs self-actualization and spiritualization.

Spiritualization involves the need to love, care for, the need to be needed, seek truth, beauty and goodness. Spiritualization means living for something greater than oneself, which most call God.

Each person is born with the power to get these needs met. The power to know enables us to find out about ourselves and others and to get enough knowledge mastery to survive and meet our basic security needs. The power to love enables each of us to love ourselves and others. Love, according to Scott Peck "is the willingness to expand and extend my boundaries for the sake of nurturing my own and another's spiritual growth.

Figure 3.1. Range of Human Powers and Needs

Basic Human Needs
Self-acceptance: Self-worth, Beingness
Security: Physical (sex, food), Touch, Warmth
Strokes: Love, Recognition, Belonging
Structure: Intellectual Meaning, Someone to depend on (trust)
Stimulation: Change, Challenge, Curiosity, Fun
Self-actualization: Identity, Creativity, To be different
Spiritualization

Intellectual
Structure
Challenge
Curiosity
Meaning
Be Different

Spiritual
Self-actualizing
Creative Love
Self-responsibility,
  Personal Power
Spiritualization —
  Being Needs
  Ultimate Needs

God
SYNERGY
True Self
ULTIMATE
STRENGTH
IDENTITY

Emotional
Self-acceptance,
  Worth
Strokes: Love and
  Belonging
Social Interest
Someone we can
  depend on
Fun
Play

Physical
Awareness of Physical
  Needs:
Fitness
Nutrition
Food
Clothing
Shelter
Sex
Touch

Basic Powers
To Perceive
To Know, Think
To Emote, Feel
To Remember, Imagine

To be out of touch with the
physical body is to be out of
touch with
E-motions.

E-MOTIONS (forms of energy) — one of our basic "Powers"
    Signals from the body telling us of a need, a loss, a satiation. The energy is used to help us *act effectively* to take care of ourselves. E-motions are direct expressions of reality as opposed to thoughts which translate or analyze our experience. Emotions give *important information* about what we need to do, what we want or how we want to change.
    Anger gives us strength and protection. Fear gives us wisdom and discernment. Sadness gives us the ability to complete the past and work through life's necessary losses. Shame lets us know we are human and limited. Shame tells us we need help and that we can make a mistake. Guilt is the "conscience former".

What is E-motion?

The power to feel allows each of us to know our own unique spontaneous reality. Emotions are tools that allow us to be fully aware of where we are in fulfilling our needs. An E-motion is an energy in motion. This energy (say the beating of my heart and tensing of my muscles in anger) allows me to prepare to meet and resolve any threat to my basic needs. Without my energy (called anger), I am powerless to uphold my dignity and self-worth.

Fear is the energy of discernment. It allows one to assess danger and be aware of danger zones in terms of satisfying one's basic needs.

Sadness is the energy of saying goodbye and completing. Life is a prolonged farewell. It is a continuous saying goodbye and completing of cycles of growth.

Grief and sadness give us the energy to complete the past. Saying goodbye to infancy and toddlerhood is essential in order to grow into the latency period of school age. Saying goodbye to school is essential in order to make one's way and take one's place in the world. Growth demands a continual dying and being reborn. Grief is the 'healing feeling'.

Guilt is the energy that forms our conscience. Without this energy, one is doomed to sociopathic and psychopathic insensitivity. Guilt allows one to stand for something and to have an internal value system that leads to action and commitment.

Shame is the energy that lets us know we are limited and finite. Shame allows us to make mistakes and lets us know we need help. Shame is the source of our spirituality.*

Joy is the energy that signals that all is well. All needs are being filled. One is becoming and growing. Joy creates new and boundless energy.

Each person has the power to want and desire. This energy we usually call the volitional faculty or will. Our will is the power of desire raised to the intensity of action. Our choices shape our reality and our life.

Finally, we have the power to imagine, which allows us to look at new possibilities. Without this power, we become rigid conformists. Human imagination is the power that has forged new frontiers and given the world innovation, advancement and progress. Our national art galleries and museums are monuments to the power of imagination. Without this

---

*This is very different from the neurotic shame induced by the poisonous pedagogy. That shame is no longer an E-motion. It has become the core of our identity.

power we would gradually become hopeless since hope always involves seeing new possibilities.

A good family matrix provides a solid ground upon which one can exercise the powers to know, love, feel, decide and imagine. Such a ground needs to be developmentally proper. This means that a person needs to have the freedom to exercise his powers to get his needs met in a way proportional to the stages of his development.

The power to know, for example, develops gradually over the first 16 years, going through phases of symbolic, pre-logical, concrete logical and finally abstract and symbolic thinking. One needs parenting sources who understand the specific way one thinks at each stage of development, so that parental expectations are balanced by healthy challenge and awareness of the child's cognitive limitations. I outlined the magical pre-logical stage in the introductory chapter. A mature person updates the magical child within himself. He comes to see his parents as the real finite human beings they are. He updates their parenting rules with reason and logic and personal experience.

I believe that all of us are born with a deep and profound sense of worth. We are precious, rare, unique and innocent. We are born with all the powers and needs I've mentioned. We are, however, immature and totally dependent on our caretakers or survival figures, a billion-dollar diamond in the rough. Our early destiny is shaped to an awesome degree by those caretakers. To continue to feel precious and unique we have to see our uniqueness and preciousness in the eyes of our caretakers. Our belief about ourselves comes from their eyes.

The foundation for our self-image is grounded in the first three years of life. It comes from our major caretaker's mirroring. Our sense of ourself needs to be mirrored by significant others who love and care and who are self-actualized enough not to be threatened by each new cognitive threshold with its expanding spontaneity and freedom. The more our major caretakers love themselves and accept all their own feelings, needs, and wants, the more they can be there to accept all the parts of their children — their drives, feelings and needs.

Parents who have good self-worth and self-acceptance are getting their own needs met. They do not have to *use their* children to have a sense of power, adequacy and security. Each parent partner is in the process of finishing their own business with their own family of origin. Separation from mother and father is being accomplished. Each is complete in the sense of having finished the past. Each has updated the destructive aspects of the poisonous pedagogy.

What is a Healthy Functional Marriage?

As I pointed out, the family is a system. It has components and principles that govern the system. *The chief component is the marital partnership.* If their relationship is healthy and functional, the children have the opportunity to grow.

A healthy functional couple commit to each other through the power of will. They *decide* and *choose* to stand by each other no matter what (for riches or poorness, in sickness and health, until death parts them). A good relationship is based on unconditional love. It's not some maudlin feeling — *it's a decision.*

A healthy functional relationship is based on equality, the equality of two self-actualizing spiritual beings who connect at the level of their beingness. Each is a whole person. Each grows because of the love for the other, which by definition occasions spiritual growth.

Each partner in a healthy functional marriage knows that in the final analysis they are responsible for their own actions and happiness. Happiness cannot be the fruition of a mature process if it is dependent on something outside itself. Life is a process of moving from environmental support to self-support. From puberty on, growing up and becoming mature means standing on one's two feet and being independent and self-supporting. No relationship is healthy if it is based on incompleteness and neediness. Healthy relationships are mature, which means equal and self-responsible.

The mature relationship image I like best is two people making music together. Each plays his *own* instrument and uses *his own unique skills,* but they play the same song. Each is a whole and complete. Each is independent and committed.

Furthermore, in a healthy and committed relationship each partner has a commitment to discipline. Each is self-disciplined and is willing to apply discipline to the relationship. Discipline involves the use of four basic techniques of easing the suffering of life's inevitable problems. Scott Peck, in his book, *The Road Less Traveled,* outlines these techniques.

They are:

1) Delaying gratification.
2) Accepting responsibility for self.
3) Telling the truth and being dedicated to reality.
4) Bracketing ego needs for the sake of spiritual growth.

Discipline is fueled by the commitment of love and is part of the commitment.

Who Are Healthy Functional Parents?

When two people in a healthy relationship decide to be parents, they can model this self-discipline and self-love for their children. They accept having children as the most responsible decision of their lives. They commit to being there for their children.

When such a relationship forms the foundation of a family, each child in the system has the safeguard of *needed age specific dependency*, as well as the security to grow through experimenting with his unique individuality. In fact, the more stable and secure the parental relationship is, the more the children can be different. As long as Mom and Dad satisfy their own needs through their own powers and with each other, they will not *use* the children to solve these needs.

Functional parents will also model maturity and autonomy for their children. Their strong identity leaves very little of their consciousness unresolved, repressed and unconscious. The children, therefore, do not take on their parents' unresolved unconscious conflicts. The parents are in the process of completeness. They model this process and do not need their children to complete themselves.

The children are then free to grow, using their powers of knowing, loving, feeling, deciding and imaging to get their own individual self-actualization accomplished. The children are not constantly judged and measured by their parents frustrated and anxiety-ridden projections. They are not the victims of their parents' "acting out" their own unresolved conflicts with their own parents.

Each person in this kind of system has access to his natural endowment.

The Five Freedoms

Family therapist Virginia Satir calls this endowment the five freedoms. These freedoms are:

1. The freedom to see and hear (perceive) what is here and now, rather than what was, will be or should be.
2. The freedom to think what one thinks, rather than what one should think.
3. The freedom to feel what one feels, rather than what one should feel.
4. The freedom to want (desire) and to choose what one wants, rather than what one should want.
5. And the freedom to imagine one's own self-actualization, rather than playing a rigid role or always playing it safe.

These freedoms amount to full self-acceptance and integration. Enormous personal power results from such freedoms. All the person's energy is free to flow outward in order to cope with the world in getting one's needs met. This allows one full freedom. This amounts to full *functionality*.

The five freedoms are opposed to any kind of perfectionistic system that measures through critical judgment, since judgment implies the measuring of a person's worth. Fully functional families have conflicts and differences of opinion, but avoid judgment as a condition of another's worth. "I am uncomfortable" is an expression of a feeling — "You are stupid, selfish, crazy" is an evaluative judgment.

The 'poisonous pedagogy' is based on inequality — a kind of master/slave relationship. The parental authority is vested by virtue of being a parent. Parents are deserving of respect, simply because they are parents. Parents are always right and are to be obeyed.

In a family governed by such rules, critical judgment is not only okay, it is a duty and a requirement. Even the most mature parents will not be able to avoid the "I'm uncomfortable" — "You are stupid, weird, crazy" syndrome. Consequently, much emotional energy that belongs to the parent will be communicated as if it belonged to the child.

A client of mine felt terrible because she had come home from work feeling frustrated, angry and hurt. Instead of saying to her children — "I need time alone. I'm angry, frustrated and hurt," — she looked at the children's unkempt rooms and began screaming at them and telling them that "they never think of anyone but themselves". She made them responsible for her frustration, anger and hurt. This is abusive judgment. It attacks the children's self-esteem.

The issue of judgment underscores what is perhaps the major process in functional families, viz, the ability of each member to communicate effectively. In fact, some theorists have looked upon good communication in the family as the ground of mental health and bad communications as the mark of dysfunctionality.

Effective Communication

Good and effective communication centers around highly developed individual awareness and differentiation. A good communicator is aware of both internal processes in themselves and external processes in others. Self-awareness involves my perceptions, my interpretations, my projections, my feelings and my desires. Other awareness involves skill in sensory observation, as well as the ability to translate words into sensory based experimental data. Sensory observation involves real contact with the other at a neurological level. Sensory observation involves seeing the other's accessing cues and hearing the other's words.

Accessing cues are things like breathing, facial expression and movement, voice tone, temper and inflection. Every neurological cue is an indicator of an internal process that is going on at the level of lived experience.

The ability to translate words into sensory based experience involves listening both to the content and the process involved in speaking. This is called active listening. Active listening is a listening for congruence. Congruence has to do with a match-up between content and process, i.e., does their body match their words? Saying I'm not angry in a loud and aggressive voice tone is incongruent. If one is not angry, they won't sound angry.

The aforementioned client failed in her awareness of her own feelings. She is, in fact, highly dissociated from her feelings. She was emotionally abused as a child and learned to numb herself through her fantasy bond defense. Being unaware of her feelings and having no knowledge of self-responsible disclosure, she responds in angry judgment and criticism. Her egocentric and magical children can only translate her outburst as a judgment on themselves. Mother's anger and frustration translates into "I am bad".

The ability to translate words also has to do with challenging much of the shorthand we use in ordinary speech. Three examples of such shorthand are generalizations, deletions and distortions.

Generalizations are useful as shorthand, as when one says, "Women are the physical child bearers". Generalizations are dangerous as when one says, "You can't trust a woman". In this case, the word "woman" needs to be translated into the concrete specific woman or women this person can't trust.

Likewise, deletions are commonplace and useful. When we are making small talk at a cocktail party, it is useful to say, "My line of work is frustrating". It is not necessary to say how specifically one's work is frustrating. However, if one wants help for his work which is a frustrating problem, it is necessary to translate that deletion into sensory information. This can be done by asking how specifically one's work is frustrating.

Distortions involve prejudices, mind-reading and cause-and-effect illusions. Making statements like, "Baptists are devil worshippers," or "Negroes have inferior brains," are **prejudicial distortions.** Statements like, "You make me sick," "You give me a headache," to another family member are **cause-and-effect distortions.** There is no real way to make another sick or give headaches simply by behaving in a certain way.

Examples of **mind-reading** are "I know what you're thinking," "I know you've never cared as much about me as I do about you". These are mind-reading distortions.

Each of these categories needs to be challenged in order to get below the surface to the experience the person is actually having or wants to have.

Good communication involves good self-awareness. This demands that one have very clear boundaries. One takes responsibility for one's own feelings, perceptions, interpretations and desires. One expresses these in self-responsible statements using the word "I". Differentiation also means that I don't take responsibility for *your* feelings, perceptions, interpretations and desires.

When one has good boundaries, one knows where one begins and ends. One discloses in concrete specific behavioral detail. "I want you to take my suit to ABC Cleaners at nine o'clock tomorrow. Will that be possible?" rather than, "My clothes need cleaning." One checks to see if the other heard it clearly or one checks to see if they understood clearly.

The last communication skill that makes for a healthy and fully functioning family is the courage and ability to give good feedback. Good feedback can take the form of confronting another with concrete sensory data on how the other looks, sounds and feels to the observer, e.g., "You seem angry. Your jaw is tight and your fist is clenched. You haven't spoken in the last 20 minutes." Feedback also involves confronting another with one's own internal response stated in sensory based concrete data, e.g., "I want to talk to you and I see you reading the paper. I feel rejected and frustrated." Confronting is important in good family relationships. It is an act of telling the truth. Caring enough to confront is an act of love.

Much more could be written on good communications. My purpose in outlining good effective communication is to show that it flows from good differentiation. Healthy partners communicate honestly with each other. They model this for their children.

To sum up, communication in a functional family will be concrete and experiential. It will be characterized by:

1. High levels of awareness about self and others.
2. Concrete specific sensory based behavioral data. A clear sense of "I" centered self-responsibility.
3. Feedback apropos of the other's unaware behavior and apropos of one's own responses.
4. A willingness to disclose what one feels, wants and knows.

Rules in a Functional Family

The rules in a functional family will be overt and clear. Husband and wife will be aware of their family differences in attitudinal, communicational and behavioral rules. These differences will be understood and accepted as neither right nor wrong. They will be acknowledged as simply different. Each partner will be working toward compromised solutions. This certainly does not mean there will never be any conflict. The capacity for conflict is a mark of intimacy and a mark of a healthy family. Good healthy conflict is a kind of contact. In dysfunctional families problems are denied. There is either fusion (agree not to disagree) or withdrawal.

Because each person is unique and because each family system's rules are different, conflict is inevitable. For example, in my family of origin we opened our Christmas presents on Christmas Eve. We opened them fast and we didn't save the paper. In my wife's family they opened their presents on Christmas morning. They liked to spend time opening their presents. Others watched while each person opened their presents. They saved the ribbons and paper.

Now who's right? Obviously no one is right. Our families represent two different sets of celebrational rules for Christmas. Celebrational rules have less voltage than parenting rules or financial rules.

How to raise the children, the right method of discipline, how to handle money, what should be spent and saved, these are rules with higher voltage. These rules lend themselves to conflict. Working out these differences is a process that takes many years.

Fair Fighting Rules

In a functional marriage the couple is committed to the process of working out the differences. They do not stay in conflict nor do they cop out with confluence (agreeing not to disagree). They strive for contact and compromise. Fighting is part of contact and compromise. Functional couples have problems and fight, and they learn how to fight fair. Fighting fair involves:

1. Being assertive (self valuing), rather than being aggressive (get the other person no matter what the cost).
2. Staying in the now. Avoiding scorekeeping. "You are late for dinner. I feel angry. I wanted everything to be warm and tasty." Rather than "You are late for dinner as usual. I remember two years ago on our vacation you, etc., etc."
3. Avoid lecturing and stay with concrete specific behavioral detail.
4. Avoid judgment. Stay with self-responsible "I" messages.
5. Honesty needs to be rigorous. Go for accuracy, rather than agreement or perfection.
6. Don't argue about details, e.g. "You were 20 minutes late," "No, I was only 13 minutes late."
7. Don't assign blame.
8. Use active listening. Repeat to the other person what you heard them say. Get their agreement about what you heard them say before responding.

9. Fight about one thing at a time.
10. Unless you are being *abused*, hang in there. This is especially important. Go for a solution, rather than being right.

When rules are covert, they present much greater possibilities of conflict. For example, rules which embody the sex roles are often not present at a conscious verbal level. Your highly successful husband who rants and raves about women's liberation may be hiding a non-verbal rule that says women are to be feared and controlled. This rule may never have emerged during the "in-love" courtship period. It may only come out after you are married as the two of you become *homemakers*. It may not emerge until after the first child. It is only then that you become Mother and he becomes Dad. As you take on these roles, your family of origin bonding comes back. These roles then emerge in full force.

When you were "in-love", your ego boundaries collapsed. When you got married, they bounced back. In functional families covert rules are brought into consciousness and dealt with. Very little will be covert and unconscious. The children, therefore, will not have to act out a bunch of 'secrets' or family system imbalances. The children will not be enmeshed in the system.

Good functional rules will allow each family member to express the five freedoms. Functional rules allow for flexibility and spontaneity. Mistakes will be viewed as occasions for growth. Shaming will be strongly prohibited. Good functional rules will promote fun and laughter. Each person will be seen as precious, unique and unrepeatable.

Good Functional Rules

Functional family rules can be summed up as follows:

1. Problems are acknowledged and resolved.
2. The five freedoms are promoted. All members can express their perception, feelings, thoughts, desires and fantasies.
3. All relationships are dialogical and equal. Each person is of equal value as a person.
4. Communication is direct, congruent and sensory based, i.e., concrete, specific and behavioral.
5. Family members can get *their* needs met.
6. Family members can be different.
7. Parents do what they say. They are self-disciplined disciplinarians.

8. Family roles are chosen and flexible.
9. Atmosphere is fun and spontaneous.
10. The rules require accountability.
11. Violation of other's values leads to guilt.
12. Mistakes are forgiven and viewed as learning tools.
13. The family system exists for the individuals.
14. Parents are in touch with their healthy shame.

One of the paradoxical aspects of functional and healthy families is that as individuation increases, togetherness grows. As people separate and move toward wholeness, real intimacy becomes possible. The poet says, "The mountain to the climber is clearer from the plain." We need separation in order to have togetherness.

Needy and incomplete people seek others to make them complete. They say, "I love you because I need you". Individuated persons who have faced aloneness and separation know they can make it alone. They seek a partner because they want to love, not because they need to be completed. They say, "I need you because I love you." They offer love out of generosity, rather than need. They are no longer fantasy bonded.

It should be obvious that the rules of a healthy, functional family described here are quite different than the components of the poisonous pedagogy.

Figure 3.2. Functional Family System Chief Components

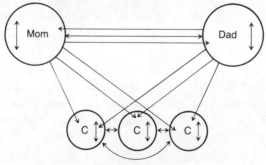

FIVE FREEDOMS

1. Whole greater than the sum of the parts.
2. System is dynamic — constantly seeks openness and growth adjusting to feedback and stress.
3. Rules are overt and negotiable.
4. Mutual Respect Balance — Togetherness — Individuation.
5. When anxiety is low interpersonally and intraphysically, the force toward individuation automatically emerges.

In Figure 3.2, I have presented a visual picture of a functional family. Each person in the drawing has a complete and whole circle as his boundary. Each person has contact with every other person. The ($\updownarrow$) indicates that each person has a good relationship with his own self. Mother and Father can let each other in because their boundaries are semi-permeable. However, the boundaries are strong enough to also keep each other out. They can say "no" to each other. They understand that while they are accountable to each other, they are not responsible *for* each other. If Mother responds angrily to Father, Father does not believe he *made* Mother angry. He knows that Mother's anger is about her own response (interpretation) and her own history (Father's voice may have sounded like her father). Each takes responsibility for his or her own responses.

Because they are committed to each other, Mother and Father are accountable to each other. Father may be concerned about Mother's angry response and choose to do what he can to respond to her. He knows and she knows he is not to blame.

Family Accountability

1. In a healthy family the Mother and Father have a disciplined love. They have the courage to do the *work* that love demands. Each loves himself and is therefore self-disciplined. Because of this they are disciplined disciplinarians with their children. They do what they ask their children to do.

   In such a family each person can pursue his own need fulfillment to a high degree. Of course, compromise and negotiation must take place from time to time. And *there will be conflict and boundary violation*. But all are accountable and committed to do the work of love, which means staying in there, fighting fair and working it out.
2. This family will have their shame available as a wonderful and healing feeling. Mom and Dad will not act *shameless*. They will not play God by issuing 'know it all' commands. They will not scream and curse. They will not criticize with over-responsible judgments or sarcastic and cutting remarks. They will exercise clear and firm boundaries as the Mom and Dad who are the architects and leaders of the family.

Was this the context from which you came into the world and enjoyed your childhood? If it was, you are indeed graced and blessed. For many of us it was not the context of our lives. For most of us it would have been, had our parents known what to do differently. For most of us, our own parents had emerged from the poisonous pedagogy. They did the best they could.

3. Let us look next at how the poisonous pedagogy dysfunctions a family system. This will give you an idea of how dysfunctional your family of origin was. As you read the next five chapters, keep an open mind. Remember that the *idealization of family and parents is a natural and an inescapable process. The issue here is not intentionality or blame.* Most parents would have done things differently if they had known that what they were doing was abusive. Most were probably abused themselves. Intention is not relevant. The issue is to discover our own actual history.

What we want is accountability. By knowing your personal history you will not be doomed to repeat it. By knowing what actually happened to you, by making the abandonment real, you can change. You cannot change what you've denied or what is embedded in unconscious ego defenses and therefore isn't real. You cannot know what you don't know. Terry Kellogg states that "by connecting with the past and making the abuse real, you can express the hurt and pain you had about the abuse. By expressing the anger or sadness, you can relieve the shame. You can then understand that *a lot of your behavior was about what happened to you and not about you.*" With that realization, a new self-acceptance and self-love can begin. It's like each of us has a real surprise in store for us, the surprise of rediscovering our own unique, valuable and precious self.

Summary

The key points covered in this chapter can be summed up using the letters of the word **FUNCTIONAL.**

F. Five Freedoms Expressed — In order to be fully functional, each human being needs to express freely the five basic powers that constitute human strength. These are: the power to perceive; to think and interpret; to emote; to choose, want and desire; and to be creative through the use of imagination.

U. Unfolding Process of Intimacy — The marriage, as the chief component of the family, needs to be in the process of becoming intimate. This process goes through the stages of: in love; working out differences, compromise and individualization; and plateau intimacy.

N. Negotiated Differences — Negotiating differences is the crucial task in the process of intimacy formation. To negotiate differences there must be the desire to cooperate. This desire creates the willingness to fight fair.

C. Clear and Consistent Communication — Clear and consistent communication are keys to establishing separateness and intimacy — clear communication demands awareness of self and the other, as well as mutual respect for each others dignity.

T. Trusting — Trust is created by honesty. Accurate expression of emotions, thoughts and desires is more important than agreement. Honesty is self-responsible and avoids shaming.

I. Individuality — In functional families differences are encouraged. The uniqueness and unrepeatability of each person is the number one priority in a functional family.

O. Open and Flexible — In a functional family the roles are open and flexible. One can be spontaneous without fear of shame and judgment.

N. Needs Fulfilled — Happy people are people who are getting their needs met. A functional family allows all of its members to get their needs filled.

A. Accountability — Functional families are accountable. They are willing to acknowledge individual problems, as well as family problems. They will work to resolve those problems.

L. Laws are Open and Flexible — The laws in functional families will allow for mistakes. They can and are negotiable.

4

Profile Of A Dysfunctional Family System

> "They are playing a game. They are playing at not playing a
> game. If I show them I see they are playing a game, I shall break
> the rules and they will punish me. I must play the game of not
> seeing that I play the game."
>
> R.D. Laing

We have seen that the chief component in the family system is the marriage relationship. Mom's relationship with herself and Dad's relationship with himself and their relationship with each other is the foundation of the family. The husband and wife are the architects of the family. Dysfunctional families are created by dysfunctional marriages. Dysfunctional marriages are created by dysfunctional individuals who seek out and marry each other.

One of the tragic facts about dysfunctional individuals is that they almost always find other individuals who operate either at the same level of dysfunctionality or at a lower level. Remember the family SPELL we discussed in Chapter 2. Each person carries the whole family within themselves. Individuals seek out the only relationships with which they have any experience. The most impactive relationships one has are those of his family of origin. You may object that you have a relationship just the opposite of your parents. The fact is that to choose the opposite is to still be dominated by the original trance. We are defined both by what we like or want and what we don't like or don't want.

The first component of dysfunctional families is that they are part of a multigenerational process. The dysfunctional individuals who marry other dysfunctional individuals have come from dysfunctional families. So the circle tends to be unbroken. Dysfunctional families create dysfunctional individuals who marry other dysfunctional individuals and create new dysfunctional families. Left to your own devices, it is very difficult to get out of the multigenerational dis-ease.

Five Generation Genogram

Let me expand on this by commenting on a family genogram. If you look at Figure 4.1, you will see a five-generation genogram. A genogram is a family generational map. It can be very useful in establishing multigenerational patterns. This genogram shows several striking patterns of dysfunctionality. First, there are five generations of alcoholism. Second, there are four generations of actual physical abandonment. Third, there was inappropriate and cross-generational bonding by both parents of the identified patient (I.P.). This is what I referred to as Surrogate Spousing. The I.P. carried on this generational pattern by marrying someone who was also a Surrogate Spouse. All the members in this genogram are co-dependent and all are in need of some treatment for emotional recovery. There are other subtleties in this multigenerational map, but they are of clinical concern. Suffice it to say, compulsivity and addiction are multigenerational phenomena.

In the last chapter we explored the components of a good marital relationship. Good functional marriages are dependent upon each partner's relationship to his/her self. If mother/wife loves herself and feels centered and growing in wholeness, she feels complete, likewise, with the husband/father. Each person feels complete and, therefore, doesn't look to the other for completion.

Without self-completion and self-value, one can hardly love another. When any natural organism is incomplete, its natural life drive is toward completion. So when two incomplete human beings come together, their

Figure 4.1. Five-Generation Genogram

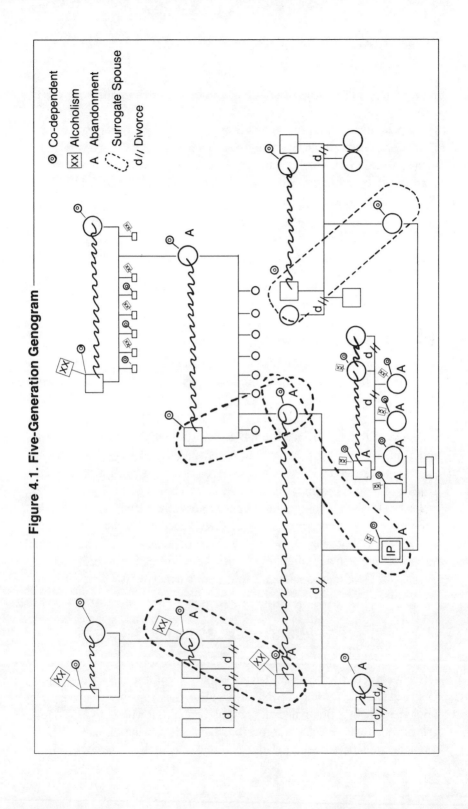

natural drive will be toward self-completion, rather than affirming each other.

If a person is in the process of self-completion, he can help the other to self-completion. In fact, a more realistic concept of marriage would be a state of union in which each partner is providing the other with the opportunity of self-actualization or self-completion. This is possibly what Goethe meant when he said:

> "Once the realization is accepted that even between the closest human beings infinite distances continue to exist, a wonderful living side by side can grow up, if they succeed in loving the distance between them which makes it possible for each to see the other *whole* against the sky. A good marriage is that in which each appoint the other guardian of his solitude."

This is also the sense of differentiation we wrote about in the previous chapter. Two people who have good differentiation are aware of . . .

1. Their feelings as distinct from their thoughts.
2. Their physical, emotional, intellectual selves as different from their partners.
3. Their own self-responsibility for their own happiness.

People with such differentiated selves are truly individuated and undependent. Being individuated and undependent does not mean that each does not need the other to love and care for. It means that while desiring to love and care for each other and to be loved and cared for by each other, each *knows* they can survive alone. Each knows he is responsible for his own perceptions, feelings, concepts and fantasies. Each knows he is responsible for his own life and happiness. Each knows that the other *cannot* make him happy. Each knows that the other is *not* his better half. Differentiation means that each partner has worked through his own fantasy bond.

Arithmetic Lesson

The notion of husbands and wives being the other's "better half" actually exposes the common fallacy of our cultural script on marriage. Our rigid sex roles promote two half-people joining together to make one whole-person, as if one-half times one-half equaled a whole. In fact, one-half times one-half equals one-fourth, which is less than one-half. So two people who marry to be completed, end up less complete than when they were incomplete. This explains a lot of the massive marriage failure that our national statistics report.

Two half-people create an *entrapment* or *enmeshment*, rather than a relationship. In an entrapment, neither person has the freedom to get out. *Each is entrapped by needing the other for completion.* As the years roll on and the fear of going it alone increases, each becomes more and more trapped. I see many entrapments in my marriage counseling. Such couples actually can't *divorce*. They are held together in an emotional symbiosis. They re-enact the fantasy bond we described in the introduction. They become bonded by their neediness. The symbol I like for entrapment is the symbol of two people in a canoe. Whenever one moves, the other is forced to move.

In a healthy relationship, each person is bonded by desire and not out of neediness. Therefore, each is in the process of becoming more or less whole. Two whole people who guard each other's wholeness come together and grow because of the guardianship of the other. Each, as Goethe suggests, provides the other the solid space (solitude) to grow. Each helps the other grow by giving up control, criticism, blame and judgment. In such a non-judgmental space one is free to exercise the five freedoms.

With such freedoms (which really amount to being loved unconditionally) one can accept oneself unconditionally. Unconditional self-acceptance is the royal road to wholeness. When one cannot feel, want, perceive, think or imagine what he is actually feeling, wanting, perceiving, thinking and imagining, one is split. The shoulds, oughts and musts become internal measuring rods which cause one to be split and alienated from self.

An inner warfare of self-talk insures a constant enervating struggle. Existence itself becomes problematic rather than spontaneous. Everything must be hassled about. Should I or shouldn't I plays like a broken record. One's self gets lost in the internal dialogue. One literally is be-side one's self. This is dysfunction.

Dysfunctionality in a family sets up shoulds, oughts and musts by which each member is measured. The poisonous pedagogy measures all perceptions, thoughts, feelings, decisions and imaginings. "You shouldn't feel that way" or "why do you want such and such . . ." or "how can you be so stupid" or "you're just a dreamer", etc., etc., etc. In such an environment, your natural powers are continuously discounted and judged as unacceptable. If you can't feel angry, your anger is split off and numbed by ego defenses. Your anger is no longer a part of you. The same is true of your sexual feelings, your fearful feelings, your sad feelings, your thoughts, your desires, your visions. As we pointed out in Chapter One, once you can't feel what you feel, your ego defenses take over and you become psychically numb.

When people marry out of deficiency and incompleteness (as I suggested, they inevitably find each other), the relationship is headed for trouble. Each needs the other for completion. In courtship each is willing to *give* because of the long range fantasy that by *giving* each will ultimately *get* the other to complete them. This giving to get is one of the most troublesome and deceptive dynamics in relationships. Giving to get is a counterfeit form of love. However, each *needy* partner is conned by the illusion that the other is actually going to fulfill their incomplete self.

Courtship is a very deceptive and confused form of counterfeit love. Being "in love" is not love. It is probably a form of genetic bonding. Nature wants babies. So people "in love" have very powerful erotic drives for each other. When we are "in love", sex is "oceanic" in its feeling. Being "in love" is characterized by strong emotion. Actually the emotion is undifferentiated from reason. One is literally "out of one's mind" when one is in love. This out-of-mind state restores the primal symbiosis of the mother/child. If one is still in a state of undifferentiation apropos of this early state, they will feel that all of the deprived emotional needs of that earliest state can be fulfilled. Such a phenomena as this is worth short-term giving up. One's very boundaries have collapsed. And so the story goes.

Power Struggles and the Need for Completion

Then comes marriage and the boundaries bounce back. Sally Hatfield is married to Bill McCoy. Now comes the power struggle between the two original families. The attitudinal behavioral and emotional rules for families swing into full consciousness. Each one feels 'at home' with their own *familiar* boundaries. Each family of origin system now vies for supremacy. The way my family did it is what *feels right*. It's what is *family-iar*. The power struggle begins and the issue of differences must be negotiated. The "selected awareness" of being "in love" has given way to the new focus on actual differences.

The ability to accept others as different in whatever way they are different depends on one's own level of differentiation. Two people with low level differentiation cannot handle each other's differences.

As the power struggle intensifies, both partners despair of ever getting the other to complete them. Either consciously or unconsciously, each begins to believe that by having a child or children, he can get completed. This belief is the beginning of the children's dysfunctionality.

Born in the soil of their parents' alienated split selves, there is no way for the children to get what they absolutely need for healthy growth. More than anything else they actually need models of good self-love and social interest. Since their parents are split and non-self-accepting, they cannot model good self-nurturing love. There *is no way for the children to learn self-love and social interest.* What they will learn is various forms of counterfeit love resulting from their parents weak incomplete ego contaminations. They will be shamed, through abandonment and ultimately they will internalize the shame just as their parents did.

When children cannot get their dependency needs met, they become dysfunctional. And this is the best scenario we can paint. Add to this physical, sexual and emotional abuse, and we're talking about severe damage to being fully functional.

All parental mistreatment and abuse stems from the parents' own needs for completion. And the parents need completion because their own needs were never met. Their own needs were never met because their needy parents were not there for them.

Parents, in abusing their own children, are struggling to regain the power they once lost to their own parents. All dysfunctional parents have been cheated out of their own feelings through their abandonment.

As children they were humiliated, laughed at, manipulated, intimidated, brushed aside, ignored, played with like a doll, treated like an object, sexually exploited or brutally beaten. What is worse, they were never allowed to express their rage, shame and hurt. Especially the hurt of why their own parents were treating them so terribly. Beneath that hurt lies the magical egocentric belief that they must be very bad to be treated this way. This is what survives in the child now become parent, *that they are bad.* As long as the parents are idealized in the fantasy bond, the child continues to blame self and feel shame.

Parents who were abused as children were not even allowed to know what was happening to them. Any mistreatment was held up as being necessary for their own good. When this mistreatment was most violent, they were told it hurt their parents as much as it hurt them. Or if that didn't work, they were taught to honor their parents no matter what. As children, their most fundamental need was their parents' protection, hence abandonment was equivalent to death. So they obeyed and denied their own awareness, (a) out of self-preservation, (b) because they possessed a magical and immature form of thinking and *because they in fact did love their parents.*

The child-rearing rules for the last 150 years, the poisonous pedagogy, made it impossible for people to remember the way they were actually treated by their parents. As adults, people act the same way their parents acted *in an attempt to prove that their parents behaved correctly toward them, i.e., really loved them and really did it for their own good.*

Alice Miller suggests that only when we have children of our own do we see for the *first time* the vulnerability of our earliest years (which has been dissociated or denied with the ego defenses that created the fantasy bond). In controlling our own children and putting them through what we went through, we struggle to regain the power and dignity we lost to our own parents.

Narcissistic Deprivation

Children *need* to have their healthy narcissistic needs met. Narcissus was the Greek God who was condemned to fall in love with his own reflection in the lake. The story is almost always interpreted in a way that makes narcissism, i.e., self-love seem bad. The story needs to be seen as a symbolic statement about emerging self-image and self-consciousness.

We humans would never know who we were without a mirror to look at in the beginning. That mirror needs to reflect ourselves as the person we really are at any given time. The original mirror is almost always the mothering person who raises us, especially in the first three years of life. The mothering person needs to mirror, admire and take us seriously. Each child needs to see his instinctual drives (orality, defecation, sexuality) and aggressive feelings mirrored in the mothering person's face. Obviously, this requires a high degree of security, self-confidence and completeness in the mothering person. When this is the case, Alice Miller writes, the child can:

1. Have his aggressive impulses so they don't upset parents' confidence.
2. Strive toward autonomy and be spontaneous because such strivings are not experienced as a threat to the parents.
3. Experience his true self — his *actual* feelings, wants, perceptions, thoughts and imaginings — because his parents do not impose moralistic shoulds, oughts and musts at a time when the child is pre-moral.
4. Learn to please himself and doesn't have to please his parents, since they are self-confident and complete.
5. Separate successfully from his parents, i.e., achieve differentiation.
6. Use his parents to meet his dependency needs, since his parents are complete and unneedy. These dependency needs are insatiable in the early years. The child needs his parents' time, attention and direction all the time during the early years.

The Drama of the Gifted Child (pp. 33, 34)

Obviously, this is a large order. Parents who never had these needs met are themselves needy. They therefore cannot give to their children what they do not have themselves. When the mothering persons have been deprived of their own healthy narcissism, they will try to get it for the rest of their lives through substitute means.

The most available object of gratification for narcissistically deprived parents is their own child or children. The children are in their control; will obey them because not to obey is equivalent to death; will never abandon them; will possibly extend their lives through achievement and performances. The child becomes the sole possession of the parents' lost narcissistic gratification.

The child thus becomes reduced to being an instrument of the parents' will. Once this occurs, the child's true self is abandoned and a false self must be created. The false self is a coverup for the being wound suffered by one's true self. If I can't have *my* feelings, *my* needs, *my* thoughts, *my* wants, then something must be wrong with *me*. I must be flawed as a person. I am worth-less than my parents' time and attention. I am worthless. This is internalized shame.

The tragedy of all this is that individuals or generations get caught up in a repetition compulsion, a vicious cycle of repeating over and over again the quest for the lost paradise, only to find that each substitute is an illusion. Compulsively seeking fame, status, new sex partners, a certainty of salvation, security in a political party, cannot give you that deep inner unity which was lost with your child self. The lost self is an inner problem, not an outer one. *Nothing* on the outside can bring back what was lost. Your lost childhood is lost forever.

The poet Omar Khayyam says,
"The moving finger writes and having writ moves on,
Nor all your piety nor wit shall lure it back to cancel half a line.
Nor all your tears wash out a word of it."

However, your tears are the beginning of your healing. And it is only through *mourning* that we can be completed and comforted. It is what many will have to do in order to leave home and break out of the fantasy bonded poisonous pedagogy.

What is crucial here is to see that dysfunctional parents reenact their own original pain on their children. It is very difficult for us to understand that every persecutor was once a victim. But understand it we must or the sins of the fathers go on and on. The abused child in the persecutor is angry and hurt. The anger is forbidden in relation to his parents. So since the anger is strictly forbidden, it is either projected onto others, turned against self or "acted out".

Dysfunctional marriages set up dysfunctional families. Dysfunctional families are the soil for abandonment. One is initiated into addiction through these dysfunctional parenting styles and the family systems they create. Addiction and obsessive compulsive disorders are symptoms of being abandoned and shamed in childhood.

Dysfunctional families have either enmeshed or walled boundaries within the system. Enmeshment is the term used to describe the violation of ego boundaries. Figure 4.2 shows a drawing of enmeshment. As you can see, all the boundaries are overrun. There is *no possibility* of intimacy in such a family because there are no whole people to relate to.

The other extreme of boundary problem is 'walled' boundaries. As you can see in Figure 4.3, the boundaries are so thick, there can be no interaction or intimacy. This family may look good on the outside. But on the inside each has lost contact with his true self. Each is playing his respective role. Each is in an 'act' and even though the boundaries are walled, each person is still ruled by the family system.

Members are playing rigid roles in enmeshed families. Their roles may be those of loving family members or good Christians. However, they are all in an act. No one is real — in touch with their real feelings, needs, or wants. Since all are pretending, no one really knows anyone else. As we

Figure 4.2. Dysfunctional Family System

Equifinality — no matter where one begins the conclusion is the same whether the subject is money, sex, in-laws, the pattern will be the same.

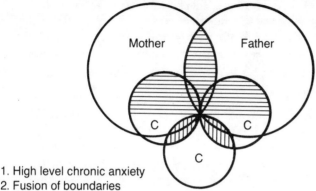

1. High level chronic anxiety
2. Fusion of boundaries
3. Confused and covert rules
4. System is rigid & static w/rigid roles
5. Undifferentiated ego mass
6. Loss of five freedoms
7. Pseudo-mutuality

Figure 4.3. Walled Boundaries

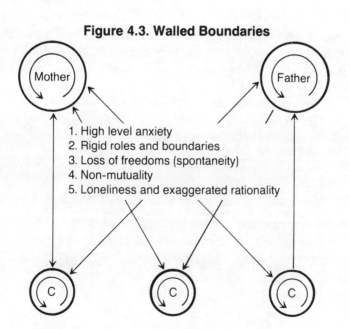

1. High level anxiety
2. Rigid roles and boundaries
3. Loss of freedoms (spontaneity)
4. Non-mutuality
5. Loneliness and exaggerated rationality

look at these families, we see a collage of images who are eternal strangers to each other. Each false self covers a core of secret inadequacy and shame. As Fossum and Mason write,

> "These people hold tenaciously and unconsciously to a narrow range of repetitive responses or games that serve to conceal, rather than reveal themselves to each other. After years everyone in the family knows each other's next line in the relational dialogue, and yet they remain imprisoned by the patterns."
>
> Facing Shame

Shame governs the entire family. The rigid roles are cover-up defenses against the shame core. Each person is in hiding and each is afraid to be his true self. All feel abandoned and alone at the deepest level. This shame is inherited generationally and is perpetrated through the rigid roles and ego defenses. Shame begets shame. The self-contempt experienced in shame is maintained through the idealization of the parents and their rules for parenting. The parents are of course shame-based themselves. Dysfunctional families are all shame-based and emotionally shut down. This sets up everyone in the system for compulsive/addictive behavior. Shame fuels addiction, which creates shame. Shame is the organizing principle in all dysfunctional families.

Boundary problems in families can be divided into three categories: the family/culture boundary; the intra-family boundaries, and the boundaries within the individual or ego boundaries. Figures 4.2 and 4.3 describe the intra-family boundaries. Feeling incomplete is an individual ego boundary problem. Not having the ability to differentiate thoughts, desires and feelings is an individual ego boundary problem. People with ego boundary problems contaminate their thinking with unresolved feelings, which cause the blocking of choice through the contamination of one's mind.

Loss of Freedom

The blocking of choice is what I call the "disabled will". Once our will is disabled, *we lose our freedom*. Since shame binds all emotions, everyone in a dysfunctional family has their freedom greatly impaired. This is perhaps the greatest casualty of dysfunctional families.

In the diagrams which follow (Figures 4.4, 4.5 and 4.6) I have tried to give you a visual picture of what happens to the power of choice when our feelings are repressed. In these diagrams I have borrowed freely from Harvey Jackins' presentation of blocked emotion in his book, *The Human Side of Human Beings*. Jackins has developed a powerful method of working through the blocked emotions from the past called Re-evaluation Counseling. He uses the diagrams I have borrowed from as the theoretical basis for his counseling theory. I have changed these drawings for my own purposes. While Jackins' focus is on the blocked emotion, my concern is on how the human will becomes disabled by the emotionally contaminated mind. I also believe that there is a higher level of consciousness beyond what Jackins describes in his drawings.

The following drawings are quite rough and surely are not intended to be scientific specimens. They will give the reader a visual glimpse of what happens to our will when the mind is blocked by emotion.

The will needs the eyes of perception, judgment, imagination and reasoning. Without this source, the will is blinded. The mind cannot use its perception, judgment, reasoning and imagination when it is under the impact of heavy emotion. The particular emotion, which is a form of energy, has to be discharged before the mind can function effectively. When the emotion is repressed it forms a frozen block which chronically mars the effective use of reasoning. Anyone who has had an outbreak of temper or been depressed has experienced how difficult it is to think under the power of these emotions.

In Figure 4.4 we see a model of what our raw intelligence looks like in an uncontaminated state. Our 3 trillion circuited, 13 billion celled computer brain is capable of a new and creative response to every new experience that occurs in our life.

Figure 4.4. Uncontaminated Raw Intelligence

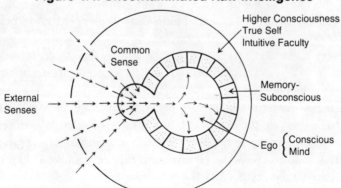

As we learn, the incoming data is given meaning and stored in our memory banks. When new information comes in, it is compared to what is already known and either stored accordingly or becomes a new bit of stored memory. When an experience is not resolved, it cannot be stored appropriately. Unresolved experience has to do with emotional discharge and meaning. The mind cannot function when biased by emotion. Our emotions are powers which give us readouts on our basic needs and move us to action.

When a child is abandoned through neglect, abuse or enmeshment, one of three transactions usually take place:

(1) Mythologies are created to explain the abandonment.
(2) The child is given reasons for the abandonment which makes no real sense and shames the child.
(3) The child is told he cannot express the feelings he has about the abandonment — usually fear, hurt (sadness) and anger.

In fact, all three transactions are aimed at repressing the child's true feelings, which are the core of his inner self.

Mythologies are meanings given to events or actions in order to distract from what is actually happening. For example, in a family dysfunctioned by work addiction, the work addict father, who is actually *emotionally abandoning his children,* is explained away by the enabling wife/mother by saying, "Your father works so much because he loves you and wants you to have nice things".

In the second case, the poisonous pedagogy has all kinds of reasons for the abuse. For example, "I'm doing this cause I love you" or "This hurts me more than you". In the third case, the emotionally blocked parents cannot handle their children's emotions. Mother's own sadness is stimulated by the child's crying. This is distressful. So Mom forbids the child to cry.

In every case, the distress experience cannot be stored *because the emotions cannot be discharged.* What occurs is a frozen pattern of blocked energy. (See Figure 4.5.)

This frozen pattern clogs one's creative intelligence. It forms a trigger which functions like the "on" button of a tape recorder. Whenever any new or similar experience happens, the old recording starts to play. Here we see the force and power of behavioral conditioning. Like Pavlov's dog, whenever stimulation occurs, the response automatically takes place. This is the basis of re-actions or re-enactments. The past so contaminates

Figure 4.5. Frozen Pattern of Blocked Energy

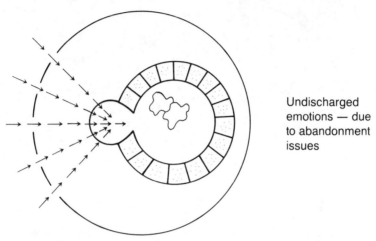

Undischarged
emotions — due
to abandonment
issues

the intelligence, that new and creative responses are not possible. Blocked emotions take over the reasoning and judgment of intelligence. And the effect is cumulative.

Whenever we are confronted with a new experience which is in any way similar to the original unresolved stress, we feel *compulsively* forced to reenact the old experience. We act compulsively; we do the exact same things that never worked before; we say things that are not pertinent and we have intense feelings that are totally disappropriate to what is actually happening.

It's like a snowball rolling downhill getting larger and larger. Once shamed, we act out of shame and create more shame. Once a false self is created to cover the secret private self, each new shaming event solidifies the false self even more. With each new abuse that precipitates anger and sadness, the old triggers are turned on and the old frozen record starts to play. This is the basis of what we refer to as over-reactions. Over the course of a number of years of repressing one's emotions, one's intelligence is greatly contaminated and diminished. The frozen patterns become chronic patterns. It is as if the "on" button becomes stuck and plays all the time. This is what I am calling "internalized shame". Figure 4.6 shows how little intelligence is left uncontaminated.

Figure 4.6. Chronic Frozen Emotions

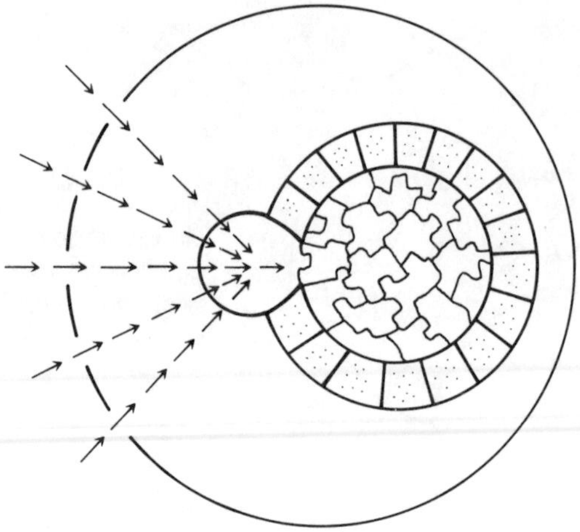

Chronic frozen emotions inhibit 90% of intelligence. When restimulated, we compulsively reenact the original stresses. The stored emotion plays like a record disc.

The Disabled Will

Such contamination seriously lessens one's decision-making process, since the will needs perception, intelligence and imagination in order to make decisions. The human *will* becomes 'disabled'.

Since the will is blind, it has no resource for its choice making. The only object left for the will to use is itself. As one wills to will, one becomes willful (literally full of will). As Leslie Farber points out in *The Ways of The Will*, the will becomes the self. With each act of willing for the sake of willing, one feels whole and complete. This is the basis of impulsiveness. To act on impulse is to will just because you can. In every 'act of will', the person feels complete. Just by willing one can get a feeling of oneness with self.

When one can only will to will, one has become grandiose. One plays God. Self-will has run riot. As Farber so brilliantly points out, *one has become addicted to one's own will.*

As children we are naturally willful, grandiose and absolutist. By not getting our developmental emotional needs met (especially the need to identify and express emotions), we are set up to become grandiose.

All adult children from dysfunctional families have the disabled will problem. The way it looks in actual life experience is:

(1) To be impulsive, to do things for no reason, to be gullible.
(2) To have trouble with decisions and to make faulty decisions especially apropos of trust.
(3) To attempt to control what cannot be controlled, e.g., an addict believes he can control his addiction, the spouse believes she can cure the addict. Parents believe they can control their children. We believe that we can control our emotions.
(4) To always look for the grand experience, the perfect wife, lover, child, parent, orgasm, etc.
(5) To be driven and compulsive.
(6) To see everything in extremes, black and white, good or bad, for me or against me, love everything about me or you don't love me.

Family Roles

What I have said thus far is that families have either rigid or enmeshed boundaries or some variation of both. The family members are selectively cut off from many of their feelings and in rigid role performances, such as The Hero, The Scapegoat, The Lost Child, etc. There are many kinds of roles.

In themselves roles are not bad and as Shakespeare wisely pointed out, we all play many roles in our lives. The roles in dysfunctional family systems are different. They are not chosen or flexible. They are necessitated by the covert or overt needs of the family as a system. They function to keep the family system in balance. If Dad is a workaholic and never home, one of the children will be Mom's Emotional Spouse since the system needs a marriage for balance.

In an alcoholic family one child will be a Hero because the family system needs some dignity. If the family system has no warmth, one child will become the emotional Caretaker and be warm and loving to everyone. If the system is ravaged with unexpressed anger and pain, one child will become the Scapegoat and act out all the anger and pain. In every case the person playing the role gives up his own unique selfhood. *In dysfunctional families, the individual exists to keep the system in balance.* This is the fate of every individual in a dysfunctional family. The whole family is dis-eased and each person gives up his true self to play a role in keeping the family together. Every single person becomes a co-dependent. Each person lives in reaction to the distress coming from chemical abuse, incest, violence, work addiction, eating disorders, the parents' rage or sickness, or whatever the compulsivity is.

In every case some form of control is being levied on the family. Control results from the disabled will and is one of the major defenses for shame. A shame-based person will attempt to control all the relationships he is in. Shame is the feeling of being flawed and worth-less. It demands that one hide and live in secret. One must guard never to be unguarded. In a moment of unguardedness, one could be exposed. This is too painful to bear. Shame-based parents control their children. Children in shame-based families play their rigid roles as a way of controlling their parents. Always being Helpful, always being a Hero, a Rebel, a Perfect Child, a Scapegoat, etc., is a way to control the family that controls you. This control madness is another way to show why dysfunctional families set their members up for an addiction. Addictions are ways to be out of control. Addictions provide relief.

Co-dependency is the major outcome of dysfunctional family systems. Suffice it to say that co-dependents no longer have their own feelings, needs and wants. They live in reaction to the family distress.

Each dysfunctional family member accepts his role. They learn what feelings their role demands and what feelings they may not have. For example, I became my family system's Hero. As a Hero, I had to be brave and strong. I had to learn to play a role of always being up and competent. In playing such a role, I had to give up my fear and vulnerability. Since these were real parts of me — I had to give up parts of myself. This role became my false self. It was an act whereby I played my enmeshed role in my alcoholic family's script. I denied my own co-dependency and came to believe that I was this super-competent person.

These roles are ways to survive the intolerable situation in a dysfunctional family. They function like ego defenses. They become part of the total family's fantasy bond. We are a happy family. We love each other. Each member plays his part to keep the system closed and rigid. Each member shares the mythology of the family trance. Each unconsciously agrees to share a certain focus and to share a certain denial. The denial constitutes the family systems 'vital lies'. Each member believes that if he exposed the lies, it would be unbearably painful and it would break up the family.

We see this most vividly when we look at incest families. The *shared secret* and the *shared denial* is the most horrible aspect of incest. Perhaps nothing so accurately characterizes dysfunctional families as denial. This denial is often referred to as the delusional thinking of the dysfunctional family trance. The delusion is to keep believing the myths and vital lies in spite of the facts, or to keep expecting that the same behaviors will have different outcomes. Dad's not an alcoholic; he never drinks in the morning, in spite of the fact that he's drunk every night.

This delusion and denial also applies to our false self roles. We become so identified with each role that we could pass a lie detector test. Our true self has been buried so long in the unconscious family trance, we think the role is who we really are.

Cultural and Subcultural Boundaries

The dysfunctional family system has a third boundary. This one exists as an invisible line around the whole family. I call it the cultural or subcultural boundary. Nationalities and religious affiliations are the strongest factors in this type of boundary. Italians, Greeks, Irishmen, etc. have their own special rules and 'vital lies'. Likewise with Pentecostalists, Catholics, Baptists, Mormons, Jews, etc. These subculture boundaries control the flow of information coming into and going out of the family. These boundaries also govern behaviors with the 'other' — the strangers, the ones outside of our clan. These boundaries can contribute greatly to the family's level of dysfunctionality.

For example, a client of mine who was a rigid Christian Fundamentalist, engaged in incest with her father because she had no right to disobey him. Her interpretation of her religion supported the poisonous pedagogy belief in parental ownership.

These subculture boundaries contribute greatly to keeping the system closed. They control knowledge and information. A major factor in getting out of a dysfunctional family is awareness about abuse and dysfunctionality. If one's religion prohibits reading psychological works as part of secular humanism, then one cannot possibly be made aware of many kinds of abuse and family dysfunction.

Thus, it is a characteristic of dysfunctional family systems that *the more they try to change, the more they stay the same*. They have no new information to break the old beliefs that form the circular feedback loops in the cybernetic system. If parents are sacred and must be honored at any cost, one cannot even look at the possibility that they were abusing you.

The overt rules that create dysfunctionality are the rules of the poisonous pedagogy. The parents become dysfunctioned as a result of these erroneous rules, which they carry within their own psyches where they play like a recorder. The parents parent themselves with these rules. Without critically questioning and updating them, they pass them on to their children. They are like carriers of a virus. Add to this parents who are in advanced stages of addiction and the voltage is intensified.

The commonalities of dysfunctional families we have been describing can be summarized as a body of covert rules that operate unconsciously to create the distress in families. These rules are:

1. CONTROL

One must be in control of all interactions, feelings and personal behavior at all times. This is the cardinal rule of all dysfunctional shame-based family systems. Control is the major defensive strategy for shame. Once you control feelings, all spontaneity is lost. Control gives each member a sense of power, predictability and security. Control madness is a form of severe disability of the will since it tries to will away what cannot be willed away, viz, the fundamental insecurity and unpredictability of life.

2. PERFECTIONISM

Always be "right" in everything you do. This tyranny of being right can be about any norms the multigenerational family system has preserved. The norm may be about intellectual achievement or moral self righteousness or being upper class and rich, etc. The perfectionistic rule always involves a measurement that is being imposed. There is a competitive aspect to this rule. There is a one-up, better-than-others aspect to this rule that covers the shame.

The members in the system anxiously avoid what is bad, wrong or inferior. The fear and avoidance of the negative is the organizing principle of life. The members live according to an externalized image. They become self-image actualized. This amounts to a chronic life of dissociation from self. One is busy observing one's own actions in a situation while internally self-monitoring, "Am I coming across okay?"

"Am I getting it right?" One is constantly comparing self with an external norm in an attempt to measure up.

No rule leads to hopelessness any more powerfully than this one. The ideal is a mental creation. The ideal is ideal, rather than real. The ideal is shameless since it disallows mistakes. Remember what I said about shame as a healthy human feeling. Shame lets us know we are finite and incomplete. Shame lets us laugh at our mistakes. Shame tells us we are always in need of feedback and human community. Shame lets us know we are not God. Shame lets us know we are human. Following the perfectionism rule leads to hopelessness.

3. BLAME

Whenever things don't turn out as planned, blame yourself or others. Blame is another defensive cover-up for shame. A person's blaming behavior covers one's shame or projects it onto others. Since a shame-based person cannot feel vulnerable or needy without being ashamed, blame becomes an automatic way to avoid one's deepest feelings and true self. Blame maintains the balance in a dysfunctional system when control has broken down.

Life's spontaneity and unpredictability inevitably break down the control rule. Blame is habitually used to regain the illusion of control. Blame is how the shaming process continues to function. As each person feels the danger of vulnerability and exposure, he shames the other with blame.

4. DENIAL OF THE FIVE FREEDOMS

Deny feelings, perceptions, thoughts, wants and imaginings, especially the negative ones like fear, loneliness, sadness, hurt, rejection and dependency needs. This follows the perfectionist rule. "You shouldn't think, feel, desire, imagine, see things, hear things, the way you do. You should see, hear, feel, think, imagine, desire the way the Perfectionistic ideal demands."

5. NO-TALK RULE

Don't talk openly about any feelings, thoughts or experiences that focus on the pain and loneliness of the dysfunctionality. This rule is a corollary of rule number four. The denial of expression is a fundamental wound to humanness. Human beings are symbolic animals who speak and express ourselves in symbols. We create new life and new frontiers through the symbolic function of the imagination.

6. MYTH-MAKING

Always look at the bright side. Reframe the hurt, pain and distress in such a way as to distract everyone from what is really happening. This is a way to keep the balance. The system remains closed and rigid. Anyone rocking the boat would upset the status quo.

7. INCOMPLETION

Don't complete transactions. Keep the same fights and disagreements going for years. This rule may be manifested two ways: One is through chronic fighting and conflict without any real resolution. The second is through enmeshment and confluence — agreeing never to disagree. The family has either conflict or confluence, but never contact. Members stay upset and confused all the time.

8. UNRELIABILITY

Don't expect reliability in relationships. *Don't trust* anyone and you will never be disappointed. Since the parents never got their dependency needs met as children, they cover up this insatiability with fantasy bonded illusions of self-sufficiency. By acting either aloof and independent (walled boundaries) or needy and dependent (enmeshed boundaries), everyone feels emotionally cutoff and incomplete. No one gets their needs met in a functional manner.

Figure 4.7 which follows sums up the profile of a dysfunctional family. This chart is a composite of the actual types of dysfunctional families I will talk about in the next three chapters. The Rigid Roles are not listed accurately; they are simply listed. I encourage the reader to use these chapters as a checklist for your own personal self-discovery. Most of our present human dysfunctions can be described by the term compulsivity. Violence, sexual disorders, eating disorders, emotional and religious addictions are the ills which destroy peoples' lives. Let us look at these now.

Figure 4.7. Profile of a Dysfunctional Family System

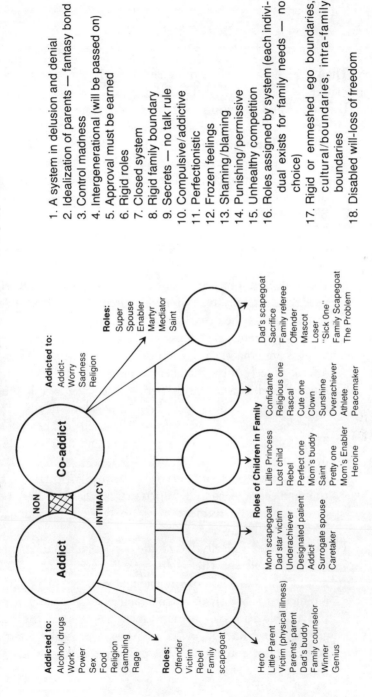

Addicted to:
Alcohol, drugs
Work
Power
Sex
Food
Religion
Gambling
Rage

Roles:
Offender
Victim
Rebel
Family scapegoat

Addict

NON

INTIMACY

Co-addict

Addicted to:
Addict-
Worry
Sadness
Religion

Roles:
Super
Spouse
Enabler
Martyr
Mediator
Saint

Roles of Children in Family

Hero
Little Parent
Victim (physical illness)
Parents' parent
Dad's buddy
Family counselor
Winner
Genius

Mom scapegoat
Dad star victim
Underachiever
Designated patient
Addict
Surrogate spouse
Caretaker

Little Princess
Lost child
Rebel
Perfect one
Mom's buddy
Saint
Pretty one
Mom's Enabler
Heroine

Confidante
Religious one
Rascal
Cute one
Clown
Sunshine
Overachiever
Athlete
Peacemaker

Dad's scapegoat
Sacrifice
Family referee
Offender
Mascot
Loser
"Sick One"
Family Scapegoat
The Problem

1. A system in delusion and denial
2. Idealization of parents — fantasy bond
3. Control madness
4. Intergenerational (will be passed on)
5. Approval must be earned
6. Rigid roles
7. Closed system
8. Rigid family boundary
9. Secrets — no talk rule
10. Compulsive/addictive
11. Perfectionistic
12. Frozen feelings
13. Shaming/blaming
14. Punishing/permissive
15. Unhealthy competition
16. Roles assigned by system (each individual exists for family needs — no choice)
17. Rigid or enmeshed ego boundaries, cultural/boundaries, intra-family boundaries
18. Disabled will-loss of freedom

All Members of the Family are Co-dependent

Summary

The key points covered in this chapter can be summed up using the letters of the word **DYSFUNCTIONAL.**

D. Denial and Delusion — Dysfunctional families deny their problems. Hence the problems never get solved. Such families also deny members the five freedoms.

Y. Yin/Yang Disorder — There is always an intimacy vacuum in a dysfunctional family. The intimacy vacuum creates the dysfunction.

S. Shame-based — Non-functional families are shame-based. The parents have internalized their shame and act *shameless* toward their children. The children often feel ashamed of the family.

F. Fixed, Frozen and Rigid Roles — Roles are created by the needs of the family as a system. Children give up their reality to take care of the needs of the system.

U. Undifferentiated Ego Mass — Members of dysfunctional families are enmeshed in each others boundaries. If Mom is scared, all feel scared. Members feel for other members.

N. Needs Sacrificed to the System — Members of a dysfunctional family cannot get their individual needs met. Individual needs are put aside for the needs of the system. There is almost always low grade anger and depression in a dysfunctional family.

C. Confluence or Conflicted Communication — The communication style in dysfunctional families is either open conflict or the agreement never to disagree (confluence). There is rarely any real contact.

T. Togetherness Polarity Dominates — Individual differences are sacrificed for the needs of the family system. In dysfunctional families, the individual exists for the family. It is difficult to leave dysfunctional families.

I. Irrevocable Rules — In non-functional families, the rules are rigid and unchanging. Such rules are usually control, perfectionism and blame. The poisonous pedagogy sets up these rules.

O. Open Secrets — The open secrets are part of the vital lie which keeps the family frozen. Apropos of open secrets, everyone knows what everyone pretends not to know.

N. Non-changing Closed System — Everyone plays their role to control the controlling distress. But the more each plays his role, the more the system stays the same. The French proverb, "Plus ca change, plus c'est la même chose" (the more something changes, the more it remains the same) sums up the dilemma of the closed family system.

A. Absolute and Grandiose Will — The major catastrophe of the dysfunctional family is that all members have their wills disabled. Control itself is a product of the disabled will. The denial of conflict and frustration creates a situation in which one wills to will. This gives one the illusion of doing something about the problem. It is a way to feel whole when one is actually split.

L. Lack of Boundaries — Members of dysfunctional families give up their ego boundaries as a way to maintain the family system. Giving up ego boundaries is equivalent to giving up one's identity.

5

Compulsive Families

Checklist For How You Lost Yourself And Became An Adult Child Of An Alcoholic Family

The open secrets. Everybody knows about them and nobody is supposed to know that everybody knows.

After 17 bitter years of long-suffering alcoholism, I put the cork in the bottle 21 years ago. In many ways the last thing I would have believed as a child was that I would become an alcoholic. I cried myself to sleep many a night because of my father's drinking and his abandonment. I laid in bed frozen with fear waiting for him to come home at night, never knowing what exactly was going to happen. I hated alcoholism and all it stood for. I obsessed about his drinking day in and day out. At 30 years old, after studying for almost 10 years to be a priest, I wound up in Austin State Hospital on a voluntary commitment for the treatment of alcoholism!

As paradoxical as it seems, *many* a child of an alcoholic becomes an alcoholic. And if they don't become an alcoholic, they marry an alcoholic or a person with some other compulsive addictive personality disorder.

This paradoxical pattern of adults who grew up in alcoholic families has focused on the truth of 'families as systems' more than any other single factor. Some 10 years ago one adult child after another began to realize that there were commonalities in their lives that seemed to have less to do with them and more to do with their families of origin. Led by Robert Ackerman, Claudia Black, Sharon Wegscheider-Cruse and Janet Woititz, the Adult Children of Alcoholics (ACoA) became a movement, which at this moment is continuing to sweep the country. With the Adult Children's movement the family systems concept took a giant step forward.

During the first decade of my recovery from alcoholism, I knew nothing of the Adult Children's phenomena. I had dabbled intellectually with family systems. I had incorporated the work of Virginia Satir, Jay Haley and Ronald Laing into my adult theology classes at Palmer Episcopal Church in Houston. But I never got the connection with my own alcoholic family of origin. I thought that my addiction to excitement, my people-pleasing and approval-seeking, my overly developed sense of responsibility, my severe intimacy problems, my frantic compulsive lifestyle, my severe self-criticalness, my frozen feelings, my incessant good-guy act and my intense need to control were just personality quirks. I never dreamed that they were characteristics common to adults, who as children lived in alcoholic families.

My compulsivity was a problem that was having life-damaging consequences. I was working, buying, smoking and eating compulsively. Even though I was recovering from alcoholism, I was still acutely compulsive. I was still an addict. This realization led me to seek further treatment for my still addicted personality.

It has been the work in chemical dependency and especially the ACoA movement that has helped me understand the nature of compulsivity and how it is set up in dysfunctional family systems. The fact that there are common characteristics of children who grew up in alcoholic families betrays an underlying structure of disorder. I've outlined some using the first letters of the phrase **Adult Children of Alcoholics.**

A   Addictive, compulsive behavior or marry addicts
D   Delusion and denial
U   Unmercifully judgmental on self or others
L   Lack of good boundaries
T   Tolerate inappropriate behavior

C   Constantly seek approval
H   Have difficulty with intimate relationships
I   Incur guilt whenever you stand up for yourself
L   Lie when it would be just as easy to tell the truth
D   Disabled will
R   Reactors rather than actors
E   Extremely loyal to a fault
N   Numbed out

O   Over-react to changes over which you have no control
F   Feel different from other people

A   Anxious — hypervigilant
L   Low self-worth and internalized SHAME
C   Confuse love and pity
O   Overly serious
H   Have difficulty finishing project
O   Overly dependent and terrified of abandonment
L   Live life as victims
I   Intimidated by anger and personal criticism
C   Control madness
S   Super-responsible or super-irresponsible

From this checklist it's clear that as children of alcoholics, we are not just reacting to the drinking of the alcoholic. What we're reacting to are the relational issues, the anger, the control issues, the emotional unavailability of the addict. These traits are a response to the trauma of the abandonment and ensuing shame that occurs in alcoholic families.

For the children this shame is primarily rooted in the broken relationship with their parents. Our index of traits shows that most of the problems ACoAs have are relationship problems. These traits also give us a clue to understanding the roots of compulsivity. The World Health Organization's definition of compulsive/addictive behavior is "a pathological relationship to any mood-altering experience that has life-damaging consequences."

The propensity for *pathological relationships* is rooted in and set up by the parental abandonment. Let us look at our index of traits.

A. Addictive, Compulsive or Marry Addicts — You are or have been in an active compulsive/addictive pattern of behavior. You are or have been in a relationship with a compulsive/addicted person.

D. Delusion and Denial — You are in a fantasy bonded idealization of your parents. You idealize your non-addicted parent. You minimize and deny your feelings and the impact on your life and/ or your children's lives of a relationship you are in.

U. Unmercifully Judgmental on Yourself and Others

L. Lack Good Boundaries — *You* take an aspirin when your spouse has a headache. You don't know where your feelings end and others begin. You let everyone touch you or let no one touch you. Your opinion is the same as whoever you are with.

T. Tolerate Inappropriate Behavior — You guess at what normal is. In your relationships you are now tolerating what you said you would never tolerate. You believe that your childhood was more or less normal.

C. Constantly Seek Approval — You are a people-pleaser and will go to almost any lengths to have people like you. In your primary relationships, you drive others crazy with your need to know where you stand.

H. Have Difficulty with Intimate Relationships — You confuse intimacy with enmeshment and contact with conformity. You believe that if you love someone, you will both like the same things. You are attracted to destructive relationships, and are turned off by healthy, stable, caring people. You sabotage any relationship that starts to get too close.

I. Incur Guilt When You Are Autonomous — You feel guilt whenever you stand up for yourself, act assertive and ask for what you want. You feel guilty that you are in recovery and the rest of your family is not.

L. Lie When You Could Tell the Truth — You find yourself lying for no good reason when it would be just as easy to tell the truth. Or you are just the opposite. You adhere to the letter of the truth.

D. Disabled Will — You are compulsive, impulsive, stubborn, grandiose, overly dramatic, controlling and have difficulty making decisions. You try to control what cannot be controlled.

R. Reactive Rather Than Creative — Your life is one reaction after another. You over-react — you say things that are not relevant, feel things that are disproportionate to what is going on. You spend so much time worrying and reminiscing over others' behavior, you have no time for your own.

E. Extremely Loyal to a Fault — You stay loyal even in the face of evidence to the contrary or you are loyal to no one.

N. Numbed Out — You are psychically numb. You deny your feelings. You don't know what you feel and wouldn't know how to express your feelings even if you did know.

O. Over-react to Changes Over Which You Have No Control

F. Feel Different from Others — You never feel like you really belong. You always feel self-conscious. You are secretly jealous and envious of other's seeming normalcy.

A. Anxious and Hypervigilant — You are always on guard. You have an intense level of nameless fear and catastrophic expectation. You have a feeling of impending doom. You are jumpy and easily startled. You enjoy your vacations most after they are over and you are showing the slides!

L. Low Self-worth and Internalized SHAME — You feel defective as a human being. You cover up with roles like Caretaking, Super-responsible One, Hero, Star, Heroine, The Perfect One. You are perfectionistic, controlling, power-seeking, critical and judgmental, rageful, secretly or openly contemptuous, gossipy and backbiting.

C. Confuse Love with Pity — You are attracted to weak people. You go to great lengths to help pitiful-looking people. You enter relationships with people you can fix. You mistake pity for love.

O. Overly Rigid and Serious or Just the Opposite — You are somber and rarely play and have fun. Life is problematic, rather than spontaneous. You are perfectionistic and super-responsible. Or you are irresponsible and never take things seriously enough.

H. Have Difficulty Finishing Things — You have trouble initiating action. You have trouble stopping once you've started. You never quite finished important things, like getting degrees.

O. Overly Dependent, Clinging and Terrified of Abandonment — You stay in relationships that are life-damaging, severely dysfunctional and damaging to you. You have trouble ending anything. You stay in a job that has no future. You are possessive, suspicious and cling to the relationships you are in — spouse, lover, children, friends.

L. **Live Life As a Victim** — You have been physically, sexually, emotionally abused. You live in a Victim Role, finding yourself victimized wherever you are. You are attracted to other victims.

I. **Intimidated by Anger and Personal Criticism** — You are manipulated by anger and criticism. You will go to great lengths to stop someone from being angry at you or critical of you. You will give up your needs to stop their anger or criticalness.

C. **Control Madness** — You fear losing control. You control by being 'helpful'. You feel frightened when you feel out of control. You avoid anyone or any situation where you can't be in control.

S. **Super-Responsible or Super-Irresponsible** — You take responsibility for everything and everyone. You try to solve other's problems even when they don't ask for help. Or you take no responsibility and expect others to be responsible for you.

From this index, researchers began to see just how dysfunctional one becomes simply by living in an alcoholic family. This index helps to focus the causes for compulsive behavior.

The alcoholic family is a compulsive family. Everyone in the system is driven by the distress caused by not being able to get his needs met. Someone compared living in an alcoholic family to living in a concentration camp. And like survivors of a concentration camp, ACoAs carry what has been compared to post-traumatic stress symptoms. In fact, if one takes a list of the disorders experienced by war veterans or any other severe trauma victims, one will find that a large number of the post-trauma symptoms match a large number of ACoA characteristics. Children who live in alcoholic families, if untreated as children, carry these characteristics of post-trauma stress into later life.

Abandonment

Because of the chronic distress in an alcoholic family, every person in that family attempts to adapt to the chronic stress. Each becomes hypervigilant, anxious and chronically afraid. In such an environment, it's impossible for anyone to get his basic human needs met. Each person becomes co-dependent.

The major consequence of this chronic stress is abandonment. Along with the actual physical abandonment by the alcoholic, the neglect of the child's basic needs is another form of abandonment. There is no one there for the child. There is no mirroring to affirm the child's preciousness and no one the child can depend on. If Dad's the alcoholic, Mom is addicted to Dad — Mom is co-dependent. She can't be there for her children's needs because she is also an addict.

As addicts, both parents are needy and shame-based. It is impossible for two needy, shame-based people to give love and model self-love.

The normal child has healthy narcissistic needs, but there is no way these needs can be met in an alcoholic family. So each child turns inward to a fantasy bond of connection with their parents (delusion and denial) and ultimately to self-indulging habits and pain killers.

A third form of abandonment comes from abuse. Alcoholic families foster every kind of abuse. Because alcohol lowers inhibitions and knocks out the rheostat between thoughts and expression, physical, sexual and emotional battering are commonplace in alcoholic families. Some estimates say that two-thirds of ACoAs are physically violated. Some 50% of incest fathers are alcoholic.

Alcoholic families are severely enmeshed. Enmeshment is another way the children are abandoned. As the alcoholic marriage becomes more entangled and entrapped, the children get caught up in the needs of both their parents, as well as the needs of the family system for wholeness and balance. Nature abhors a vacuum. When the family system is unbalanced, the children attempt to create a balance.

In my family my dad was never there. By about age 11, he was for all practical purposes gone. I was the oldest male. The system needed a husband. I became my mother's emotional husband (Surrogate Spouse). My mom did not decide this, the system demanded it. I also became my brother's "Little Parent" since the system needed fathering. At 13 I was giving him an allowance.

In another family I worked with as the drinking husband's alcoholism intensified, the oldest daughter became Mom's Scapegoat. Mom had been pregnant with her at the time of her marriage. In fact, she was the reason Mom and Dad got married. As Mom realized Dad was an irresponsible alcoholic, she turned her anger onto the girl child.

Another child was not planned. He was the accidental third child in a very dysfunctional marriage. He felt the emotional abandonment in the womb. He became a 'Lost Child' in the family. Literally the parental message he got was "Get lost, child, we can't handle another child."

In alcoholic families the discipline is modeled by *unself*-disciplined disciplinarians. The rules of the poisonous pedagogy offer justification for a lot of the so-called discipline. Very little of it is really discipline. It comes out of the parents' irritation and rage about their own life. Most of the time it has nothing to do with the child, i.e., it doesn't come from his behavior or help the child improve. Punishment occurs frequently and is usually inconsistent. The parents model this inconsistency.

What all this adds up to is that the children, who need their parents' time, attention and direction for at least 15 years, do not get it. They are abandoned. Abandonment sets up compulsivity. Since the children need their parents all the time, and since they do not get their needs met, they grow up with a cup that has a hole in it. They grow up to have adult bodies. They look like and talk like adults, but there is within them an insatiable little child who never got his or her needs met. This hole in the soul is the fuel that drives the compulsivity. The person looks for more and more love, attention, praise, booze, money, etc.

The drivenness comes from the emptiness. And since one cannot be a child again and cannot go back and have a mom or a dad, the needs cannot be filled *as a child.* They *can* be dealt with as they are recycled in adult life. But they can only be dealt with *as an adult.*

The Compulsive Family in General

I've used the alcoholic family as a prototype of the compulsive family. Historically the studies in chemically dependent families began to reveal the dysfunctional structure of other types of families. Through studying alcoholism and the alcoholic family, a whole range of compulsive/ addictive patterns emerged to explain other dysfunctional families.

The pattern was clear. Shame-based compulsive people create needy marriages and engender families in which children are shamed through abandonment. The victimized children from these marriages become equally compulsive and continue the cycle.

The poisonous pedagogy, with its master/slave inequality, is intensified in families parented by addicts. However, *these addicts were set up for addiction by being discounted and having their needs denied by the poisonous pedagogy. The original culprit is the poisonous pedagogy.*

Power, control, perfectionism, criticism, contempt, blame, rage are all ways that shame is interpersonally transferred. Parents who are covering up their shame with their own fantasy bonded ego defenses, their own rigid roles and their addictions become *shameless*. Acting as if they know it all, criticizing, controlling, condemning, blaming and punishing, these parents play God. Such shameless behavior necessitates that the children carry the shame.

Let's take rage for example. Rage is common in alcoholic families. It is also a common addiction in itself. A rage-aholic can dysfunction a family every bit as severely as an alcoholic father. Rage serves a self-protective function by insulating the self against exposure and by actively keeping others away. For example, father goes on a drunken spree. He misses several days of work. When he goes to work, his boss chews him out. As he comes home he feels the shame of his behavior. He sees his son's bicycle lying in the front yard. He seeks out his son and begins raging at him, using his poisonous pedagogical rights. This spontaneous behavior enables father to feel good about himself (doing his fatherly duty) and lose all contact with the pain of his own shame. The son, however, takes on father's shame by being shamed. Rage is a strategy of defense aimed at making the son feel shame in order to reduce the father's shame.

Since there is so much shame present in an alcoholic family, the interpersonal transfer of shame goes on continuously. The poisonous pedagogy actually supports the parents in their strategies of interpersonal transference of shame. Power, control, blame, criticism and perfectionism are encouraged and promoted by the poisonous pedagogy.

Children idealize parents through the fantasy bond and therefore they will pass the rage, hurts, loneliness and shame of their own abandonment onto their own children. Instead of *passing it back where it belongs, they pass it on.*

You've probably noticed, *I use the words compulsive and addictive synonymously*. The word addiction is often limited to those disordered relationships to chemical substances (nicotine, foods, drugs) that have their own intrinsic addictive potency. While there is some clarity in such a distinction, it can cover up other addictive behaviors, such as addiction to work, rage, adrenalin rush, sex, etc. I would bet that the chemical structure of the mood alteration resulting from the excitement of sex, gambling, work achievement, religious ecstasy, the feeling of righteousness, being in love, is similar to the chemical change resulting from drugs. As far as I'm concerned, all addictions are ways to avoid unacceptable feelings. That avoidance leads to life-damaging consequences.

As we've discovered the crisis in the family is the fostering of shame by means of abandonment. This shame sets up the compulsive/addictive behavior which dominates our culture. I've already given some statistics on the extent of alcoholism, eating disorders, physical violence, incest and sexual abuse. The majority of our culture is addicted because we still use the parenting rules of 150 years ago in a world that has been ravished by those rules.

Compulsive/Addictive Behavior

I believe that our greatest human problems focus on compulsive/addictive behavior. Addictions narrow our minds and disable our wills. We are driven and out of control. Our life is no longer a conscious choice but a multigenerational accident. We are no longer free.

It is false thinking to believe that addiction is only about dope fiends in dark alleys or belligerent and stumbling drunks. *Addiction touches the lives of most of the people in our culture.*

In my own work as president of the Palmer Drug Abuse Program, I found a very stereotyped conception of addiction. While we were dealing with teenagers abusing chemicals, we were also dealing with their parents and families. All around me I found work addiction, religious addiction, eating disorders, co-dependent people addicts, parents addicted to their children, cigarette addicts, rageaholics, etc.

I knew I had to expand the definition of addiction. I knew that if people could identify their own compulsivities — their own life-damaging relationships with mood-altering experiences, I could create a community of concern about *our common crisis.*

An addiction is *any* pathological relationship with *any* mood-altering experience that has life-damaging consequences. The pathological relationship part is set up by the abandonment issues. The inability to relate in a healthy manner is the result of shame, since shame is always the result of broken relationships. Once the interpersonal bridge is broken with caretakers or survival figures, children believe that they do not have the right to depend on anyone. They quit trusting themselves and others. They are set up for the fantasy bond and self-indulging patterns of behavior. They are set up for pathological relationships.

Pathological implies a delusional quality to the relationship. Delusion and denial are the essence of addictive compulsive behavior. In denial one denies that what one is doing is really harmful, either to self or others. In delusion we keep believing that what is happening is not happening in spite of the facts. Firestone's 'fantasy bond' is a form of delusion and denial. In my opinion, all addictions are fantasy bond reenactments.

The fantasy bond is re-enacted in several ways. It can come with the grandiosity of being in love; the ecstasy of feeling good and righteous; sexual conquest and orgasm; the *full-filled* feeling of eating; the altered state of consciousness induced by starving; the magical possession of money and things; the high of drugs. In all compulsive/addictive behavior, the illusion of connection is restored. One is not alone; one has overcome separation and aloneness. Delusion and denial keep away the 'legitimate suffering', which comes with feeling the pain of emptiness and aloneness. Addicts minimize the effects of their compulsivity in their life. They rationalize the life-denying consequences of their behavior.

Compulsive/addictive behaviors are not about being hungry, thirsty, "horney" or needing to work. They are about mood-alteration. They help us manage our own feelings. They distract us or alter the way we are feeling so that we don't have to feel the loneliness and emptiness of our abandonment and shame.

The mood alteration that comes from distraction is mostly unrecognized in our culture. We promote hard work and competitive achievement. We are a God-fearing worshipping nation. We are sports-minded and have an array of entertainment which the whole world seeks and envies. All of these activities *can become* addictions. They are all ways that we can become involved in adrenalin rush and excitement and distract ourselves from whatever we are feeling.

Gambling (which claims some 10 to 13 million addicts) is perhaps the most dramatic. For gamblers "the action is the distraction". The fact is that any activity can distract and therefore mood alter. Work addiction and religious addiction are major addictions in our country.

Emotional Addictions

Emotions themselves can be addictive. We can substitute one emotion for a less painful emotion. Men are frequently taught to substitute anger for fear. Most everyone has met an angry man. Such men have internalized their anger. Men are supposed to be warriors. Warriors have to be super strong and totally adequate. Any hint of inadequacy would make one less a man. Men are afraid of feeling inadequate and can cover that feeling up with anger. Anger feels powerful. Inadequacy feels weak.

I came home from work one summer evening and my wife greeted me at the door with the news that our air conditioner had stopped working. It was in the middle of summer, humid and unbearably hot. A voice in my head tells me, "Real men know how to fix mechanical things." Since I can't fix anything mechanical, I feel inadequate. I don't even know where our air conditioner is. So instead of saying, "Gee honey, that's awful. Let's go to a hotel and call someone to get it fixed," I say angrily, "What did you do to it now? Can't I count on you for anything?" Anger feels potent, fear feels wimpy. This example shows you how anger works as a mood alterer.

Any feeling can be an addiction for other feelings. Women often cry when they are angry. One person may be a full-fledged sad addict. I'm sure you've met a 'sad sack' — a person who is always sad. That's an addiction. Chemicals, activity and emotions are powerful ways not to feel what one is feeling. Remembering that abandonment is the set-up for compulsivity helps us to see why we want to mood alter. When abandoned, we feel rejected, lonely, sad and angry. And, of course, we feel shame. Later as shame is internalized, we get all our feelings shamed. So to feel is to feel shame, loneliness, sadness, hurt and anger. Deep internalized shame is excruciatingly painful. Therefore, we want to mood alter.

Thought Disorders

There are also other ways to be compulsive. Certain thought disorders are excellent ways to distract and cut off emotions. Obsessive worrying, ruminating, getting engrossed in minute details, generalizing and abstract thinking, are all ways to cut off one's feelings.

Obsessive thought patterns play a major role in all compulsivities. The thought patterns in sexual addiction are called lusting. A sex addict may be in his head for hours lusting before he begins his ritualized behavior — cruising, going to get pornography, looking for a child to victimize. The lust is an addictive part of the addictive process.

The most crucial aspect of any compulsivity is the *life-damaging aspect of it*. Life-damaging means that the compulsive, addictive behavior causes personal dysfunction. The compulsivity blocks the person from getting his needs met through his own basic human powers. The compulsivity takes up all his energy. His choices are narrowed. His freedom is lost. His will has become disabled. The person is driven and his life is powerless and unmanageable. Without freedom one is dehumanized. Shakespeare wrote:

"Oh, God, that man should put an enemy in his mouth.
That we should with joy, pleasure, reveal, and applause transform
ourselves into beasts."

Without choice we have become like animals living from the outside. Compulsivity is a state of inner barrenness. We become totally externalized, 'without any self-reflection and interior life'. How could one have an inner life when he feels flawed and defective as a human being? This shame core keeps the addict from going inward. The true self is lost and hides behind a masked false self.

Compulsivity is also about bad habits that become vicious over a period of time. Philosophers speak of habits as second natures. Good habits are virtues which are strengths added to our personhood. Bad habits are vices and have the power to control our lives and take it over. Habits are a very dominant part of the euphoric type of mood alterers such as drugs, sugar and sex. Drugs and food also have the added factor of having their own intrinsic chemical power. These chemicals are in themselves addicting.

I've never in 15 years of working with teenage drug abusers found a single one who was what I'd call *only a chemical addict.* As powerful as many of the current market drugs are, especially cocaine and crack, I've never yet worked with an addict who didn't have the 'hole in his soul'. I've been in my personal recovery for 21 years, and I've never yet known a person in recovery from chemical abuse who didn't have abandonment issues.

Perhaps nothing is more important for adult children of dysfunctional families than to connect their abandonment violation with the behavioral dysfunctions and problems that abandonment causes. For example, in the checklist I've given for ACoAs, each of the behavioral characteristics is a response to being violated. Abandonment violates our rights, our boundaries and our needs.

Our violated *true self stays in hiding* because we have lost the connection between what happened and the response to what happened. Since the fantasy bond idealizes our persecutors, we can only conclude that our neurotic, dysfunctional behavior is about us and not them.

As Terry Kellog has said, "It's really helpful when we hear about the responses to violence, to know very simply that these responses are about what happened to us and not about who we really are." This insight is the beginning of any recovery process. Once we see it, we demythologize our idealized parents and can see that *we are not bad, flawed or defective.*

At this point, I'd like to sum up this chapter by presenting a profile of four types of compulsive families. Each family is a composite profile of people I've actually counseled, people who have shared in my workshops and people from my own experiences. Each will be disguised in such a way as to protect his personal ego boundaries. At the same time, these profiles will reflect what is happening in real flesh-and-blood family systems. The four types of compulsive families are: chemically addicted; eating disordered; religiously and work addicted. I will be talking about sexual addiction physical violence, emotional battering and co-dependence in the chapters which follow.

Chemical Addiction: The Blue Family

Jesse is the father of this family. He is an alcoholic and sex addict. These two addictions often go together. He was inappropriately bonded with his mother and was abandoned by his own father. He had two stepfathers. They were both alcoholic. One was physically abusive to Jesse and his mother. His mother carried the poisonous pedagogy in denying her son his sexual feelings as well as his anger. Jesse is very passive aggressive. He was taught that real men don't cry and are not afraid. At 16 Jesse met Jessica and got her pregnant and they married.

Jessica was inappropriately bonded with her father since her mother was the adult child of an alcoholic, an incest victim, and addicted to sickness, being bedridden most of her life.

Jessica's father was sanctified by Jessica and her seven sisters. Actually, Jessica's father was an enabler, allowing his wife to stay addicted by walking on eggs and living in *reaction* to her feelings, needs and wants. Jessica's family looked very respectable. They were staunch churchgoers. Only appropriate feelings were ever shown.

Jessica and Jesse had three children. Their first child (the reason they married) Gweneviere was born to her 16-year-old mother She was not wanted and felt this from birth. She became the Lost Child, as well as Superachiever and Super-responsible first child. She was Mom's Scapegoat and felt this conflict all her life. She went to work early. She married and divorced two addicts and now lies in chronic depression and isolation. She hates men as her mother, aunts and grandmother did. She is still lost and very confused about how to change her life.

Jack was born 13 months later. He was the first male in two generations and bore the unconscious sexualized rage of two generations of man-haters. He became the family Caretaker. Jesse abandoned all the children with his active alcoholism. Jack bonded inappropriately with Jessica and played the role of Surrogate Spouse.

Jack was also Super-responsible and a Superachiever. He also took the role of Caretaker by being grandmother's, aunts' and Mom's helper. He later 'acted out' his alienated rage for having to be Jessica's emotional spouse and the family caretaker by becoming alcoholic himself. He started drinking in secret at age 13 and by age 15 was seriously addicted having had several alcoholic blackouts. In spite of this, Jack developed a Hero role by being the class president and salutatorian in high school.

After one year of college Jack decided to be a celibate minister. This ensured both his inappropriate bond role and hero role. His active addiction destroyed his ministry. He got help in A.A. and sobered up. He married pregnant, reenacting Jesse and Jessica's marriage. He had two children and lived in non-intimacy for seven years. Jack later found ACoA and continues in it until now.

The third child, Jacob, was also a Lost Child — being an accidental pregnancy. He came at the apex of Jesse and Jessica's ever accelerating dysfunctionality. He was a third child and carries the loneliness and sadness of the marital relationship. Jacob was also the Protected one, Gweneviere and Jack becoming 'Little Parents' hoping that Jacob would not experience the pain of the family's trauma. In fact, Jacob felt so totally abandoned that he still reenacts the abandonment by running away and totally disappearing. He married at 17, pregnant, reenacting Jesse and Jessica's marriage. He also married an adult child, and had three children, as his parents did, later abandoning them as his father had done to him. His oldest daughter became the Super-responsible One and Little Parent to her sisters, and later parent to her own parents. The other two daughters both became serious drug addicts.

The foregoing is a classic example of how alcoholism controls the lives of all the people in the family. Each child becomes doubly addicted — both to Jesse's alcohol and Jessica's co-dependency (her addiction) to Jesse. All of these people are enmeshed, having to give up their own uniqueness and individuality. The whole family needs to be treated.

Someone estimated that each drinking alcoholic affects the lives of 50 people. To see the alcoholic family multigenerationally is the best example I know of to show how alcoholism impacts the family.

Eating Addiction: The Orange Family

Jake Orange is the perfect product of the poisonous pedagogy. He is authoritarian, rigid and controls his emotions. He also attempts to control the emotions of all those around him. Jake is an overachiever. He is also a work addict and has made millions of dollars. Jake is exactly like his father.

Jake married Jonelli, who had a rigid and authoritarian mother. Jonelli is the perfect lady. She graduated from Southern College and was elected Miss Southern Belle. She would be physically striking were it not for a weight problem. Although not obese, she struggles with a fat/thin obsessive eating disorder. She stays so preoccupied with fat/thin thinking, she can avoid her low-grade depression, which is really anger at herself. She is angry at herself for never standing up to her mother, for staying in a marriage she wanted to leave after two months.

Jonelli is also addicted to Jake. She constantly obsesses on how awful he is. She spends hours talking to lady friends about him. She has no time to be in touch with her own feelings.

Jake and Jonelli have four children. Two girls and two boys. The girls are 14 and 12, the boys are 8 and 2 years old.

The 14-year-old, Priscilla, is anorexic. Her weight fluctuates between 60 and 85 pounds. She is very much in denial and minimizes that there are any problems. Her anorexia broke out coincidentally with the mother having an affair and being caught by the father. The anorexic condition has lasted for two years. The younger sister is beginning to act out by getting in trouble in school. The eight year old is isolated, non-athletic and obese. The two-year-old boy was wanted by the father as another chance. Jonelli is extremely depressed over the child. After some treatment, Priscilla has started to eat, but she is secretly bulimic.

Priscilla is the service bearer for the family. She serves to unify her parents' marriage. She carries her mother's unexpressed rage and has taken control of the family. Her mother's rage is equated with food. Priscilla fears this rage. Therefore, if she eats, she will have to feel the rage. The starvation and vomiting keep her mood altered. She carries the rigidity and severe authoritarianism of her childhood by her severe and austere self-management.

The father still attempts to control but is obviously shaken and deeply frustrated by his real inability to control anything. He often feels suicidal. This is a classic picture of an eating-disordered family. The mom's weight problem is about unexpressed anger, which covers her hurt and sadness about her own childhood. She has reenacted that childhood by marrying someone controlling like her mother.

To the anorexic daughter food equals feelings. So that starvation is the way not to feel the terrible rage which covers the loneliness, pain and sadness that this family feels at the unconscious level. The anorexic daughter also controls the father, as well as the entire family. She has made certain that her mother and father will not divorce. The third child is a Lost Child. He was an accidental pregnancy. He carries the loneliness and isolation of the marriage. He is ninety pounds overweight and eats to fill the emptiness he feels. Everyone in this family is addicted and is in need of treatment.

Let me turn the discussion now to a type of compulsive family that looks good on the outside but carries their pathology at a very covert level. In alcoholic and eating disorder families, the pathology is more overt and obvious. The families look bad and are clearly in trouble. The children play obvious roles to balance the system.

In the next two examples the parents look good and are not obviously in trouble. Their behavior is acceptable according to societal standards. The family pathology is more covert, more hidden, and the members of the family feel more confused and crazy.

In one of our sample profiles, Mom is a religious addict. It is very difficult to be in a conflict with someone who is on a pedestal, who looks and acts holy. In our second example, Dad is a highly successful public figure. He looks like a perfect 10 in the American way of making it. Yet both families are extremely dysfunctional.

The children are caught up in the covert family system. Since one of the functions of children in a system is to make the covert explicit, the children act out the pathology.

Religious Addiction: The Purple Family

Pevilia Purple is married to Biff. Biff is a traveling salesman. He has had several affairs and is a sex addict. He is the classic 'good old boy'. He gets by on his job just enough to be the manager of a large territory. But he is really lazy, a jock at heart, who would really rather pitch softball than be intimate with anyone.

Pevilia is emotionally Biff's mother. She provides beautifully by keeping an immaculate house and by being a consummate cook. She continually nags, lectures, quotes scripture, bitches and on occasion goes hysterical. Biff gets out of the house every chance he can, even though he's only home for three weekends a month. Pevilia is totally controlling of everyone and everything within her view. She is avidly religious. She has changed churches several times. The reason is always that the church is not true enough to the Bible. She has finally found a spiritual guru who she thinks is a true messenger of God. She studies the Bible daily with this self-appointed Biblical authority. He is attached to no denomination, as denominations are of the devil. His followers claim that he has affected several miraculous cures.

Pevilia takes two of her daughters, Susie and Sue Ellen, with her to Bible Class daily. They are 9 and 12. The 12-year-old, Sue Ellen, was sexually abused by her 16-year-old drug-addicted brother, Raldo. Raldo was in therapy for homosexuality for six years and has been in drug programs for the last three years. He is incorrigible and has now dropped out of school. There is another boy, Billy, who is four years old and another older daughter, Maggie, who is 19 years old.

Maggie is a perfect daughter. She is in first year college. While she is not a born-again Christian like her mom, she is a rigid Christian. She has dated one boy from Sunday School for five years. She has literally never been kissed. She was a straight "A" student, the valedictorian of her high school class. She tries to be perfect.

The young son, Billy, is prone to violent outbursts of temper. This is usually blamed on the 16-year-old who is also rageful. Biff, who also rages, has had actual fist fights with Raldo over the years. Biff has never liked him and makes no bones about it.

Pevilia herself was in therapy for nine years until she realized that therapy was a form of secular humanism. She got counseling for her marriage, spending three years basically talking about Biff. She has been involved in trying to control Raldo's therapy for years. She has been advised to put him into an in-house treatment center, but she can't bear to do this to him. She enables him by giving him money, writing phony excuses while he was in school and defending him. The sexual abuse of his sister was completely hushed up and has been a family secret until Sue Ellen started 'acting out' with obsessive compulsive behavior concerning venereal disease. If she passes a bar or strip joint, she goes into hysterics over the possibility that venereal germs have soiled her.

In spite of all of this Pevilia smiles incessantly. She thanks God for sending her such misfortune and has been told over and over again how much God must love her.

Pevilia doesn't dialogue with her children or with anyone for that matter. She always knows what is right and firmly but gently lets them know. When the children are hurting, she consoles them with scriptural quotations and moral exhortations.

This family is a compulsive family. Mom is addicted to the ecstasy she feels when she experiences her sense of righteousness in prayer, moralizing Biblical readings or in religious services. She uses this feeling of goodness to distract herself from how lonely, how disappointed, sad and angry she feels. She plays the role of being good and righteous — Saint Mom. The children call her a saint. Mom is also severely co-dependent. She obsesses on her husband and children. She stays in her head worrying so much of the time that she doesn't have to feel her own loneliness and emptiness.

The husband was raised by a domineering and controlling mother. His mother divorced his father at an early age and bad-mouthed the father for years to come. Any time Biff wanted money or anything that cost money, mother would blame his father. She sexually abused Biff by continuously demeaning his father to him. She categorized his father with all men "who think with their penis". Biff became an irresponsible kind of person — always messing around and always looking for fun.

The oldest daughter, Maggie, takes some of the heat off the parents' marriage by being the 'Perfect One'. She's like a robot, always saying the right thing. She is goal oriented and superachieving.

The drug-abusing son, Raldo, is the family Scapegoat. He acts out the covert rage of his parents. He takes the heat off the non-intimacy and utter loneliness of his parents' marriage. He carries his father's secret sexual addiction, as well as his father's unresolved sexual abuse and acted it out with his sister. His purported homosexuality has to do with his father's unconscious abandonment issues with his own father, as well as Raldo's actual abandonment by his father, Biff. Raldo seeks the nurturing of a man. He also distracts the family with the homosexual issue.

Sue Ellen is the family victim. She's the third child and is totally confused. Her role is to take care of her parents' marriage. She does this by being a victim. The times of greatest closeness between Pevilia and Biff are when they deal with Sue Ellen's issues. The fourth child, Susie, is a Lost Child. She was an accidental pregnancy. Pevilia refuses to use any birth control methods. She says they are non-Biblical. Susie tries to be perfect and not bother anyone. She plays alone a lot and is referred to by Biff as his 'good child'. Pevilia calls her a gift from God.

Little Billy already carries the system's rage and acts it out. He is athletic and gets special attention from Dad when Dad is home.

Pevilia sometimes wonders in the secret, most honest, recesses of her heart whether she really is specially loved by God. In fact, she feels completely confused by the disproportionate grace that life seems to offer. She would never talk about her doubts.

This family is seriously sick and everyone in it needs treatment.

Work Addiction: The White Family

Mickey and Matilda White live in the most luxurious section of their city. They are millionaires. Each has been married before. They have two children of their own and each has a child by a previous marriage.

Mickey is the president of a large manufacturing company founded by his grandfather who died at age 89 'after a hard day's work'. "He worked every day of his life" is a frequently heard family quotation.

While Mickey is sick of hearing this, he still likes to quote it in public when talking about the White Enterprises. Mickey's dad is still alive and also comes to work daily. Both Granddad and Dad were womanizers and modeled this to their sons as a way to be a real man.

Mickey has five brothers, three are partners in the company. The youngest is totally screwed up with alcoholism, and the second son is a religious fanatic. Mickey started out with a lot of pressure to do as well as his father and grandfather. At first, he worked in a socially acceptable manner, working from nine to five and occasionally on Saturday. Slowly over the years, he's worked longer and longer hours. Nine to five became five to nine. Saturdays are entertainment days with clients. And even though Mickey says he loves his family, Sunday is a dreaded day.

Mickey's daughter by a previous marriage has been diagnosed as a borderline personality. She's been in several of the most lavish psychiatric treatment centers. Currently she's on psycho-active drug treatment.

Mickey's first wife was 'a raving bitch' who constantly accused him of sleeping around. She overprotected their child and has used the child to take sides against her father. Their child witnessed the most violent emotional fights between her mom and dad. Mickey's work intensified during his divorce and during his joint therapy sessions with his daughter.

Matilda is altogether different. She was raised as a perfect lady. She graduated cum laude in a fine Eastern school. She does volunteer work at several hospitals and is past president of the Junior League. She constantly defends her husband to their teenage sons and to her daughter. The children, ages 13, 12 and 10, love their dad and love to be with him. Except he's never there. He breaks promises about going fishing and playing golf. The boys are set up not to have their anger by being told that Dad works so hard for them. Mom constantly points out all the toys and luxuries they have as a result of Dad's working so hard. They feel guilty when she tells them this.

The oldest son is a star athlete. Dad makes some of his games. The youngest son is awkward, non-competitive and non-athletic. Both sons are failing in school.

Mickey believes in strong discipline. He often states how the 'teenage drug crisis' could be solved with hard work and strong physical discipline.

Mickey appears self-assured, even arrogant at times. But underneath he is shame-based. He was not a good athlete, nor was he academically bright. He punched out a friend who ridiculed him for not having the capacity to make it without his father's money. He has always been afraid he couldn't make it on his own. His father was physically abusive (in order to make a man out of him). Mickey was verbally shamed as a child.

Mickey and Matilda have been sexually dysfunctional for most of their 15-year marriage. The dysfunction is basically 'disorder of desire'. Neither has any real desire for the other. They never talk about it. Matilda is the perfect wife in every other respect. She is a wonderful hostess and charms her guests with generous hospitality.

Her child, Suzette, who is 13 years old, admitted to her therapist that she's been compulsively masturbating for nine years. She also has some obsessive/compulsive cleaning disorders, going through ritual washings before and after school.

Mickey is the most celebrated layman in his religious denomination. He and the whole family have gone to church every Sunday. They look like a perfect family. Recently the oldest son has refused to go to church. Sundays are becoming a battlefield.

At home Mickey stays busy all the time. He's always doing something. Basically his belief is that he is what he does. His wife is severely co-dependent. She never refers to herself. She always speaks in the plural. She stays busy all the time — worrying, driving the children places, instructing the maids, doing volunteer work, planning parties. She stops her children from having any emotions other than two positive ones — joy and go-getter determination.

The children are all underachievers, the oldest son being the exception in sports. He is the family Star and like his dad he only feels okay when he is performing.

Matilda's daughter has severe depression and is actually thought disordered. The younger son is a Lost Child as well as Dad's Scapegoat. Mickey vows he will not lose his temper at him but does so over and over again. Mickey's daughter is the Scapegoat for the entire blended system. Mickey is idolized by all the children. Each, however, is shamed by not being *worth* Dad's time.

Mickey is a severe work addict and Matilda enables him by continually defending him. The whole family is compulsive and needs treatment.

In all these examples, the poisonous pedagogy operates in a destructive way. Obedience demands the denial of feelings. Punishment along with obedience demands that one suffers in silence. The *no-talk and no-feeling expression rules* govern all of these families. Since the problems are denied and minimized, they cannot be solved. As the children are forced to repress their emotions, they lose touch with their vital selves. They lose touch with their own reality. To be in denial of feelings is to be in a state of numbness and withholding. Functionality calls for vitalization and spontaneity. These families are emotionally dead. They no longer even feel their shame. They have internalized it.

Because each person was deprived narcissistically, he continues in the repetition compulsion. The repetition compulsion forms the endless cycles of 'acting out' the primary pain and woundedness of emotional deprivation. It is the repetition compulsion which, more than anything else, underscores the hopelessness of addiction. The repetition compulsion is the continual 'acting out' of the original pain in a vain attempt to be connected and overcome alienation and aloneness. Each new cycle promises the intimacy and original connection of love that one needed as a foundation of growth and self-acceptance. And each new cycle ends in a deeper sense of loneliness and depression coming from the pain and sadness of loss. As each new layer of shame is accrued, a more grandiose and delusional false self is strengthened. As each cycle of repetition compulsion is enacted, the hopelessness and powerlessness engenders despair. There is no way out, there is no exit. I remember, in my active alcoholic days, thinking I'll just have to drink until I die.

Denial keeps it going. The idealized parents and family demand a 'bad me' and a negative self-image. It can't go both ways. Either hitting, screaming, criticizing, judging, punishing, bribing, guilting, isolating are for my own good and acts of responsible love. Or they are sick products of a diseased set of rules that are carried unconsciously from generation to generation. If they are responsible acts of love — *then I have to be bad.* If I can demythologize them and see them as destroyers of psyches that lead to spiritual bankruptcy, then I can be restored to my innocence and preciousness.

My parents and I are both the victims of destructive rules. As we can now see the set-up, we can change these rules and our family structures.

Summary

The key points covered in this chapter can be summed up using the letters of the word **COMPULSIVE.**

C. **Children of Alcoholics as Guidepost for Understanding the Compulsive Family** — The common traits possessed by adult children of alcoholics have provided the greatest proof for the family systems approach. ACoAs have also offered immense insight into the structure of compulsive families. ACoAs are helping us to grasp how compulsivity is set up in dysfunctional families.

O. **Out of Control and Controlling** — One of the strange paradoxes of compulsive families is that while the members are out of control with their compulsivity, the family system is dominated by control. The control domination can result from one member (Dad's drinking) or from a strict rule of control.

M. **Major Responses to Alcoholism** — The checklist in this chapter offers the most common traits exhibited by adults who have grown up in alcoholic families. These traits are natural responses to the violation being imposed by the alcoholic and co-alcoholic's behavior.

P. **Pathological Relationships** — Compulsive/addictive behavior is a pathological relationship to any mood-altering experience that has life-damaging consequences. The pathological relationship is rooted in the original pathological relationship of abandonment. Compulsivity is set up in families by abandonment.

U. **Unmet Dependency Needs** — The abandonment creates an environment where there is no one there to depend on for the fulfillment of one's basic dependency needs. A person thus grows up with an insatiable child living inside him. The child needed his parents for the first 15 years of his life. Since we cannot go back and actually be children again, these needs are insatiable.

L. **Loss of Vitality and Spontaneity** — When one has to give up his own feelings, needs and wants, he develops a false self.

This false self is a mask and is unreal. When one is living life as someone else, he loses his vitality and spontaneity. This is a set up for compulsivity. The only way one can feel alive is when he is in compulsive/addictive behaviors.

S. Shame-Based and Shameless Caretakers — Compulsive families are created by shame-based people. Shame is the fuel of the compulsive/addictive behavior. Shame-based people defend against shame by acting shameless. They act shameless by using cover-ups for shame like control, superior power, perfectionism, criticism, contempt and rage.

I. Idealization of Caretakers — Fantasy Bond — Shameless caretakers transfer their shame to those they take care of. Their superior power and control, coupled with children's cognitive egocentrism, result in the child carrying the caretaker's shame. Children naturally idealize parents (create a fantasy bond) and are vulnerable prey to their shame-based caretakers 'shameless' cover-ups.

V. Violation of Self — Once children take on their caretaker's shame, they feel flawed and defective within themselves. A flawed, defective person must develop a defensive false self. This sets the person up for compulsivity. All members of a compulsive family are shame-based. All become co-dependent.

E. Expanded Notion of Compulsive/Addictive Behavior with Examples — In this chapter I have expanded the common notion of compulsive/addictive behavior. Addiction is usually limited to ingestive addictions. In my model, the words compulsive and addictive are the same. I include the activity addictions (work, gambling, entertainment, buying), as well as feeling and thought addictions in the total definition of 'compulsive/addictive disorder'. I offer four examples of compulsive families illustrating chemical, eating, religious and work compulsivity.

6

The Persecuted

Checklist For How You Lost Your Self And Became An Adult Child Of A Sexually Or Physically Abusing Family

"The abused children are alone with their suffering, not only within the family, but also within themselves. They cannot share their pain with anyone. They cannot create a place in their own soul where they could cry their heart out."

Alice Miller
For Your Own Good

"It was my older brother. He would expose himself to me and make me touch him. I worried about him all the time. I stayed outside as long as I could. It was like being hunted. I felt like an animal. I finally gave up. I would let him do whatever he wanted to. I felt soiled and contaminated. I thought of suicide everyday of my life. I couldn't be with people. I wondered why people were interested in things — why they laughed or wanted to go to school. I would wander in fields in order not to be. I just wanted 'not to be'."

These statements were uttered by Cathy, a 46-year-old woman. Never before had she told anyone. I had counseled with her 10 years earlier concerning the death of her 13-year-old son. He had been killed in a car wreck. I had also counseled with her after her second husband had terrorized her verbally. Cathy has been depressed all her life. She was physically abused in her first marriage and has been the victim of psychological battering in her second marriage. She bears the classic wounds and manifests the classic patterns of an incest victim.

Incest is defined by Webster as "sexual intercourse or inbreeding between closely related individuals . . . when they are related . . . within degrees wherein marriage is prohibited by law or custom."

I agree with Susan Forward that the definition should be expanded to include people who "perceive themselves to be closely related (including step-parents, step-siblings, half-siblings and even live-in lovers if they have assumed a parental role." (*Betrayal of Innocence*)

I understand incest to include overt, covert and emotional types of sexual abuse. I differentiate molestation from incest. Molestation is a sexually abusive act performed by a stranger. The effects can be equally as damaging.

Incest is always the most shaming of any form of violence. It takes less incest to produce shame than any other form of abuse. All sexual abuse involves some shaming because of the victimization and physical boundary violation. But incest has the added element of betrayal by a supposed loved one. Incest, like all abuse done to magical and cognitively immature children, has the effect of the child's believing it was their fault. No child can think that their parents are bad. If Daddy can't be bad and the child *feels icky and bad,* then it must be the child who is bad.

Children certainly feel bad living in compulsive families but cognitively they cannot grasp that their parents are dis-eased addicts. The child needs the parent for survival. Children also internalize their parents at their worst. What this means is that when the parent is acting in the way that is most threatening to the child's survival, the child records this most vividly. A raging drunk and out-of-control violent father is much more dangerous to survival than a verbally scolding mother. The child adapts to the threat and internalizes it for the sake of survival.

Incest dramatizes in the most powerful way the tragedy of the abandoned child. Incest is a form of violence — the violation of a child's sexuality. This amounts to the violation of one's very being, since sexuality is something we are, rather than something we have.

The incest drama is played out on the stage of an innocent child's naive trust. It is fueled by a natural sense of respect and desire to please. It reaches its denouement in the idealization of the parent at the expense of a ruptured and soul-murdered self that will never be the same again. It is no wonder the incest taboo is found in all human societies.

Dissociation

Incest clearly focuses on the major problem of abandonment. This problem can be expressed as the disconnection between the act of victimization and the response to being victimized. Because the violation is so profound, the defense is equally profound. 'Instant numbing' is my phrase for it. The technical word is dissociation. In dissociation the victim literally goes away. The violence is so intolerable that the victim leaves their body. They ultimately lose the connection with the memories of what happened. This is why incest is often hard to deal with. The survivor often has no conscious memories of what happened. It is also why the prosecution of offenders is difficult. A terrified child being hassled by an adult lawyer on a witness stand is at a profound disadvantage.

Fortunately the victim's body does retain the *feelings* of what happened. These 'body memories' are what allow the healing work, called debriefing, to take place in therapy. The debriefing process is the process of connecting the memories and the feelings. Because the memories are dissociated from the feelings and because the feelings are so intense, the victim experiences life as unreal. The victim feels crazy. They think there is something wrong with them. They have lost the connection with what was done to them.

When anyone is violated, the first feeling response is raw fear and terror. One wants to run away from the threat and fear. One is helpless and out of control. The more the situation is intolerable, the greater the need to dissociate. The body records and imprints the terror. Later the feelings of hurt, anger, abandonment and shame are recorded. The victim then dissociates from the memories, depersonalizes the offender, especially if it's their parent or relative, and feels a sense of unreality. Later they may have recurring nightmares or other sleep disorders. They may experience blip memories that come like a momentary flashback. Or they may just feel crazy without any true psychosis.

The increased intensity of traumatization may cause a split personality or even multiple personalities. Since the victim is dissociated from the memories, they feel like these symptoms are about them. Their defenses have severed the relationship of their feelings with the traumatizing event. In reality, these defenses are *natural responses* to the violence.*

The debriefing work that must be done with sexual abuse victims involves having them go back into the memories. The emphasis is on getting in touch with the concrete sensory-based details as much as is possible. This allows the victim to connect with what actually happened. In this way they connect the feeling responses to the sexual violation itself. They become aware that what they feel and the way they behave is about *what happened to them and not about them.*

The poisonous pedagogy plays a major role in the tragedy of incest and sexual abuse in general. I believe *it implicitly* gives permission for sexual abuse by promoting a kind of ownership of children. It is the ownership principle that justifies the inequality. If children must obey and honor their parents at any cost, then the parents implicitly have the right over their children's bodies.

I have two clients who were abused exactly on these grounds. One was taken in the bathroom by her father at age 14 and told to spread her legs so that he could see if she was still a virgin. He was purportedly very religious and was doing his parental duty. Another, at age 11, was tied spread eagle to the bed while her mother examined her for a vaginal rash with the father watching. Since he was her parent he had a right to be there.

While I risk over-simplifying a complex problem, I believe the master/ slave presuppositions of the parenting rules I've been discussing lend themselves to the parents taking possession of their children's bodies.

Cheryl McCall's *Life* Magazine article of December, 1984, begins with the words: "There are perhaps 34 million of us in America — adult women who were victims of sexual abuse." This figure is consistent with figures quoted by others in the field (Kinsey, *Psychology Today* Survey). These figures shock most people because the common conception of sexual abuse is limited to a kind of 'horror story abuse'. Horror story almost always means sexual intercourse (physical penetration). Most people have the idea that if there is no physical penetration, then there

---

*Much of the information in this section has been taken from lectures by Renee Frederickson, an expert on sexual violation.

is no sexual abuse. *Nothing could be further from the truth.* Infants, toddlers, preschool children are abused with great regularity without any physical penetration.

There is almost no good data on male sexual abuse. The figure often quoted is one out of 12 males are abused by the time they are finished adolescence. My own opinion is that the figures would be much higher if people understood the whole range of sexual abuse. What follows is a checklist of traits that are common psychological and behavioral responses to sexual violence. No one of these traits alone indicates sexual violation. Several are necessary before one would begin to make a case for sexual abuse.

A   *Age inappropriate behavior*
D   *Denial, delusion, dissociation, depersonalization*
U   *Unreality*
L   *Loneliness, isolation*
T   *Terrors, excessive fears, phobias*

C   *Compulsive disorders, addictions*
H   *Hostility, sexualized rage*
I   *Internalized shame*
L   *Live life as a victim*
D   *Delinquency, criminality, prostitution*
R   *Reenacts abuse*
E   *Employment and work problems*
N   *No talk rule — keeping the secret*

O   *Offender status*
F   *Feelings somatized*

S   *Split personality (multiple)*
E   *Eating disorders*
X   *X'd out identity — confused identity*
U   *Underlying depression*
A   *Aggressive and seductive behavior*
L   *Loss of sexual identity*

V   *Violated sexual boundaries*
I   *Intimacy problems*
O   *Objectification of self and others*
L   *Love confused with sex*
E   *Excessive dependency and clinging*
N   *Nightmares and sleeping disorders*
C   *Cross generational bonding*
E   *Early childhood symptoms*

A. Age Inappropriate Behavior or Knowledge Inappropriate to Age

In children the behavior could be the child making coital movements trying to insert penis into someone or something; touching or trying to touch grown up genitals; humping animals or toys; girl child putting things in her vagina. Later the behavior involves early promiscuity, early masturbation, early prostitution or frequenting prostitutes, the high school lover boy or slut. Later it may appear as sexual dysfunction either in or out of marriage. 'Disorder of desire' in marriage is a common symptom of emotional incest.

D. Denial, Delusion, Dissociation, Displaced Feelings, Depersonalization, Psychic Numbness

These are all ego defenses. The dissociation is an out-of-body kind of defense. The victim goes somewhere else mentally and imaginatively. This is the major cause of memory loss. The feelings are often displaced or the experience can be displaced as the child can, for example, start seeing monsters in the hall or having hallucinations. The child often depersonalizes the incest offender when a relative is involved. Denial and delusion are the result of the child believing *he is bad* and idealizing the family or parents. Even if idealization does not occur, the child still feels he is bad.

U. Unreality

The victim feels that his 'now' experience is not real. He has no understanding of so-called normal reality. Finds it hard to understand why people are interested in the things they are interested in. Loses interest.

L. Loneliness, Isolation and Withdrawal

Person withdraws physically. Wants to be invisible. Often is not noticed unless acting out seductively. Tends to run away from things. May run away from home, school, any conflict or problems. Wants to run away from life. Often thinks of suicide.

T. Terrors, Excessive Fears, Phobias, Anxiety, Hypervigilance

The major consequence of being violated is raw terror. The person who has felt helpless and victimized is traumatically and chronically stressed. This nameless terror may manifest as a phobia or many phobias.

C. Compulsive Disorders, Addictions

The major addictive range includes: co-dependency, drug, (alcohol) addiction, eating disorders, sex addiction.

H. Hostility, Sexualized Rage, Passive-Aggressive Behavior

Anger patterns depend on whether one becomes a victim or offender. Offenders will be aggressive and rageful. Victims will be more passive-aggressive. The victim will usually experience the rage at the end of a relationship.

I. Internalized Shame

The victim will internalize the shame and feel soiled, flawed and defective as a human being. He will act in a self-destructive manner, e.g., drug addicted, smoking, overeating — all forms of chronic suicide. The shame core is covered up with excessive control, perfectionism, rage, power, criticalness and being judgmental. It is also covered by the ego defenses (dissociation, displacement) and by rigid roles.

L. Lives Life as a Victim

The victim trusts untrustworthy people and ends up being victimized. Is attracted to other victims and confuses love and pity.

D. Delinquency, Criminal Behavior, Prostitution

Behavior may appear in childhood as aggressive and destructive — setting fires, destroying property, hitting and stealing. Later it appears as delinquency, breaking the law. In some studies 85% of prostitutes were sexually abused as children. A high percentage of female drug addicts were also sexually abused.

R. Reenacts the Abuse

The victim may reenact it on others or reenact his own victimization. Multiple relationships, marriages, affairs which end with offender/victim polarity, are often outcomes of sexual abuse.

E. Employment and Work Related Problems

Often sexual abuse victims go from job to job and have inconsistent work habits. Seem to have lost their effectiveness. This frequently begins in school. Underachievement or authority related problems.

N. No-Talk Rule

Known as *Keeping the Secret*. The secret is perhaps the major factor in the sexual abuse victims rupture between the violence and the responses to violence. Many have *never told anyone* about what happened. Often if they tell, they are told to keep the secret for the sake of keeping the family together. Or they may be told that they imagined what happened. The no-talk rule keeps the victim from *expressing the feelings* about what happened and, therefore, working through the violence.

O. Offender Status

Victims often identify with their offender as a way of feeling less helpless. They bond with them and almost literally become them. They then reenact the offense onto others.

F. Feelings are Somatized

Since the feelings cannot be expressed, they are often somatized. The victim gets sick and therefore can feel as bad as he really feels. Sickness may come out in the same areas of the body that the original abuse occurred — such as vaginal rashes or pain, sore throat, anal or bowel dysfunction, upper respiratory asthma, chronic chest congestion, sore back.

S. Split Personality (Multiple Personality)

When a victim is in his normal social role, he acts very differently from when he is at home in private. The private at-home self reenacts what happened at home '— but now with safety since it is not the fearful parent or relative — but one's husband, spouse, lover or children. When the distress has been of the 'horror story kind', a person can develop several personalities.

E. Eating Disorders

I mentioned this earlier under the general topic of compulsivities. Obesity is one of the common ways a sexual victim protects himself. Fat is considered a sexual turn-off so it protects the victim. Fat is insulation. It is as if one could build a fence around oneself. Often the victim puts the weight on in the area the abuse was done.

X. Crossed Out, Confused Identity

The victim feels different from others. Feels like he is defective merchandise. Victim also often feels crazy without any concomitant psychosis.

U. Underlying Depression

Victim carries the post-traumatic stress disorder. The act of violence is shocking. The betrayal makes it more shocking. A chronic sense of sadness and grief ensue.

A. Aggressive and Seductive Behavior

Often the sexual abuse victim feels that the only way he is desirable is sexually. He therefore uses sex as a way of gaining control. The seduction behavior also has the symbolic sense of getting control of the offender and getting it over with. Sexual victims and offenders find each other with unbelievable regularity.

L. Loss of Sexual Identity and Functionality

This is the opposite of the victim only having identity by being sexual. Since sex is the very core of our being, to be violated sexually is to be violated in the very core of one's identity. Another consequence of the violation is sexual dysfunction. The victim may later experience impotence, frigidity, disorder of desire, flashbacks while in the act of sex. May need sado/masochistic fantasies in behavior in order to function.

V. Violated Sexual Boundaries

Sexual abuse violates the core of one's being — one's physical, emotional, spiritual boundaries. One has one's door knob on the outside with little control over who comes in. Violated boundaries are like a country without borders or laws. The response to such violations is to either have sex with everyone or with no one (walls).

I. Intimacy Problems

The betrayal and chronic shock set one up in a kind of emotional numbness. The fear of closeness is the fear of betrayal and pain. This comes up over and over again in marriage and relationships. Victims often move away from real love, affection and closeness and are attracted to an abusive rejecting person. Victims have an impaired ability to evaluate the trustworthiness of others. Victims are enmeshed in the family violence and often seek enmeshed relationships. Victims set up old fantasy bond dilemmas. If only I give more, try harder, give more sex, then maybe he'll really love me. They often reenact this dilemma with offender type spouse or relationships.

O. Objectification of Self and Others Sexually

Once violated a person withdraws into self. The withdrawal into self and self-indulging habits and painkillers is the opposite of having friendships and mutuality. Once a person is used, he becomes an object. Since there is no nurturing parent there for the child, the child objectifies himself. Thumb-sucking, early masturbation are self-indulging and objectifying habits. Once a person objectifies himself, he tends to project that outwards onto others. Sexual objectification is an outcome of sexual abuse. Our whole society wholeheartedly supports sexual objectification. A good woman person is a 10. Pornography glorifies genitals at the expense of personhood.

L. Love Confused with Sex

Victims of sexual abuse often confuse love with sex. They believe they are only loveable if they are sexually desirable. They believe they must be the best possible sex partner or else they will be abandoned and rejected.

E. Excessive Dependency and Clinging

Because the abandonment and shame destroy the interpersonal parent/child bridge, the child has no one to depend on. Their natural developmental dependency needs are neglected. They, therefore, grow up with an excessively needy child within them. Clinging is a defensive strategy to avoid abandonment.

N. Nightmares and Sleeping Disorders

The victim has often been violated in his own bed at night. Night terrors, recurring nightmares, sleeping excessively after one has gone to sleep and fearing to go to sleep may all be the result of sexual violence.

C. Crossgenerational Bonding and Role Reversal

Children are victimized by being drawn into the family systems needs for balance. If Mom and Dad's marriage is sexually and emotionally barren, Dad may make his daughter his little princess. He may later have sexual fantasies of her. Even though they are never acted on, the child has to carry the covert fantasies. Daughter definitely becomes Dad's emotional spouse and takes care of his emotional needs or his affectionalized sexuality.

E. Early Childhood Symptoms

Along with age inappropriate knowledge of behavior, several other phenomena may be the result of early sexual abuse. These phenomena are unexplained bruises, age regression — starting to wet or soil self after potty training is over, public display of age regression, playing with or smearing feces at an inappropriate age, night terrors or sleep disorders, bowel disorders, vaginal disorders (pain, rashes), traumatic response (e.g., shrieking or screaming to vaginal exam), prolonged bed-wetting, prolonged thumb-sucking, dramatic mood changes, aggressive, sudden and unprovoked behavior, self-mutilation and suicidal thought or talk, picking at skin or scabs until they bleed, hitting self, cutting self, slapping self, wearing two or more pairs of underpants and refusing to change, somatic complaints, sore throats, stomachaches, gagging, asthma, upper respiratory disorders.

The checklist is by no means exhaustive. If you have no memories of sexual abuse, this list can give you an idea about whether you are an adult child of a sexually abusing family. This is especially important in view of the fact that our common understanding of sexual abuse is extremely limited. One out of one hundred people have been through the kind of horror story abuse that hits the newspapers, the crisis hotlines and the child protection agencies. This is bad enough! If one out of a hundred people had a serious disease, we would be vaccinating everyone against it.

Sexual abuse involves whole families. It can be divided as follows:*

1. Physical Sexual Abuse

This involves hands-on touching in a sexual way. The range of abusive behaviors that are sexual include sexualized hugging or kissing; any kind of sexual touching or fondling; oral and anal sex; masturbation of the victim or forcing the victim to masturbate the offender; sexual intercourse.

2. Overt Sexual Abuse

This involves voyeurism, exhibitionism. This can be outside or inside the home. Parents often sexually abuse children through voyeurism and exhibitionism. The criteria for in-home voyeurism or exhibitionism is whether the parent is being sexually stimulated. Sometimes the parent may be so out of touch with his own sexuality that he is not aware of how sexual he is being. The child almost always has a kind of icky feeling about it.

One client told me how her father would leer at her in her panties coming out of the bathroom. Others speak of having no privacy in the house, much less the bathroom. I've had a dozen male clients whose mothers bathed their genital parts up through eight or nine years old.

Children can feel sexual around parents. This is not sexual abuse unless the parent originated it. It all depends on the parents. Here I'm not talking about a parent having a passing sexual thought or feeling. It's about a parent using a child for his own conscious or unconscious sexual stimulation.

3. Covert Sexual Abuse

(a) **Verbal** — This involves inappropriate sexual talking. Dad or any significant male calling women "whores" or "cunts" or objectified sexual names. Or Mom or any significant females deprecating men in a sexual way. It also involves parents or caretakers having to know about every detail of one's private sexual life, asking questions about a child's sexual physiology or questioning for minute details about dates.

Covert sexual abuse involves not receiving adequate sexual information. I've had several female clients who didn't know what was happening when they began menstruating. I've had three female clients who did not know that their vagina had an opening in it until they were 20 years old.

---

*I have taken this classification from the work of Pia Mellody. She is a pioneer in our ever-expanding understanding of the range and consequences of sexual abuse.

An overt kind of sexual abuse occurs when Dad or Mom talk about sex in front of their children when the age level of their children is inappropriate. It also occurs when Mom or Dad make sexual remarks about the sexual parts of their children's bodies. I've worked with two male clients who were traumatized by their mother's jokes about the size of their penis. Also female clients whose fathers and stepfathers teased them about the size of their breasts or buttocks.

(b) Boundary Violation — This involves children witnessing parents in sexual behavior. They may walk in on it frequently because parents don't provide closed and locked doors. It also involves the children being allowed no privacy. They are walked in on in the bathroom. They are not taught to lock their doors or given permission to lock their doors. Parents need to model appropriate nudity, i.e., need to be clothed appropriately after a certain age.

Children are sexually curious. Beginning at around age three or between ages three to six, children start noticing parents' bodies. They are often obsessed with nudity. Mom and Dad need to be careful walking around nude with young children. If Mom is not being stimulated sexually, the nudity is not sexual abuse. She simply is acting in a dysfunctional way. She is not setting sexual boundaries.

The use of enemas at an early age can also be abusive in a way that leads to sexual dysfunction. The enemas can be a body boundary violation.

4. Emotional Sexual Abuse

Emotional sexual abuse results from crossgenerational bonding. I've spoken of enmeshment as a way that children take on the covert needs of a family system. It is very common for one or both parents in a dysfunctional marriage to bond inappropriately with one of their children. *The parents in effect use the child to meet their emotional needs.* This relationship can easily become sexualized and romanticized. The daughter may become Daddy's Little Princess, or the son may become Mom's Little Man. In both cases the child is being abandoned. The parent is getting his needs met at the expense of the child's needs. The child needs a parent not a spouse.

Pia Mellody, who runs a pioneering co-dependency treatment unit at The Meadows in Wickenberg, Arizona, gives the following definition of emotional sexual abuse. She says when "one parent has a relationship with the child that is more important than the relationship he has with his spouse," there is emotional sexual abuse.

Sometimes both parents emotionally bond with a child. The child tries to take care of both parents' feelings. I once worked with a female client whose father would come and get her in the middle of the night and put her in bed with him in the guest bedroom. He would do this mainly to punish his wife for sexually refusing him. The daughter has suffered greatly with confused sexual identity.

Cross-generational bonding can occur with a parent and a child of the same sex. A most common form of this in our culture is mother and daughter. Mother often has sexualized rage, i.e., she fears and hates men. She uses her daughter for her emotional needs and also contaminates her daughter's feelings about men. I have had cases where mothers physically sexually abuse their daughters.

This issue is whether the parent is there for the child's needs, rather than the child being there for the parents' needs. And while children have the capacity to be sexual in a way appropriate to their developmental level, *whenever an adult is being sexual with a child, sexual abuse is going on.*

Some sexual abuse also comes from older siblings. Generally sexual behavior by same age children is not sexually abusive. The rule of thumb is that when a child is experiencing sexual "acting out" at the hands of a child three or four years older, it is sexually abusive.

Sexual Offenders

Let us now look at a profile of sexual offenders. Here we encounter some verification of the notion that the poisonous pedagogy predisposes the offender for the possibility of sexual abuse.

Incest offenders are sexually excited by children and ostensibly see nothing wrong with gratifying themselves at the expense of children. This is not true in every case. But more often than not, *the offender sees the child as having no rights.* Most offenders have been victimized themselves. Half have been sexually abused; the other half abused in some other way. Most often the other abuse is physical. Almost all offenders are sex addicts, although all sex addicts are not pedophiles. Most are emotionally retarded and feel inadequate in an adult world. They turn to children to get respect, affection and sex. The offenders are often alcoholic or chemically addicted. They have poor impulse control — especially over sexual matters. Most had poor relationships with the parent of the same sex and have a very shaky image of what it is to be a male or female.

Child sexual abusers live a secret life, hiding their behavior from spouses, colleagues and closest friends. Lucy Berliner, a Seattle therapist, quoted in Cheryl McCall's article, says, "Most of us think of child molesters as hideous, until we find out we know one." They are members of our club, or elders in the church. In fact, a disproportionate number of sex offenders are outwardly religious. Many are work addicts and religious addicts.

Incest Family Systems

Male sex offenders are by far the most dominant. Of four million known offenders only 5% are women. Males are the most dominant part of the sexual addiction population. Women are mostly co-dependents of sex addicts. This is true of the incest family. The mother is always in a collusive role when the father is victimizing the children. *Just as in the other compulsive families, there is the addict and the co-addict spouse or co-dependent.* The spouse either tolerates the abuse actively or passively.

Active collusion means that the spouse participates in the abuse either actually or by knowingly allowing it to happen.

Passive collusion is about the spouse being so bonded to the offender, either by addictions or by being abused, that she is out of touch with what's going on.

In an incest family all the members are seriously dis-eased and need treatment. Even if you were not the one being abused in your family, you still carry the covert secrets of the family system. The children function to make the covert overt in the family system. The children "act out" the unconscious of the family and the family "secrets". This acting out can even occur in a future generation. Two clients of mine are carrying unspoken sexual secrets from past generations.

Rothgahr comes from a rigidly religious family. His father was authoritarian and controlling. He is the sixth child of nine children. Second and sixth children often bond with mother. Bonding means taking on mother's emotional issues — both conscious and unconscious. Rothgahr's mother is an incest victim who never resolved her victimization. She's never done the debriefing work. Therefore, Rothgahr carries her unresolved sexual secret through bonding. He came to me because he was frightened of dreams and actual fantasies he was having about molesting children.

Rothgahr is what Patrick Carnes, in his book *Out of the Shadow*, calls a Level I sex addict. Level I involves womanizing, manizing, compulsive masturbation, pornography with or without compulsive masturbation, cruising and prostitution. Carnes sees voyeurism, exhibitionism, indecent liberties and phone calls as Level II sexual addiction, with rape, incest and molestation as Level III sexual addiction.

The levels have to do with the increasing risks of the sexual behavior apropos of culturally sanctioned behavior. Levels II and III always involve a victim and are punished by law. Level III is the most victimizing and incurs the greatest legal punishment.

My client was a womanizer. He was terribly disturbed by his molestation fantasies. He wasn't even aware that he was a sex addict confusing Level I with just being a "good old boy". My belief was that he was carrying his mother's unresolved incest issues. This was the basis for his molestation fantasies. He was also acting out the "internalized shame" produced by his religiously addicted family. This was the basis for his sexual addiction.

Another client, Ophelia, has the same bonding issues. She carries her mother's unconscious unresolved incest. She has dealt with her sexual terrors by totally shutting down sexually. She is a rigid and devout Catholic. She has abstained from sex for 40 years, refusing to date or remarry out of commitment to her faith. She inappropriately bonded with her three sons. Each son is a sex addict and carries her sexualized rage. Each has been devastated sexually by her repressed sexuality. She was often exhibitionistic with her sons. She behaved this way unconsciously, i.e., without having any consciousness of what she was doing and how this would impact her son's sexual lives.

Incest families are common in our culture. The sexual victimization is carried on through the offender/collusive victim incest family system. Offenders were once victims who bonded with their offenders out of helplessness. They continue to reenact the abuse on their offspring. They do to their children what they wish they could have done to parents who abused them. The fantasy bond keeps the child in the adult idealizing the parent and feeling bad and shamed. And the cycle goes on.

The Adult Children of Physical Violence

I'll never forget Hub. He was one of the most striking men I've ever met. Physically handsome and incredibly bright. He had been close to making a fortune on several occasions. He knew how to do everything except complete the deal. He would always "almost make it". He had been married several times. I had met two of his wives. They were not what I'd ever have suspected. Both were markedly unattractive and both hated men, myself included, as I learned in the counseling sessions.

Hub was an ACoA and like a lot of ACoAs he had been physically abused as a child. It is estimated that two-thirds of ACoAs are victims of physical violence. When I first asked Hub about his childhood, he told me that his dad had knocked him and his brother around a lot. "But," he quickly added, "we deserved it."

It took me several sessions to get the gory details. The knocking around often consisted of his father dunking Hub's head in the toilet and slapping him across the face several times. And as if this wasn't horrible enough, his father would urinate before sticking Hub's head in the toilet. The usual offenses that *deserved* such punishment were things like spending his lunch money on candy, not making his bed and talking back to the maid.

Many researchers believe that physical abuse is the most common form of abuse. I believe that almost everyone has been through at least an episode of physical abuse. The reason for this is the belief, fostered by the poisonous pedagogy, that corporal punishment is a useful way to teach children to respect their parents and be obedient. Violence against children (and women) and the condoning of that violence is part of an ancient and pervasive tradition.

No form of abuse is more binding than physical violence. The victim bonds to the abuser out of terror — terror for his or her life. The offenders are usually more developmentally retarded than any other abuser. Impulse control is learned from about two years old on. So the spouses and children in violent families are living under the reign of an adult person whose behavior is not even as mature as a well adjusted two year old.

The profile of a physically abusing parent includes the following: isolated; poor self-image; lacks sensitivity to others feelings; usually physically abused himself; deprived of basic mothering; unmet needs for love and comfort; in denial of problems and the impact of the problems; feels there is no one to turn to for advice; totally unrealistic expectations of children; expects the children to meet his needs for comfort and nurturing; when children fail to meet his needs, interprets this as rejection and respond with anger and frustration; deals with children as if they were much older than they are. Interestingly, in the category of biological parents, biological mothers are offenders about 5% more than fathers.

There is no good data on the extent of physical abuse. The usual data covers those cases which are reported. It excludes those not treated by a physician, those cases treated by a physician but not identified as abuse, and those cases identified as abuse but not reported. It's estimated that there are 200 unreported cases for every case reported.

The ownerships of children by parent, and the belief that children are willful and need their wills broken accounts for the rationale of spanking children.

The Bible is also often quoted to support this practice. The rod spoken of in the Bible was originally the shepherd's rod. It was an oak stick about three feet long tipped with flint or metal to beat away the wolves and to guide the timid sheep over difficult wadis (stream beds). The shepherd's rod was later expanded into the rod of authority by Moses. The rod symbolized God's presence and was mostly used to gently guide the people along right paths. Almost nowhere in scripture is there any widespread permission to spank children. A few isolated texts have been made into an entire pedagogical edifice. Society was also totally non-democratic in Biblical times.

Physical violence against children has been going on for a long time. R.J. Light, in an article in *The Harvard Educational Review* dated November, 1973, claims that in Colonial America, a father had the right not only to kill his children, but to call on colony officers to assist him. It was common to flog children without provocation to break them of their willfulness.

Our commonly quoted nursery rhyme about the old woman who lived in a shoe attests to the common acceptance of physical spankings. I remember as a child wondering what the point of this nursery rhyme really was. What a splendid way to end the day — porridge without bread and a sound whipping.

Physical violence is the norm in dysfunctional families. This includes actual physical spankings; having to go get your own weapons of torture, belts, switches, etc.; being punched, slapped, slapped in the face; pulled on, yanked on, choked, shook, kicked, pinched; tortured with tickling; being threatened with violence or abandonment, being threatened with being put in jail or having the police come; witnessing violence done to a parent or sibling.

This last is a major issue in homes where wives are battered. A child witnessing his mother being battered is equivalent to the child being battered. A witness to violence is a victim of violence.

I recently spoke at the Mayor's conference on battered women. In my city, Houston, the figure on battered women is one out of four. The subject of battered women is being documented at an alarming rate.

Bonding to Violence

Bonding to physical violence is perplexing and paradoxical. One would think that the trauma of it is so great that one would never get near it again. Actually, the exact opposite is closer to the truth. Being beaten and humiliated is so shaming that one's sense of self-worth diminishes. The more one is beaten, the more one's self-worth diminishes. The more one thinks they are lowly and flawed as a human being, the more *one's choices diminish*. One becomes bonded to violence.

Learned Helplessness

Another theory attempting to explain the paradoxical bonding to violence is the theory of learned helplessness. This theory was developed by Martin Seligman. He hypothesized that dogs subjected to noncontingent negative reinforcement could learn that their voluntary behavior had no effect on controlling what happened to them. If the original kind of stimulus was repeated, the dog's motivation to respond was lessened.

Various types of experiments have been done to support this hypothesis. These have included dogs, cats, birds, rats, mice, fish, primates and humans. Some animals learned to be helpless at a faster rate and became more helpless across a greater number of situations. For some the learning only occurred in one situation, others generalized it and were helpless in all areas of stressful behavior.

Seligman's study is the most illustrative. His research team placed dogs in cages and administered electrical shocks at random and varied intervals. The dogs quickly learned that no matter what response they made, they could not control the shock. In the beginning, the dogs tried various movements in an attempt to escape. When nothing they did stopped the shocks, they ceased any voluntary action and became submissive. Later the researchers changed the procedure and attempted to teach the dogs that they could escape by crossing to the other side of the cage, the dogs still remained passive and helpless. Even when the door was left open and the dogs were shown the way out, they refused to leave and did not avoid the shock.

The earlier in life the dogs received such treatment, the longer it took to overcome the effects of this so-called learned helplessness.

A graphic illustration of learned helplessness was reported in a Florida paper recently. It seems that 100 nice hotel beds and rooms were made available for some of the street people in a Florida city. Only four people took the offer.

When applied to the physical battering of women and children, this theory helps us to see why battered children and battered wives come to believe that they are helpless. The children tend to set up the exact kind of relationships later on, and the wives do not attempt to free themselves from the battering relationship.

The belief in helplessness is the most important aspect of this phenomena. The battered child or wife becomes determined by a negative cognitive set, a negative belief system. They really come to believe that the situation is hopeless. This is the reason victims of violence do not attempt to free themselves from the battering relationships.

Children are actually as helpless as they believe themselves to be; women believe they are but they usually are not. Children victimized by physical violence tend to generalize the feeling of helplessness. They feel helpless in other adverse situations. Such children become "externalizers". They believe that most of the events that occur in their lives are caused by factors outside their control.

Often the physically abused child is in a family where the mother is being battered. A girl child victimized by witnessing her mother's violation grows up to believe that she cannot escape being battered. She believes with her mother that women cannot escape men's overall coercion.

A boy child may become the victim of the mother's repressed rage and be battered by her. If he witnesses his father's violence, he may grow up to believe in male supremacy and in the stereotyped picture of male supremacy in the family. Boy children more often than girls identify with the violent offender and become offenders. Bonding with the offender is a way to overcome the feeling of helplessness and powerlessness. The person bonding with an offender literally loses his own reality and becomes the offender. In that way he feels he can survive. Every offender was once a victim who bonded with his offender. Battering husbands and parents were once helpless victims.

I was fascinated at my own intense response to the movie *Rambo*. Obviously massive numbers of others were fascinated with it, too. In this movie Rambo is hunted by the abusing and unjust authority figures, represented by the Sheriff and his deputies. Rambo subsequently kills them all and totally annihilates the town where he encountered them. The abusive treatment of Rambo touches the abused and revenge-seeking child in all of us. While my law-abiding adult is horrified by Rambo's mass killings, my child cheers him on.

Boundaries and Abuse

Both incest and physically abusive families tend to be dominated by the rules of the poisonous pedagogy. The family profiles show strong and rigid boundaries around the family. The boundaries are often established by strong religious beliefs, as well as the belief in following perfectionistic and rigid rules. Thus the whole family is oriented toward an "externalizer"- type boundary dynamic. The hurt and pain is coded in the family secret. The child is forbidden to talk out of obedience to the adults. No new information can come into the family because of the rigidity of the system and the male hierarchical control. The religious rules often call anything outside the family religion (usually fundamental-istic or highly authoritarian) "secular humanism". Anything psychological is looked upon with suspicion. Hence, the very material that could give new permissions and offer guidance is rejected.

Physical violence affects a level of shame second only to sexual abuse. Being slapped, jossled, pinched, shoved, etc., is often done in public. It may be in public places or in front of brothers and sisters or older children. Shame is the feeling of being exposed before one is ready to be exposed. Shame is often associated with being looked at — having eyes on you before you're ready to be seen. Shame is associated with being caught naked, with one's pants down, as it were. Children are frequently made to take their pants down to get spanked.

Many other debilitating consequences flow from the shame. To feel flawed as a person lessens one's motivation to initiate action. To believe that there is nothing one can do to control one's life greatly reduces one's ability to learn and to solve problems. Thus the range of responses from which one can choose is greatly narrowed by shame. One's will becomes disabled; one becomes blind to options. A deep profound chronic depression sets in.

Look at the following checklist. Many of the symptoms of adult children of physically and sexually violent families are identical to the symptoms of people who have been chronically stressed like war victims or victims of concentration camps. Using the letters on the phrase, **Adult Children of Physical Violence,** check out whether you may have lost your true self through physical violence.

A *Abuse feels normal*
D *Delusion and denial*
U *Unreality*
L *Loss of the ability to initiate or solve problems*
T *Trust issues*

C *Criminal behavior*
H *Hostility and internalized rage*
I *Intense jealousy and possessiveness*
L *Loneliness, alienation, isolation*
D *Dissociated and depersonalized*
R *Rigidity*
E *Eating disorders*
N *Numbed out and apathetic*

O *Objectification of self and others*
F *Fixated personality development*

P *Prostitution and sexualized rage*
H *Hypervigilant and fear of losing control*
Y *Yearning for parental approval*
S *Shame-based*
I *Illness — real or imagined*
C *Co-dependent*
A *Acting-out behaviors*
L *Loss of boundaries*

V *Victim role*
I *Incensed at parents*
O *Offender status*
L *Low grade chronic depression*
E *Externalizer*
N *Nightmares or dream repression*
C *Compulsive/addictive behavior*
E *Extremely split*

A. Abuse Feels Normal

You continue to live in abusive situations. You feel that there are no other choices. This is your lot.

D. Delusion and Denial

You idealize your parents. You minimize their physical punishments. You have never thought that you could leave the physically abusive relationship you are in. You still think you can control the physical abuse by being more perfect or by pleasing your offender.

U. Unreality

You often feel like things and events around you are unreal. You can't understand why people are so interested in certain aspects of life. You have little real interest in anything.

L. Loss of the Ability to Initiate Things or Solve Problems

You can't get started, have trouble completing thought processes, can't seem to see any alternatives and feel confused a lot.

T. Trust Issues

You trust no one. When you have risked trusting, your judgment was bad. You don't trust your own perceptions, feelings or thoughts. You're not attracted to those who seem to be truly trustworthy.

C. Criminal Behavior

You are or have been in trouble with the law. You were a delinquent. You secretly steal or have stolen in the past. You feel that nothing is wrong with cheating or stealing if you can get away with it.

H. Hostility and Internalized Rage

You are angry a lot and inflict your nasty moods on to others or you are terrified of anger and manipulated by it. You are passive aggressive. You feel like lashing out at everyone.

I. Intensely Jealous and Possessive

You control your spouse and children. You are possessive and jealous. You are offended at the slightest withdrawal of their attention.

L. Loneliness Alienation Isolated

You feel lost. You feel different from other people. You feel like you don't really belong. You feel crazy without any attendant psychosis.

D. Dissociated and Depersonalized

You don't have control over your physical self. You are disconnected from your body. You don't know when you are tired, hungry or "horny". You are cold and distant. You do not have warmth or intimacy with anyone. You have no memories from childhood. You have catastrophic fantasies. You are paranoid. You have lots of accidents.

R. Rigidity

Operating with fixed and rigid rules. Your body is rigid and without much feeling. You are inflexible.

E. Eating Disorders

You don't know when you feel empty or hungry. You eat to fill up. You eat to feel full. You repress anger and eat to cover it up.

N. Numbed Out and Apathetic

You are numb. You deny your feelings. You feel apathetic and listless. You have low energy.

O. Objectification of Self and Others

You do not experience others as persons but as objects to be used. You treat yourself as an object. You indulge yourself usually in secret. Long history of thumb-sucking. Early and chronic masturbation. You objectify sex partners: You see a woman as a set of breasts, rather than as a person.

F. Fixated Personality Development

You are emotionally a child. You are extremely needy. You have impulse control problems. You are insatiable in your need for affection and expression of love. You are fixated at the age your physical abuse started.

P. Prostitution and Sexualized Rage

You are now or have been a prostitute. You were manipulated and used physically by your parents. You have open or secret contempt for the opposite sex.

H. Hypervigilant and Fear Loss of Control

You live in a state of readiness for attack. You feel jumpy and are easily startled. You have attacks of sudden fear or panic. You fear losing control.

Y. Yearn for Paternal Approval

You continue to seek your parents' approval and love. You do things you think will please them, only to be disappointed over and over again.

S. Shame-based

You feel inadequate and flawed as a human being. You feel that what happened to you in childhood you deserved. You think you are bad and deserve all the bad things that have happened to you. You are self-destructive and have tried to mutilate yourself on occasion. You feel you are almost always wrong.

I. Illness — Real and Imagined

You have been sick a great deal in your life. You go to doctors often. You have been told that there is no organic cause for a lot of your physical illnesses. You have lots of headaches, stomachaches, backaches. You are accident prone.

C. Co-dependent

You have no sense of your own reality. You do not know what you feel, need or want. You have great trouble making decisions. You have a great need to control other's behavior.

A. Acting-Out Behaviors

You commit a lot of violent behaviors. You do to your children what was done to you. You do to other people what was done to you. You reenact either as offender or victim what was done to you in childhood.

L. Loss of Boundaries

You have very poor physical boundaries. You let everyone touch you, or put up walls so that no one touches you. You have sex when you don't want to. You have sex with people you don't want to have sex with. Or you won't have sex with anyone.

V. Victim Role

You continually end up being a victim. You feel you can't control being victimized.

I. Incensed at Parents

You hate your parents. You resent them and obsess on the wrong they did to you. You haven't seen them in years. You see them as little as possible.

O. Offender Status

You have been called an offender. You beat your wife. You beat your children. You violate other's rights. You break the law and feel no compunction. You rage at those around you. You have little empathy or sympathy.

L. Low Grade Chronic Depression

You have been depressed as far back as you can remember. You have intermittent thoughts of suicide. You believe you are helpless to change the course of your life.

E. Externalizer

You believe that most of the events that occur in life happen outside of your or anyone's control.

N. Nightmares or Dream Repression

You have recurring nightmares or you never dream. You have occasional memory blips — like a scene flashes on the screen and disappears. You never know whether it really happened or not.

C. Compulsive/Addictive Behaviors

You are an addict. You are compulsive and impulsive.

E. Extremely Split

You have at least two personalities. You are one way on the outside and another way at home. No one can believe you are so different at home. You have several personalities. You are confused about your own identity.

The reader may be beginning to see the overlap in these responses to violence. Being violated is being violated. The first level response is fear. Fear for one's life and fear because one is out of control. A second level response is hurt at the betrayal inflicted by supposed loved ones.

The final level is anger, shame and isolation. Because the violence is so painful, ego defenses are activated and the person numbs out. The numbed-out state is what sets people up for compulsive/addictive behavior and acting out. All our checklists so far have variations of these elements in them.

Sexual and physical violence are devastating forms of abandonment. The child is left alone. The child is a victim of his parents' or caretaker's shameless needs. They are used and abused. Sexual and physical violence is about the silence of nights spent holding in screams, holding back tears, holding in one's very self.

Summary

The key points covered in this chapter can be summed up using the letters of the word **PERSECUTED.**

P. **Physical Violation — Body as the Ground of Our Being** — Physical and sexual abuse violate the ground of a person's being. Our body image is our most fundamental boundary. When one's body is violated, the core of the self is injured.

E. **Extent of Incest and Sexual Abuse** — Because the common conception of sexual violation is the "horror story" kind, few people are aware of the many other forms of sexual abuse. In this chapter we looked at four base categories of sexual violation: physical, overt explicit (voyeurism, exhibitionism); covert (verbal and boundary violation) and emotional (cross-generational bonding).

R. **Responses to Physical and Sexual Violence as Normal Behavior** — Because physical and sexual abuse are so traumatic, the dissociation from the trauma is intense. Memory loss is common in these forms of violence. The victim loses the connection between the violence and the response to violence. Victims come to believe their reactive behavior is their normal behavior. They condemn their behavior as crazy and neurotic. In reality it is a *normal* reaction to violence. Learned helplessness and bonding to violence are outcomes of this disconnection.

S. **Set-up for Physical Violation Results from Poisonous Pedagogy** — The poisonous pedagogy promotes a master/slave kind of ownership relationship between parents and children. This belief in ownership implicitly opens up the possibility of physical and sexual abuse.

E. **Entire Family System Involved in Incest and Physical Violence** — There is always a collusive role played by the spouse of the offender. The non-abusing parent either consciously or unconsciously permits the victimization. All other members are being severely affected by the abuse. All are co-dependents.

C. Checklists — These checklists for sexual and physical violence offer victims a way to connect the violence with the natural reactions to the violence. In identifying the behavioral reactions they can better determine what happened to them.

U. Universality of Physical Abuse — In this chapter I pointed out that the battering of women and children is part of an ancient and pervasive tradition. Even with the woman's movement, one out of eight women are still being battered.

T. Typical Offenders — The common characteristics of both sexual and physical offenders are: poor self-image; lack of sensitivity to others feelings; shame-based; abuse in some way themselves; unrealistic expectation for children; in delusion and denial; isolated.

E. Ego Defenses — Special emphasis was placed on dissociation as an ego defense. This defense allows one to leave one's body when it is being violated. One learns to completely cut off feelings and physically numb out. This sets victims up for compulsive/addictive behavior.

D. Denial (Keeping the Secret) — The greatest problem with physical/sexual victimization is that victims cannot *express* their fear, hurt and anger. The incest victims are in a true Catch-22. If they tell, they risk losing their family.

7

The 'Bad' Child

Checklist For How You Lost Your SELF And Became An Adult Child Of Emotional Violence

"If a child lives with criticism, he learns to condemn.
If a child lives with hostility, he learns to fight.
If a child lives with shame, he learns to feel ashamed."

Dorothy Law Nolte

Pia Mellody suggests that children are born with two basic questions: Who am I? and How do I do it? The latter question pertains to the child's getting his basic needs met and making his way in the world. The most dominant need that any child has is to move from the complete environmental support of infancy and childhood to the self-support of maturity.

In order to grow, children need their parents' attention, time, affirmation of their feelings, direction, and good modeling.

In many ways children also offer parents a chance to learn and grow.

As a child meets each developmental level, the parent will have that same developmental level need triggered. Infancy is an opportunity for any parent to be aware of how they fared with their own infancy needs. Children offer parents a chance to look at the rich emotional life that they once had and could have again. Alice Miller writes in *For Your Own Good:*

"Children need a large measure of emotional and physical support from the adult. This support must include the following elements:

1. Respect for the child
2. Respect for his needs
3. *Tolerance for his feelings* (italics mine)
4. Willingness to learn from his behavior . . .
   a. About the nature of the individual child
   b. About the child in the parents themselves
   c. About the nature of emotional life, which can be observed more clearly in the child than in the adult because the child can experience his feelings much more intensely and . . . undisguisedly than the adult."

This text reminds me of the lines from Kahlil Gibran:

"Your children are not your children . . . you may strive to be like them but seek not to make them like you. For life goes forward not backward."

Maybe this is what the scripture means when it exhorts us to become as little children. Instead of learning from our children, the poisonous pedagogy exhorts us to mold and train them like animals. It asks us to crush their vitality, spontaneity and emotional expression.

At any given moment we are having emotions. While our emotions are not all of who we are, they are our vital connection with life as it is now. Our emotions are one of our basic powers. They tell us of a need, a loss, a satiation. They are the oil gauge on our car telling us how it goes with our basic needs. Such needs are the fuel without which our lives cannot run in any functional manner.

Anger, Sex and Emotional Energy

I have been offering you checklists to see how you may have lost your precious and incomparable inner child. The checklist I now propose applies to everyone. It's my opinion that everyone has been violated emotionally. When it comes to emotional development, the poisonous pedagogy is clear. Strong feelings are harmful and weak. They mar rational clarity and they must be controlled. The two emotions that are especially dangerous are anger and sexual feelings. I can't imagine a person in a modern American home who was allowed to have their sexual or anger emotions for very long.

Anger is essential as the core energy of our strength. Without the energy of anger, one becomes a doormat and a people-pleaser.

Anger is an *emotion* often confused with *behaviors* like hitting, screaming, cursing. The latter are behaviors based on judgment. They are not emotions.

Without sexual emotions and the mature age appropriate behaviors based on them, the human race would die out in 100 years. Sexual emotions promote and preserve the species. Angry emotions protect and preserve the individual.

E-motions are energies in motion. If they are not expressed, the energy is repressed. As energy it has to go somewhere. Emotional energy *moves* us as does all energy. We are moved to tears when we've lost something dear to us. We are moved to action when we feel our shame. We are moved to joy when our needs are being met. Without our emotions we can't know where we are with our basic needs. Without our basic needs we cannot live as functional human beings. To deny our emotions is to deny the ground and vital energy of our life.

Because our emotions are forms of energy we can only stop them by mustering counterenergy. We do this with muscle tension, shallow breathing, fantasies of punishment, abandonment or critical self-talk. This tensing, internal talking and shallow breathing is the way we physically numb out. After years and years of practice, we can literally no longer feel our emotions. Psychic numbness is the soil out of which our addictions are born. Our addictions are the way we feel alive.

In my drinking days, I felt much more alive and sane when I was drinking than when I was sober. As the chemicals relaxed my muscles, I could feel my feelings. I felt high. Being high or euphoric is the way we are supposed to feel when we are fully functional. Drunk I felt alive, sober I felt numb and dead.

Emotional violation is the most common core of our current cultural crisis. Our massive addiction and family violence are rooted in the denial and repression of our affective life. This repression of emotion is supported by our schools, our churches and our legal system.

Figure 7.1. Ego Boundaries

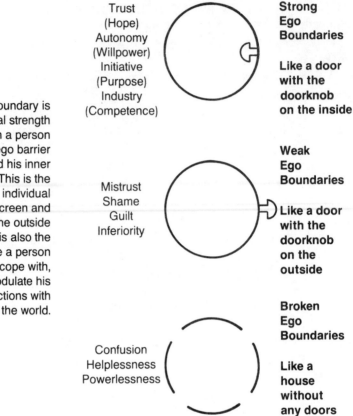

Ego boundary is the internal strength by which a person has an ego barrier to guard his inner space. This is the means the individual uses to screen and interpret the outside world. It is also the structure a person uses to cope with, and modulate his interactions with the world.

Trust
(Hope)
Autonomy
(Willpower)
Initiative
(Purpose)
Industry
(Competence)

Strong
Ego
Boundaries

Like a door
with the
doorknob
on the inside

Mistrust
Shame
Guilt
Inferiority

Weak
Ego
Boundaries

Like a door
with the
doorknob
on the
outside

Confusion
Helplessness
Powerlessness

Broken
Ego
Boundaries

Like a
house
without
any doors

Epigenetic Development

Human development occurs epigenetically. This means that one stage builds upon the previous one. There is a time of developmental readiness. Nature has her developmental rhythms. At a certain age the human organism moves toward muscle development, walking and talking. At approximately 18 months, children start saying "No, let me do it." At three and one half years, they start asking "Why?" At six years they get obstinate again. At 15 they puberty on us and begin moving away from home. Each stage marks a crisis. Each crisis is a time of potential growth, as well as a time of heightened vulnerability. If the developmental tasks are not accomplished at the proper time and in the proper sequence, the organism goes on without developmental strength.

The strength of our ego boundaries is the result of each properly resolved developmental crisis. If the crisis is resolved and the need is met, the ego grows in strength. If the developmental task is not met, the ego does not obtain the structure it needs for the next developmental task. It is weakened and when the need is not met at all, it is broken.

In Figure 7.1 I've tried to show three symbols of ego structure. These ego structures are what I referred to earlier as ego boundaries. A child needs to develop strong ego boundaries to move into adolescence. If a person can become solidly a child, while he is a child, he then has the foundation to enter adolescence on his way to becoming an adult. If we cannot be children while we are children, we become adult children. Jean Jacques Rousseau said this well when he wrote:

> "Nature wants children to be children before they are men. If we deliberately depart from this order, we shall get premature fruits which are neither ripe nor well flavored and which soon decay. We shall have youthful sages and grown-up children. Childhood has ways of seeing, thinking and feeling, peculiar to itself; nothing can be more foolish than to substitute our ways for them."

Emotional abuse is a form of psychological battering. Psychological battering includes all other forms of abuse as one cannot be physically or sexually violated without being also psychologically battered.

In what follows I'll limit my discussion to the neglect of developmental dependency needs. Hopefully, the reader is aware that emotional violence is involved in all abuse.

Mirroring, Echoing, Affirming

The child's earliest needs are for a warm loving person to be there to mirror, echo and affirm them. This means that in the first 15 months of life (called the symbiotic stage) the child needs a face with accepting eyes to reflect his self. Whatever is in the mothering person's eyes becomes the core and foundation of the child's identity.

Alice Miller has argued that the infant child's inner sensations form the core of his self. These earliest sensations come from the mother's feeling about the child. Since the child is non-verbal, everything depends on feelings. This early feeling of self is the core out of which identity will be formed. This earliest need is called the healthy narcissistic need. If parents never got their narcissistic needs met, they will use their children as objects of narcissistic gratification. The child intuits very early on that he must take care of the parents' emotional needs if he is to survive.

I have a client, let's call her Gwenella, who was born to take care of her mother's grief for her brother who died one and a half years before my client was born. The facade of laughter and happiness that Gwenella came to counseling with was truly deceiving. She had been in a terrible marriage for 18 years, taking care of a cocaine-addicted spouse. Both of her children were acting out with drugs. When she finally took off her smiling, little Mary Sunshine mask, she began weeping buckets and hasn't stopped yet.

Touching, Warmth, Strokes, Belonging, Attachment

If our survival mothering figure is defended against her emotions and cut off from her spontaneity and warmth, we will not be touched in the way we need to be. Children need to be touched in order to establish a sense of warm contact. Such warm contact tells us that there is someone out there who we can trust and depend on. Our hope for getting our dependency needs met depends on this. If we can feel the touch and the warmth of an emotionally available person, we can begin our life with a sense of trust. We can believe that the world is friendly and warm. We can depend on what's out there to get our needs met. If our mothering person is not there for us emotionally, we will feel the coldness and mistrust the world. We will have to create a fantasy bond, an illusion of connectedness, in order to go on.

Stroke deprivation can literally kill a child in the earliest stages of life. As we grow older our need for physical strokes is extended into the need for emotional strokes. Emotional strokes mean getting attention, being prized and valued and having our growth achievements applauded.

When we cannot get these strokes in a healthy manner, we will do whatever we have to do to get them. Strokes are a *basic* need. Strokes are to the psyche what food is to the body. Children who do not get strokes in a healthy way, get them in unhealthy ways. Being *singled out* as bad, causing trouble, being the family failure are all forms of recognition.

Selfness, Self-value, Self-acceptance, Self-actualization

We need to be valued for the special person we are. We need to see all of ourself in the eyes of our caretakers as we interact with them. All our emotions, all our needs, all our drives need to be echoed back to us so we can get a sense of ourselves and establish an inner unity. If parts of us are accepted (when we giggle and coo) and other parts are rejected (when we have a temper tantrum or cry too loud), then those parts get split off. Each time we feel those parts of ourselves, our internalized parental eyes and later voices reject them. These rejected parts of self (most often our sexuality, anger and aggressiveness) operate underground. They continue to grow outside our consciousness and have a life and power of their own.

Anger, for example, can explode on us without warning. People often say "I don't know what came over me today," or "I lost it today," meaning I lost my temper. I got out of control. The same is true for sadness or fear.

Growing up I was not allowed to have anger. It was one of the seven deadly mortal sins. A well-meaning Catholic nun passed an x-ray of a diseased lung around the room and told us that's what your soul looks like under mortal sin. I vowed never to get angry again. I was urged to be nice. I was compared (a form of shaming) to a rat fink down the street named B.W. "Why can't you be nice like B.W.," I was told. B.W. actually set fires to garages, but was a saint around adults.

I also grew up, like most males, being told, "Real men don't cry" and "Don't be afraid. There's nothing to be afraid of."

Even when I was joyous, I couldn't be joyous too long because "there were starving children in Latin America." If you can't be glad, mad, sad or afraid, you have to pretty well shut down.

Your true self indeed must shut down and a false self is created. This false self meets the needs of both the parents and the covert needs of the system for balance. When a child can experience his own emotions, he can individuate in the proper developmental sequence. But as Fossum and Mason write:

> "When children begin to fill the parents' needs and shut down emotionally, they cannot rely on their own emotions and become consciously and then unconsciously dependent on the parents for thoughts and feelings. This dependency is soon transferred to the outside world." *Facing Shame*

Autonomy, Difference, Space, Separation

Children have a need to be different. They have a need for physical space. In fact, the need for physical space is the foundation for a person's physical boundary. Never did a child of mine do a task exactly like I showed them or asked them to do it. They did it their way. And as frustrating as that often was, it's the way God and nature intended it.

Each person is unique, unrepeatable and incomparable. Each has a basic need for individuality, autonomy and difference. This need emerges at about 15 months. This is the beginning of the long journey of separation. After symbiotic bonding, we begin separating. This is a painful process (as evidenced by temper tantrums).

The Terrific Twos mark the beginning. In this period a child learns that his name is "Don't". The child starts saying "No" and this is wonderful. If we would allow children to say no the way nature and God designed it, we wouldn't have as many molested children and we wouldn't have to have a national campaign trying to teach teenagers to just say "No". Child molesters are like hunters going after prey. They know to look for the most needy and the *most obedient* child on the playground.

The great danger in the autonomous stage is shame. The child needs to learn a sense of shame and doubt. These are important limits. Shame is the emotion that lets us know we are finite. It tells us we will and can make mistakes. It lets us know we are in need of help, that we are not omnipotent. Shame is what tempers the child's omnipotent willpower. However, too much shaming begins the process of turning the child's need to exercise his will and manipulate the environment against himself.

As Erik Erikson writes in *Childhood and Society*:

> "He will overmanipulate himself. He will develop a precocious conscience. Instead of taking possession of things in order to test them by purposeful repetition, he will become obsessed by his own repetitiousness . . . he learns to gain power by stubborn and minute control . . . Such hollow victory is the infantile mold for the compulsive neurosis. It is also the source of later attempts to govern by the letter, rather than by the spirit."

Too much shaming creates the internalized shame that is covered by obsessive control and perfectionism. Here one can see the generational cycle in full swing. The compulsive controlling parent shames the child who will be an adult with a compulsive controlling immature child inside.

Shame results from all forms of abandonment. Actual physical abandonment is shaming. As a child my father was never there. I felt worth-less than his time. We have seen how physical and sexual abuse are shaming. All forms of psychological abuse are shaming: yelling, belitting, name-calling, labeling, criticizing, judging, ridiculing, humiliating, comparing, contempting are all sources of shame. Shame-based parents are models of shame. How could shame-based parents possibly teach their children self-love?

The most destructive aspect of shame is the process whereby shame moves from being a feeling to being a *state of being (i.e., internalized)*. This comes about when one's emotions, needs and drives are shamed. I've discussed how one's emotions get shamed. When I'm taught that anger is a deadly sin, I am ashamed when I am angry. My anger gets bound by shame. What this means is that when I feel anger, I also feel shame. Likewise with fear, sadness and joy.

In the system I grew up in the only emotion you could have without shame was guilt. Guilt is an important emotion. In healthy family systems, guilt is the conscience former. It makes one accountable and responsible. Guilt is developmentally more mature than shame. It presupposes the presence of some internalized values. Guilt is the feeling of regret one has about behavior that violated a sense of personal value. Fossum and Mason in *Facing Shame* write:

> "While guilt is a painful feeling of regret and responsibility for one's actions, shame is a painful feeling about oneself as a person."

Repair and reparation are closed off in internalized shame. Shame is about one's identity not about the transgression of one's values.

What I grew up with was neurotic guilt. Neurotic guilt is a mask veneer of co-dependency. Neurotic guilt occurs in dysfunctional family systems which are enmeshed. In such systems each person is playing their rigid role in order to keep the closed system in balance and each is giving up his uniqueness in order to perform his false self role in loyalty to the system. Neurotic guilt denies one any sense of uniqueness. In fact, in dysfunctional families any attempt to leave the system, to give up one's rigid role, to individuate, to differentiate, to be unique and different is met with anger and rejection. Anyone in a dysfunctional family trying to be his own unique self will feel guilt. It's important to see that this guilt *is a symptom of the dysfunctional system.*

Remember that the individuals in a dysfunctional family exist for the family. The family does not exist for the individuals.

Internalized shame also results from one's drives being shamed. A curious three-year-old will start finding parts of his body. I can envisage the following scenario.

One day little Farquahr finds his nose. He calls it by name, which greatly excites Mom. Mom calls Grandma over who promptly asks Farquahr to show her his nose. He proudly responds and receives beaucoup strokes. Later on he finds his ear and gets the same response. Likewise with his elbow, fingers and navel . . . and then one Sunday with all the family in the living room (and maybe even with the preacher visiting) he finds his penis. To his little mind, "If the nose got 'em, this is really going to get 'em." Not so. Never has little Farquahr been removed so fast from a room. He has never seen such disdain on his mother's face (not even as bad as when he covered his bedroom wall with shit). He gets it, "There will be no genitals in this family." From that moment on his sexual feeling and drive will be shamed. His sexuality will have to live in secret. It certainly cannot be a part of an open spontaneous, vibrant family life. And we wonder why "disorder of desire" is the most common sexual dysfunction in marriages. And why Masters and Johnson found 68% of marriages sexually dysfunctional. How can one live in a family where genital sex is totally secretive (or banal) for 20 years and then when one gets married, one expects to have everything sexual be open and vibrant? Many people can only be excited sexually as long as it's illicit. It's when it's licit, part of family life, that many people turn off. What a tragedy! Sexuality is the most shamed of all our human drives.

Children also get their aggressive drives shamed. They are curtailed in their rambunctiousness. They are curtailed in their curiosity and desire to explore and learn. Often their drives to eliminate are shamed in potty training so that they wind up like me, having to run water in bathrooms so that no one will know I'm doing the dastardly thing. And God help me if I'm caught in public with a need for number two. That is a catastrophic nightmare. Once the drives are shamed, each time a person feels a natural urge or drive he will also feel shame.

Likewise with all the needs I'm describing. If no one was there to touch you, and you were shamed for wanting to be close and touch, when you felt the need to touch you would also feel shame. Lots of men have been shamed in their need to hug, cuddle and touch. They learn to project or use the ego defense of conversion when that need comes up because they were shamed for being needy. Real men don't need.

When I project my need to be touched, I usually do it by looking at someone, usually a female, and saying "You look like you need a hug." As a counselor I can get away with hugs all day. Who really needs to be hugged is me.

A lot of men convert the need to be touched and be close into sexuality. They sexualize their affectional needs. They come home from work. They feel the need to be warm and close so they say "I'm horny."

Women have been shamed for their sexual needs — even more so than men. So women learn to be ashamed of their sexual needs. They will affectionalize their sexual needs. They may be hugging and close and start to feel sexual. Then they feel shame and cut off those feelings. All needs can be shamed and in dysfunctional families they usually are. If one cannot be who he is and no one is really there for him, then any feelings, needs or wants he has are not okay.

Pleasure, Pain, Stimulation

Children need pleasure and fun. They need to be stimulated by age-appropriate challenges. Children also need to experience their legitimate suffering. Overindulging and oversubmissive parents are abandoning and abusing their children by not letting them experience the normal amounts of pain that life brings. Pain is the vehicle of growth and the carver of wisdom. "Without a hurt, a heart is hollow," the song says. "The deeper that sorrow carves into your being, the more joy you can contain," writes the poet. It is abuse of the first order to protect a child from this source of growth, courage and wisdom.

Overperfectionistic and overly punitive parents deprive their children of the fun, laughter, joy and spontaneity which are a right of childhood. The stern authoritarian, often somber religious parent cuts off these life-giving and spontaneous emotions. I'm continually amazed at what happens to the "good news of salvation" in some churches. Instead of joy, freedom and celebration, there is black somber salubrious gastric indigestion. Children growing up in such families are being severely deprived of the joys of childhood.

Dependability, Predictability

Children need their parents to be dependable. They need to count on them being there as they test their personal limits. This testing of personal limits is a requirment for identity formation. It demands that there be a reasonably healthy solid person there for a child to push against.

For example, when the two-year-old ventures out in exploration and autonomy, he needs the mothering person to be there. He may say let me do it but if Mom leaves the room, he'll follow her and do it where she's in his peripheral vision. He needs to find his boundaries and self-identity within the limits of safety. This will hold true all the way through adolescence. An adolescent needs to test and experiment and have a Dad and Mom with a pretty firm identity who he knows is there. If Dad is needy and wants his son to show him how grateful he is for all Dad has done (I'm struggling with this now with my 17-year-old), then the son has to *interrupt his identity formation* to take care of needy Dad.

The need for dependency is the need for predictability and meaning. Children need their parents to be there for them in a reasonably predictable manner. In dysfunctional families, the children never know what to expect. Dad may be getting drunk — that's why he's not home. Mom may be hysterical or hypochrondriacal. The children have to walk on eggs. They never know what's coming next. The rageaholic father may have an outburst at the most unexpected times.

Adult children often use their children as a substitute for their own parents. Hence the child can become the "object of an endless number of contradictory wishes and expectations that cannot possibly be fulfilled." (Alice Miller)

In such an atmosphere the children have no time to tend to their own feelings, needs and wants. They must be hypervigilant. They are constantly on alert to what may be happening next in the family. Much more could be said about the developmental dependency needs. There are more subtle and cruel forms of emotional abuse, such as double binds, out-and-out cruelty, torture and corruption.

My thesis is that the job of parents is to be there for children. This is why I wouldn't let anyone under 30 have a child. I'd also have extensive mental health tests and childrearing instruction be prerequisites for parenting. Since there's a fat chance that this will ever happen, no one need worry about me getting my way. I'm 50 now and I'm ready to be a parent, I think!

There are *no bad children.* Children are born precious, unique and incomparable. We must fight to protect children so that each child has the right to a good childhood.

I certainly don't believe that everyone always stays good and pristine. And I believe that evil is the most obvious fact in the universe. There are bad people — but there would be far less if more children had a healthy emotional environment to grow up in.

Children are confused by the moralistic measures imposed on them at an early age. We ask two year olds if they've been a "good" boy or a "bad" boy. We call them good boys or good girls when they please us. We call them bad boys and girls when they displease us. Such distinctions are parents' projections and come from the moralistic presuppositions of the poisonous pedagogy.

Lawrence Kohlberg at Harvard has spent the better part of a lifetime, researching moral development in children. His studies are built on the monumental work of Jean Piaget, who spent 50 years studying how children's minds work. He's written a dozen books and one hundred plus

Figure 7.2. Human Development

Erikson — Emotional	Kohlberg-Moral	Piaget-Mental
Ages 0-15 months — Symbiotic **Trust v. Mistrust** Mirroring, touching, warmth, pleasure, pain, sadness, fear, dependability **HOPE**	**Ages 0-7/8 years** **Pre-Moral** The good is what I do and like — what is pleasurable —	**Ages 0-2 years** **Sensory-Motor** Conquest of the object out of sight is out of mind
Ages 15 months - 3 years **Separation** **Autonomy v. Shame & Doubt** Curiosity, space, separation, anger **WILLPOWER**	The good is what I do and like and can get away with.	**Ages 2 - 7/8 years** Pre-Logical Magical Egocentric Transductive Logic Mind is Like a Slide Projector Conquest of the Symbol
Ages 3 years to 7 years **Primary Identity** Initiative v. Guilt Sexuality **PURPOSE**		
Ages 7/8 to Puberty **Industry v. Inferiority** Learning • Social Skills Co-operation **COMPETENCE**	**Ages 7/8 to Puberty** 1. Avoid Punishment 2. Hedonism and Concrete Reciprocity — You scratch my back — I'll scratch yours	**Ages 7/8 to Puberty** Logical Thinking Concrete Literal Co-operation — Social interest
Puberty **Identity v. Role Diffusion** Builds upon previous identifications with parental models **FIDELITY**	**Puberty** Mutuality and Interpersonal Relations Acceptance By Others	**Puberty** **Abstract Logic** Conquest of thought, think about thinking, future is a problem Ideals, Idols — Value Formation

articles showing us his researched data on the stages of mental development. Kohlberg's data suggests the following: From birth to seven years old, children are pre-moral. The good is what they want and like. Only at about age seven do they begin to think logically, although their logic is limited to the concrete literal. With proper challenge they move from thinking that the good is what you can get away with to a kind of concrete reciprocity — you scratch my back and I'll scratch yours. Only in adolescence are they cognitively capable of altruistic thinking. In adolescence morality is dominated by interpersonal conformity. Only later on is the mind capable of mature thinking. The good is worthy of being done. The good has intrinsic value. One does good because good is good to do. One does good because of principles and beliefs that one adheres to. It takes 25 years for one to get to this level of thinking. According to Kohlberg many adults never make it.

Figure 7.2 is a summary of the work of Erik Erikson, Lawrence Kohlberg and Jean Piaget on the emotional, moral and mental stages of human development. As far as I know, these are the best guidelines we have based on research and clinical data. No one accepts them as absolute but they constitute the best norms we have so far. Parents who model goodness and firmly establish behavioral consequence for anti-social behavior provide a much more stable moral foundation for their children than do spankings, and punishing and moralistic labeling. To label children bad throughout the first seven years is abusive and does damage to their self-worth. Calling children "bad", spanking and punishing them for being bad causes them shame. Shame-based people feel flawed and defective as human beings. If anything sets people up to be immoral, it's shame.

Look at the following checklist for adult children of emotionally violating families.

A   *Abandonment fears*
D   *Denial and delusion*
U   *Undifferentiated emotions*
L   *Loneliness and isolation*
T   *Thought disorders*

C   *Compulsive/addictive behavior*
H   *High-level anxiety*
I   *Intimacy problems*
L   *Loss of affect and energy*
D   *Drive and needs are shamed*
R   *Resentment/guilt cycle*
E   *Emotions in shame binds*
N   *No expression of emotions — no talk rule*

O   *Overly controlling*
F   *False SELF*

E   *Empty and narcissistically deprived*
M   *Manipulating and gamey*
O   *Overindulged and oversubmitted to*
T   *Terrorized and tormented*
I   *Insatiable inner child*
O   *Overly perfectionistic, rigid, authoritarian*
N   *Needy and wanting*
A   *Abused physically or sexually or both*
L   *Lack of emotional coping skills — lack of communication skills*

V   *Violated emotional boundaries*
I   *Internalized anger, sadness, fear, joy, shame*
O   *Offender/victim ambiguity*
L   *Loss of inner self-unity*
E   *Enmeshed in caretaking others' feelings*
N   *"Now" phobic*
C   *Corrupted through bad modeling*
E   *Emotional constraint (with or without dramatic outbursts)*

A. Abandonment Fears

You have great difficulty separating. You stay in relationships long after it is healthy to do so. You hoard things and cannot seem to let go of anyone or anything.

D. Denial and Delusion

You are fantasy bonded to your family of origin. You defend your parents against any suggestion that they did less than a sterling job. You continually try to please your parents and win their love. But no matter what you do, it is never quite enough.

U. Undifferentiated Emotions

You never know quite what you feel; you don't know how to express your emotions. You cry when you're angry; you get mad when you're afraid. You somatize your feelings, i.e., have unusual amounts of sickness. You feel through others.

L. Loneliness and Isolation

You are unconnected and things sometimes seem unreal. You feel lonely and never quite feel like you belong.

T. Thought Disorders

You detail to the point of boring other people. You generalize a lot and often obsess on things that you can't do anything about, like the Iranians, the government, the Communists. You obsess on little things, you ruminate and worry excessively. You stay in your head (intellectualize, explain, analyze) a lot and discuss your problems, rather than doing anything about them. You are always reading about your problems, learning why you are the way you are.

C. Compulsive/Addictive Behaviors

You use euphoric type substances to change your feelings. You use activities to distract you from your feelings.

H. High-Level Anxiety

You are chronically anxious. You don't know exactly what you fear, but you imagine the worst. You catastrophize.

I. Intimacy Problems

When you start feeling close to someone, you sabotage the relationship. You're attracted to emotionally unavailable people. When you could be close to someone, you are not interested. You cling to a relationship once you're involved.

L. Loss of Affect and Energy

People experience you as cold and mechanical. You are incongruent. You say you're happy, excited, angry, etc., but you don't look or sound happy, excited, angry, etc. You are numb.

D. Drives and Needs Are Shame-Bound

When you feel horny, hungry, want to be touched or need something, you feel ashamed. ·

R. Resentment/Guilt Cycle

You feel resentment about your duties to your family of origin or to current family, but you feel guilty when you're not taking care of those duties. You feel resentment because you cannot pursue your own individual interests. And you feel guilty anytime you do act differently in your own self-interest.

E. Emotional Shame Binds

When you feel any emotion, you feel shame.

N. No Expression of Emotions Rule

You grew up in a family where no one expressed how they felt. You were supposed to mind read. You were supposed to know your parents loved you, even though they never told you or that other members of the family were mad, hurt, sad or afraid. It was simply not okay to express or talk about your feelings.

O. Overly Controlling

You try to control everyone and everything around you. You try to control other people's behavior. You try to control what can't be controlled. You control your emotions and feel shame when you can't.

F. False Self

You pretend a lot. You gauge your behavior by how it looks — by the image you believe you're making. You wear a mask, play a rigid role and hide your emotions. You say you're fine when you feel hurt or sad. You say you're not angry when you are.

E. Empty and Narcissistically Deprived

You feel empty and go from one experience to another trying to be satisfied. No matter how much you do or how much you get, you never feel satisfied.

M. Manipulating and Gamey

You use your energy to play games with people. You manipulate to get your needs met, rather than being straightforward about it.

O. Overindulged and Oversubmitted to

You pamper and indulge yourself. You are constantly irritated because people don't respond to your needs. You are demanding and impatient and expect others to see to it that your needs are met. You blame others for everything that goes wrong in your life. You never feel that you are responsible for what's happening.

T. Terrorized and Tormented

You feel frightened most of the time. You are easily startled and shaken. You panic easily. You torment yourself with self-judgment. You are self-deprecating.

I. Insatiable Inner Child — Immature

You look like an adult and walk and talk like an adult, but you really feel like a child.

O. Overly Perfectionistic, Rigid and Authoritarian

You endlessly strive to do everything right. You constantly monitor yourself. You are critical and judgmental.

N. Needy and Wanting

You feel needy and look to others to fill your needs. You married to be taken care of. Your wants are never filled or you don't know what you want.

A. ABUSED PHYSICALLY OR SEXUALLY

L. Lack of Emotional Coping and Communicational Skills

You feel overwhelmed by strong emotions. You are frightened when you are around someone with strong emotions. You can't communicate what you feel or clarify what others are feeling.

V. Violated Emotional Boundaries

You don't know where you end and others begin. When your friend, spouse or children feel an emotion, you feel the exact emotion. You have no empathetic ability because you actually start feeling what others feel. You are intimidated by anger. You are manipulated by fear, sadness and anger.

I. Internalized Anger, Sadness, Fear, Shame, Joy, Guilt

You are an angry person; you don't feel anger. You are a sad person; you don't feel sadness. Internalizing feelings mean that they no longer rise and fall like feelings but function like the broken on button of a machine. They are frozen; they are a state of being. When shame is internalized, all the emotions are bound in shame.

O. Offender/Victim Ambiguity

In relationships you bounce back and forth between being a victim and being an offender.

L. Loss of Inner Self-Unity

You are alienated from some of your feelings. They function autonomously at times. For example, you find yourself losing your temper at unplanned times. You say "I don't know what came over me." The same with sadness, fear or sexual feelings.

E. Enmeshed in Caretaking Others' Feelings

You feel others' feelings and continually act in ways that will make others feel better. If they are angry, you change your behavior so that they will feel better. If they are sad, you will do things to take away their sadness.

N. "NOW" Phobic

You feel remorse about the past and wish you could do it over. You fantasize about the future saying, "Things will be better when it comes." You live in the past or future but never in the now. Memory and imagination are ways to avoid your present feelings.

C. Corrupted Through Bad Modeling

You trust no one. You live in paranoid expectation. You feel you should take whatever you can. You hate Negroes, Whites, Asians, Europeans, etc. You hurt and shame people whenever you can.

E. Emotional Constraint (with or without Dramatic Outburst)

You are physically numb and you feel and express no feelings. You are psychologically numb and you express your feeling in dramatic outbursts. In the latter way you get them over with quickly.

Summary

The key points covered in this chapter can be summed up using the letters of the phrase **BAD CHILD.**

B. Basic Dependency Needs — All children need someone they can depend on; have someone to mirror and echo them; to be touched; have their feelings affirmed; to be taken seriously and to be stimulated and challenged.

A. Attention, Direction Time and Good Modeling — Children need caretakers who give them time, attention, direction and good modeling. To be able to do this, parents need to get their own needs met.

D. Dependency Need Neglect — When a child's dependency needs are not met at the proper time and in the proper sequence, the energy of that developmental stage gets blocked. This blocked energy arrests emotional growth. One becomes an adult with an unfulfilled inner child.

C. Checklist for Emotional Violence — The list outlines the various reactions that normally result from emotional violation and neglect. The list is offered to help victims of emotional violence see that their behavior is more about what happened *to* them, than it is *about* them.

H. Hole in the Soul — The phrase "hole in the soul" is used to metaphorically describe the neglect of development dependency needs. This is the emotionally abused part of every adult child. It forms the core of the repetition compulsion.

I.   Internalized Shame — Shame moves from being a feeling to being a characterological state of being in three ways: (1) By shame-based modeling; (2) By being shamed (neglect, abuse); (3) By having one's feelings and drives shamed.

L. Loss of Affects — When feelings are not affirmed, they are split off from one's sense of self. One is be-side oneself. The energy which needs to be available for direct coping with the world is lost to the inner warfare of keeping the prohibited feelings in check. One loses all spontaneity.

D. Developmental Charts — The work of Erikson, Kohlberg and Piaget are outlined, showing the proper age level for emotional, intellectual and moral development.

8

The Most Common Family Illness — Co-dependence:

Checklist For How You Lost Your SELF And Became An Adult Child Of Any Dysfunctional Family

"There is nothing so rare as an act of your own."
Henry Thoreau

"You do not need to be loved, not at the cost of yourself . . . Of all the people you will know in a lifetime, you are the only one you will never leave or lose."
Jo Courdet
Advice From a Failure

Co-dependence is the most common family illness because it is what happens to anyone in any kind of a dysfunctional family. In every dysfunctional family, there is a primary stressor. This could be Dad's drinking or work addiction; Mom's hysterical control of everyone's feelings; Dad or Mom's physical or verbal violence; a family member's actual sickness or hypochondriasis; Dad or Mom's early death; the divorce; Dad or Mom's moral/religious righteousness; Dad or Mom's sexual abuse. Anyone, who becomes controlling in the family to the point of being experienced as a threat by the other members, initiates the dysfunction. This member becomes the primary stressor. Each member of the family adapts to this stress in an attempt to control it. Each becomes *outerdirected* and lives adapting to the stressor for as long as the stress exists. *Each becomes co-dependent on the stressor.*

Hans Selye has described what he calls the general adaptation syndrome in humans; any demand that is made on the organism that becomes a threat is adapted to in several ways. In the face of the threat, the body prepares to fight or take flight. The heartbeat increases; the muscles tense; the blood is taken from the sections of the body that don't need it; the muscles of the bowels and bladder are constricted or released in order to have greater mobility; the blood is sent to the upper muscles and legs. The persons become hypervigilant.

This state of readiness was intended by nature to be a *survival state*. In dysfunctional families, it is often the normal state. When a threat actually occurs in the forms of abandonment I have described, the person responds with *survival behaviors*. Such behaviors include denial, dissociation, repression, withdrawal (flight responses) or anger, identification with the persecutor and reactive and reenacting behavior (fight responses). These survival behaviors are the traits I have been describing in the checklists.

Survival Behaviors

When the stressor stops (Dad quits raging, drinking, working, eating), the person still carries the impact of the stress. In dysfunctional families, the stress often goes on for years. The degree of stress ranges in intensity from mild (chronic fear) to severe (traumatic events). The adult child of a dysfunctional family learns to survive by developing certain patterns of behavior. These behaviors are the survival behaviors which were the *actual* responses to the violence. As the child from the dysfunctional family grows up, these survival behaviors continue even though they are now disconnected from the original source of distress. These *survival behaviors feel normal since they are the patterns one used every day of his early life in order to survive.* As an adult they are not only unnecessary, they are actually unhealthy. While once they were protective, now they are destructive.

Robert Firestone has compared these defenses to the body's physical reaction in forming pneumonia. In pneumonia, the body's defensive reaction is more destructive than the original assault. The presence of organisms in the lungs evokes cellular and humoral defenses that lead to congestion that can destroy the organism. Firestone writes:

> "In a like manner, defenses that were erected by the vulnerable child to protect . . . against a toxic environment may become more detrimental than the original trauma. In this sense one's psychological defenses become the core of one's neurosis."
>
> *Fantasy Bond*

Survival behaviors are hard to give up. They are old friends who served us well. *We did survive.* But we survived by developing a kind of *power* that resulted from sacrificing ourselves. We learned to control people by becoming Caretakers, by being Stars, Heroes, and Heroines, by being Lost Children, by being Perfect, by being the Problem, or the Rebel or the Scapegoat, by being Surrogate Spouses, by being Our Parent's Parent, by being Little Parents, etc. In every case we developed a dependency on things outside ourselves to the point of self-neglect. We gave up our own reality in order to take care of our parent(s) or the needs of the family system. In short, we survived by having our true self abandoned. We survived by not being there. We learned all the defenses in order to cover up the pain of being shamed, alone and self-ruptured.

In the end our survival behaviors left us powerless and spiritually bankrupt. Co-dependency is a set of survival behaviors which are unhealthy patterns of learned behavior. Co-dependence can be defined as *a recognizable pattern of fixed personality traits, rooted in the internalized shame resulting from the abandonment that naturally happens to everyone in a dysfunctional family system.*

According to Dr. Timmen Cermak in his book, *Diagnosing and Treating Co-dependence,* co-dependence is now clearly definable enough "to warrant the diagnosis of mixed Personality Disorder as outlined in

DSM III." This means that co-dependence has significant enough clinical status to be recognized and labeled as an emotional disease entity in its own right. Dr. Cermak has done extensive work on integrating the psychiatric and chemical addiction models.

Co-dependence is always a symptom of abandonment as I have defined it, including neglect, abuse and enmeshment. Co-dependence is a loss of one's inner reality and *an addiction* to outer reality.

I like the word used by the Spanish existentialist José Ortega y Gasset, "otheration". In describing the essence of man, Ortega y Gasset contrasts the life of man from the life of animals. Man, he says, lives from within himself (*ensimismamiento*), while animals live constantly on guard against the outside. Their life is dominated by the outside. They must be constantly on guard against the threats from the outside. They must guard against the ever present dangers to their life. They must constantly stalk and look for food. If they cease their endless vigilance, they will die. The life of an animal is "otheration" (*alteración*). "Otheration" is a good description of co-dependence.

The discussion and labeling of co-dependence has had an interesting history. Originally the word co-dependence was limited to the study of alcoholic families. It was first used to label the spouse of the alcoholic. Later as family systems thinking came to be used, the whole family was seen as co-dependent.

As the definition of addiction was expanded to include the wider range of addictions (activities, feelings, thoughts), the awareness dawned on observers that *any type of dysfunctional family exhibits the same co-dependent structure.*

In my television series I extended the discussion to include our entire society. I argued that all the people in our society have been raised by the rules of the poisonous pedagogy. And these rules create dysfunctional families. The co-dependence, which is naturally fostered in our families, is the crisis of our day. We are in the death throes of an epoch.

The utter atrocities of Nazism have shown us clearly what the inherent potential of destruction in the parenting rules we have been using for the last 150 years. These rules are non-democratic. They are based on inequality of power and unequal rights. They promote the use and ownership of some people by others and teach the denial and repression of emotional vitality and spontaneity. They glorify obedience, orderliness, logic, rationality, power and male supremacy. They are flagrantly anti-life.

These rules are carried by family systems, by our schools, our churches and our government. They are a core belief of the modern "consensus reality".

Society itself thus becomes the ultimate dysfunctional family system. As a system it follows the principles of a general system theory.

Society (culture) has a life of its own, distinct from the lives of those within it. Society or culture is a closed system. Like the individual families we have examined, the society as a closed system dictates the roles (sex roles) and behaviors the individual can choose from. The society as a closed system calls forth certain characteristic behaviors and processes in the individuals who make it up. Our current society encourages co-dependence and in many ways views it as normal.

A good example of our cultural numbing and co-dependence is sexual addiction and sexual abuse. A large amount of Level I sexual addiction is considered normal. This includes multiple affairs, pornography and compulsive masturbation.

Most of us are so emotionally dead that it takes "horror story" sexual abuse to get us outraged. Emotions move us to action. Without emotions we are zombie-like. As we redefine child abuse (especially sexual abuse), we realize it has been going on for centuries. Perhaps 60 million of our people have been sexually abused. This abuse results from sexually addicted families. There are disastrous consequences to everyone even in so called mild sexual abuse. Sexual shaming is the major factor in this. Sexual shaming occurs regularly in our families, churches and schools.

We have millions upon millions of incest families. They are the "symptom bearers", the identified patients of a sexually diseased culture.

Sex in our society is either secretive or banal. It is never the mysterious and sacred core of our beingness. We watch our entertainers promulgate the objectification of sex, laughing and giggling at the jokes about the size of penises, breasts and buttocks. Individuals are reduced to genitalia — women are cunts and pussies; men are measured by the size of their cocks.

Free sex, wife-swapping, sport fucking (I just realized I'm not supposed to say fuck even though it's okay to say kill) are part of the sickness. But the real culprit is endorsed by the repression and denial of sexuality. The poisonous pedagogy does this. The repression of sexuality is what sets up the wild and shameful sexual acting out.

Many of the traits that have emerged as components of co-dependency are traits that in one way or another are culturally normal.

Sociologists have clearly outlined the process of "consensus reality" formation. They have shown how what we consider normal is what we all agree on.

For example, Erich Fromm pointed out that during the Viet Nam War, it was normal to hear someone say that the way to end the war was to drop a hydrogen bomb on Hanoi. If the same person had suggested that the way to end air pollution was to level all the factories, most would think of him as crazy. The two suggestions are actually identical. Because all the birds are flying in the same direction doesn't mean it is the right direction.

Co-dependent Traits of Society

Some of the so-called normal co-dependent traits of our society are:

Our Notion of Marriage

I was watching a man play a $25.00 slot machine in Las Vegas recently. His very obeisant wife was coyly standing next to him. Every once in a while he reached in his pocket, grabbed a handful of nickels and generously gave them to his wife. He saw me watching him and introduced himself to me, then asked if I'd like to meet his "better half". It was hard for me to believe that he believed she was his better half!

This notion of two halves making the perfect marriage is an extremely dysfunctional notion. As we already know ½ x ½ equals ¼ and two incomplete people cannot make a relationship. A good relationship demands that there be two whole people who *choose* to be in the relationship and know that each *can live without the other*. The opposite of this is an enmeshment or entanglement, wherein both persons involved are convinced they cannot make it without the other. We are taught at an early age to call this inseparable relationship *true love*. Women especially are taught that their destiny is to find their true love and give their life to him. *What is described as true love is actually an addictive relationship.* Two people come to believe that they can't live without each other. Such a relationship is jeopardized if either partner starts to grow or change.

Our popular music also reinforces that two halves make one whole notion. These songs glorify suffering and promote the idea that happiness and completedness lies in the other person. Some examples are songs like: "Stand By Your Man"; "She's The Sunshine of My Day" . . . "Lord She Took Me In and Made Me Everything I am Today"; "Good Hearted Woman" who "love him in spite of his wicked ways" and "Last Blues Song" where it says, "I'm getting high on feeling low." We could go on and on. We grew up with these songs. We heard many of them during our adolescence when our identities were being formed.

Music has a profound impact on the nonverbal unconscious part of our brain. Just at the time when love and relationships are being focused, our unconscious is being grounded in beliefs that we are nothing unless somebody loves us or that we can't survive without a love partner.

The marriage relationship is the foundation and architect of the family. Little wonder millions of adult children have been robbed of their childhood because they were enmeshed in their family systems intimacy vacuum.

Our Notion of Love

The belief about marriage conditions our notion of love. Our cultural beliefs about love are actually forms of addiction. Many religious preachers teach a form of passive dependent love. They teach that the highest act of love is self-sacrifice. The highest love is to set aside one's own physical, emotional and intellectual needs to serve and take care of others. They teach long-suffering and martyrdom as two of the major ways to attain goodness. Acting good and acting righteous are more important than actually *being* good. Acting loving is more important than being loving.

Helping and giving up one's self for others can often be a way to attain moral superiority. Helpers are always helping themselves. Taking care of others is a way to feel powerful and in the moment of helping, one can overcome one's feelings of emptiness and powerlessness. The feeling of goodness or righteousness is a euphoric feeling. Feeling righteous is a powerful way to mood alter. I have some personal experience of this.

I was in seminary for a number of years studying to be a Catholic Priest. I wore a Roman collar and a black robe. I preached goodness and righteousness. I was a counselor and spiritual advisor. Certainly, I would not discount *all* that I did. I acted out of the best awareness that I had.

Nevertheless it was a rude awakening for me when I began to realize *how helping and caretaking can be a subtle disguise for self-glorification.* My shame-based inner self could feel like I was really okay when I was preaching and helping. I ultimately had to realize that this was a counterfeit form of love.

Being in love is perhaps the most addictive of all. "In love" is not "love". It is a state of biological bonding. One's boundaries collapse and there is a profound mood alteration. Stanton Peele, in his book *Love and Addiction* writes:

> "An addictive experience is one which absorbs a person's consciousness, and as with analgesics, relieves the sense of anxiety and pain. There's perhaps nothing quite as good for absorbing our consciousness as a love relationship of a certain type."

Scott Peck has written brilliantly about our culture's various forms of counterfeit love. His book *The Road Less Traveled* offers an enlightening, and for many, surprising discussion of this matter. Love, according to Dr. Peck, is a form of work. It involves commitment, the overcoming of laziness and the overcoming of fear through the courage to risk exposure and rejection. Love is therefore not a feeling — it is an act of the will and a decision. *All true love begins with self-love.* The work and discipline of love flow from a true sense of self-value. We have to know how to value ourselves before we can value others.

Rationalism — The Denial of Fun, Emotions and Spontaneity

Most families, schools and churches teach the control of too much fun, spontaneity and emotions. The schools I went to taught me to learn "not to talk", to stand straight in line, not to ask too many questions, to memorize great quantities of material, to learn a number of things I've never used again (solid geometry, years of Latin, diagramming sentences). I was discouraged from laughing at school and certainly never in church. To be excited, noisy, happy, full of energy was reprimanded as bad. When I was sick (especially' at home), quiet, depressed, obedient, orderly, I was rewarded and called good. Children are seen as good and well-behaved when they obey silently and promptly.

Our schools and churches are still highly rationalistic. Reason and logic are desirable; emotions are weak and suspicious. We do not educate the right hemisphere of our brain. Right hemispheric activity includes intuition, music creativity and holistic thinking. Our logic is still Aristotelian. This logic is characterized by black and white kinds of thinking and judgment. If you believe in one thing, you must by that fact reject its opposite. There is no synthesis — no area of grey.

Rationalism has been clearly refuted for 150 years. Kant, Hegel, the entire Existentialist Movement, Einstein, Whitehead and countless others have refuted the rationalistic bias that favors logic and linear left brain thinking at the expense of felt thought (poetry), intuition and creativity.

Existentialism has offered a whole corrective model based on right brain thinking and the phenomenology of human experience. Einstein, Heisenberg and others have completely surpassed the simple mechanistic universe of Isaac Newton. Brilliant and innovating scholarly approaches to Biblical studies have exposed *any literalistic approach* to the Bible as simplistic and downright lazy. The catastrophe of Black Nazism has brought the modern world to a flaming and ignominious death.

Dishonesty and Pretending as Correct Behavior

The poisonous pedagogy promotes obedience without content. One should pretend to be grateful, rather than to be honestly ungrateful. One should pretend to be loving, rather than honestly unloving. We are taught as children to accept the family's "vital lies". We are not to notice what is happening. We are to pretend it is not happening. Rather than asking directly for what we want or saying what we think and feel, we are to play roles and pretend.

We are taught to be nice and polite. We are taught that these behaviors (most often lies) are better than telling the truth. We are taught above all to pretend we are not feeling the things we are feeling. Our churches, schools and politics are rampant with teaching dishonesty (saying things we don't mean and pretending to feel ways we don't feel). We smile when we feel sad; laugh nervously when dealing with grief; laugh at jokes we don't think are funny; tell people things to be polite that we surely don't mean, like we'll have to get together some time.

Glad-handing and lying politicians have basically destroyed most people's trust in our national leadership. Presidents, politicians and so-called religious leaders have succumbed to their sexual and adrenalin addictions. If not those addictions, they've shown us work addiction and the addiction to Heroism. All in all it's not a pretty picture. Something's wrong in a society where 60 million are seriously affected by alcoholism; 60 million are sex abuse victims; 60% women and 50% of men have eating disorders; one out of eight is a battered woman; 51% of marriages end in divorce and there is massive child abuse. We are an addicted society. We are severely co-dependent.

My belief is that co-dependence is the disease of today. All addictions are rooted in co-dependence, and co-dependence is a symptom of abandonment. We are co-dependent because we've lost our selves.

When I put the cork in the bottle, I still had to deal with what Vernon Johnson calls the *ism* of alcoholism. I was still a compulsive personality. I worked the 12 steps on my alcoholism, never on my co-dependency. Consequently, I soon developed other addictions. I smoked, drank 12 cups of coffee a day. I became addicted to the adrenalin rush of working and making money. I struggled with sugar binges and dieting. My belief is that substance addictions are diseases of diseases.

Menninger, for example, described alcoholism as "a man on fire running into the sea to put out the fire, but drowning". The alcohol is the substance used to deal with the loneliness and pain. But like fever which is a symptom of an organic disorder, when the fever gets to be 107°, it will kill you. The alcohol which one is using to heal the shame and loneliness, itself becomes the killer. In this sense alcohol is a disease of a disease.

In the case of alcohol and other chemical abuse (drugs and food) we have to stop using the ingested substance in order to even be able to get to the underlying disorder — the co-dependence. The co-dependence is the disease underneath any substance addiction.

In the activity addictions it is easier to see the co-dependence. Any co-dependent person has internalized shame and has strong feelings of low self-worth. Co-dependents try to make themselves indispensable by taking care of others. They are willing to do whatever it takes to be loved or worthwhile. Co-dependents often choose professions of caretaking and financial achievement, throwing themselves into their work to the point of workaholism and burnout. Co-dependence is core addiction. It is a diseased form of life. Once a person believes that his identity lies outside himself in a substance, activity or another person, *he has found a new god, sold his soul and became a slave.*

Co-dependence is a "conflict of Gods". One has no 'inner life'. Co-dependence is at bottom a spiritual problem. It is spiritual bankruptcy.

Adult Children of Dysfunctional Families

In the checklist that follows, see if you identify yourself in several of the following traits. If you do, it's likely that you are co-dependent and are carrying your family dysfunction. I have used the phrase **ADULT CHILDREN OF DYSFUNCTIONAL FAMILIES** to present these traits. This checklist is a kind of summary of all that we have looked at up until now.

A   *Abandonment issues*
D   *Delusion and denial*
U   *Undifferentiated ego mass*
L   *Loneliness and isolation*
T   *Thought disorders*

C   *Control madness*
H   *Hypervigilant and high level anxiety*
I   *Internalized shame*
L   *Lack of boundaries*
D   *Disabled will*
R   *Reactive and reenacting*
E   *Equifinality*
N   *Numbed out*

O   *Offender with or without offender status*
F   *Fixated personality*

D   *Dissociated responses*
Y   *Yearning for parental warmth and approval*
S   *Secrets*
F   *Faulty communication style*
U   *Underinvolved*
N   *Neglect of developmental dependency needs*
C   *Compulsive/addictive*
T   *Trance — carrying the family spell*
I   *Intimacy problems*
O   *Overinvolved*
N   *Narcissistically deprived*
A   *Abuse victim*
L   *Lack of coping skills (underlearning)*

F   *False self — confused identity*
A   *Avoid depression through activity*
M   *Measured, judgmental and perfectionistic*
I   *Inhibited trust*
L   *Loss of your own reality*
I   *Inveterate dreamer*
E   *Emotional constraint*
S   *Spiritual bankruptcy*

A. Abandonment Issues

You were physically abandoned by one or both of your parents. Your parent(s) was there, but not emotionally available to you. You were physically, sexually or emotionally violated by someone in your family. Your developmental dependency needs were neglected. You were enmeshed in your parents' neediness or in the needs of your family system. You stay in relationships far beyond what is healthy.

D. Delusion and Denial

After reading this book, you still think you had a great childhood and that your family was the good old American Family!

U. Undifferentiated Ego Mass

You carry feelings, desires and secrets of other people in your family system.

L. Loneliness and Isolation

You have felt lonely all or most of your life. You feel isolated and different.

T. Thought Disorders

You get involved in generalities or details. You worry, ruminate and obsess a lot. You stay in your head to avoid your feelings. You read about your problems, rather than taking action.

C. Control Madness

You try to control yourself and everyone else. You feel extremely uncomfortable when you're out of control. You mask your efforts to control people and situations by "being helpful".

H. Hypervigilant and High Anxiety

You live on guard. You are easily startled. You panic easily.

I. Internalized Shame

You feel flawed as a human being. You feel inadequate and hide behind a role or an addiction or character trait, like control, blame, criticism, perfectionism, contempt, power and rage.

L. Lack of Boundaries

You don't know where you end and others begin — physically, emotionally, intellectually or spiritually. You don't know what you really stand for.

D. Disabled Will

You are willful. You try to control other people. You are grandiose. With you it's all or nothing.

R. Reactive and Reenacting

You react easily. You feel things that are not related to what is happening. You feel things more intensely than the event calls for. You find yourself repeating patterns over and over.

E. Equifinality

No matter where you begin, your life seems to end at the same place.

N. Numbed Out

You don't feel your feelings. You don't know what you feel. You don't know how to express what you feel.

O. Offender With or Without Offender Status

You are actually an offender, or you are not an offender, but you do in fact play that role sometimes.

F. Fixated Personality

You are an adult, but your emotional age is very young. You look like an adult, but feel very childlike and needy. You feel like the lifeguard on a crowded beach, but you don't know how to swim.

D. Dissociated Responses

You have no memories of painful events of your childhood; you have a split personality; you depersonalize; can't remember people's names or even the people you were with two years ago. You are out of touch with your body and your feelings.

Y. Yearn for Parental Warmth and Approval — Seek It in Other Relationships

You still try to gain your parents' approval. You yearn for the "perfect relationship". You have an exaggerated need for others' approval. You fear offending others. You find emotionally unavailable partners (just like your parents were), who you try to make love you. You will go to almost any lengths to care and help your partner. Almost nothing is too much trouble. Having had little nurturing yourself, you find people who need nurturing and take care of them.

S. Secrets

You carry lots of secrets from your family of origin. You've never talked to anyone about how bad it was in your family, and you carry lots of secrets about your own life. You also carry lots of sexual secrets which you would not want to tell anyone.

F. Faulty Communication

You have had trouble communicating in every relationship you've been in. No one seems to understand what you say. You feel confused a lot in communicating with others. When talking to parents no matter how good your intentions are to be sane and clear, it winds up the same — conflicted and confused.

U. Underinvolved

You stand on the sidelines of life wishing you were a participant. You don't know how to initiate a relationship, a conversation, an activity. You are withdrawn and would rather bear the pangs of being alone than risking interaction. You are not spontaneous. You allow yourself very little excitement or fun.

N. Neglect of Developmental Dependency Needs

You have a hole in the cup of your psyche. You never seem to be satisfied. No matter how much you anticipate something, soon after it is over, you feel restless and unsatisfied. You are childish and feel like a child a lot of the time. You cry when someone says really beautiful things about you. You feel like you don't really belong a lot of the time.

C. Compulsive/Addictive

You have been or are now in an active compulsive addictive behavior(s).

T. Trance

You still carry the family trance. You are fantasy bonded and still idealize your parents. You still play the role(s) you played in your family system. Nothing has really changed in your family of origin — same dialogue — same fights — same gossip. Your marriage or your relationship is just like your parents.

I. Intimacy Problems

You have trouble in relationships; you've been married more than twice; you choose partners who embody the same emotional patterns of your primary caretakers. You are attracted to seductive psychopathic partners; you are *not* attracted to partners who are kind, stable, reliable and interested in you. You find "nice" men/women boring. When you start getting too close, you leave a relationship. You confuse closeness with compliance; intimacy with fusion.

O. Overinvolved

You are drawn to people who are needy. You confuse love with pity. You are drawn to people who have problems that you can get involved in fixing. You are drawn toward people and situations that are chaotic, uncertain and emotionally painful.

N. Narcissistically Deprived

You feel empty and childishly helpless inside. You compensate with addiction to chemicals, food, prestige, money, possessions, heroism, sex, power, violence, passive dependent persons, children, etc., as a way of feeling important and worthwhile.

A. Abuse Victim

You were physically, emotionally, sexually abused as a child. You have become a victim in life and play that role in all areas of your life. You feel hopeless about changing anything. Or you were abused and have become an offender. You identified with the abusing parent or caretaker and act just like he does.

L. Lack of Coping Skills (Underlearning)

You never learned how to do many things necessary for a fully functional life. Your methods of problem-solving do not work but you continue to use the same ones over and over. You learned ways of caring for your wounds that, in fact, perpetuated them. There are a whole set of models of what's normal that you have never seen. You have no real knowledge of what is normal. Your bottom line tolerance is quite abnormal.

F. False Self — Confused Identity

Your self worth depends on your partner's success or failure. When you're not in a relationship, you feel an inner void. You feel responsible for making your partner happy. You take care of people to give yourself an identity. You wear masks, calculate, manipulate and play games. You act out rigid family roles and/or sex roles. When your partner has a stomachache, you take Pepto-Bismol.

A. Avoid Depression Through Activity

You get involved in unstable relationships. The more you are active and in your head, the more you can avoid your depression.

M. Measured, Judgmental and Perfectionistic

You have unrealistic expectations of yourself and others. You are rigid and inflexible. You are rigid and judgmental of yourself and others. You are stuck in your attitudes and behavior, even though it hurts to live the way you do.

I. Inhibited Trust

You really don't trust anyone, including your own feelings, perceptions and judgments.

L. Loss of Your Own Reality — Damaged and Weak Boundaries

You take more than 50% responsibility, guilt, and blame for whatever happens in a relationship. You know what others feel or need before you know your own feelings and needs. Rather than take any risk of abandonment, you have withdrawn and refuse to get involved. Any change in the status quo of a relationship is experienced as a threat by you. You feel embarrassed by what others do and take responsibility for their behavior.

I. Inveterate Dreamer

In your relationships you are in touch with your dreams of how it could be, rather than with the reality of your life and situation. You live according to an ideal image of yourself, rather than what your true reality is. You have a grandiose and exaggerated notion of yourself. You fantasize and catastrophize and exaggerate the seriousness of decisions and events.

E. Emotional Constraint (with or without Dramatic Outburst)

You believe that controlling your emotions is a way to control your life. You attempt to manage your life and your emotions. You have dramatic outbursts of emotions that have been repressed for long periods of time. You have inappropriate outbursts of emotions. (You yell at your children after holding in your anger all day at work.) You compulsively expose your emotions. You go to great lengths to verbalize every feeling as soon as it enters your awareness. You do this so that you won't have to feel them for very long.

S. Spiritual Bankruptcy

You live totally oriented to the outside believing that your worth and happiness lies outside of you. You have no awareness of your "inner life" since you spend all of your energy avoiding your shame-based inner self.

In all the families we have examined so far, all the members are co-dependent. Every dysfunctional family we have seen has certain structural similarities. Those similarities are as follows:

(1) A dominant dysfunction causes a threat to which all other members respond. The adaptations to the threat cause the system to close up in a frozen and rigid pattern.
(2) The frozen pattern is maintained by each member playing one or more rigid roles.
(3) There is a high level of anxiety and confusion.
(4) All members are shame-based and shame is the organizing principle of all dysfunctional families.
(5) The more the system tries to change, the more it stays the same.

(6) All dysfunctional families are held together by variations of the rules of the poisonous pedagogy.

(7) All members have lost their own reality. Each is out of touch with his own feelings, needs and wants. Each is a false self, who has given up his individual uniqueness for the sake of loyalty to the system.

Fortunately millions are identifying themselves as co-dependents. ACoA, CoA, Al-Anon, and Co-dependency groups are starting up everywhere. Many major treatment centers have set up programs to treat co-dependence.

It's crucial to experience the powerlessness and unmanageability that results from being co-dependent. In what follows I offer you a guide for taking a *written first step for co-dependence.* I have borrowed the format for this guideline from Pia Mellody's work at the Meadows. I have expanded Pia's format using the letters of the word co-dependence to outline the essential traits of co-dependence. Each trait is rooted in 'internalized' shame and constitutes the powerlessness of the disorder. This powerlessness leads to behaviors which cause one's life to become unmanageable. Examples of these behaviors are listed on the righthand side of the page.

I encourage the reader to write out your own personal examples. If you identify with being a people-pleaser, write out a concrete specific example of a time when people-pleasing cost you something. By writing out the details, you connect with the emotions involved. 'You cannot fail with detail', is a therapeutic slogan. The emotions are what move you to change. Feeling the pain of your co-dependent behavior will move you to do something about it.

I invite you to take this first step now.

GUIDELINE FOR WRITTEN 1ST STEP FOR CO-DEPENDENCE

SPIRITUAL BANKRUPTCY

Adult symptoms of Abandonment

Powerlessness
Core Self is Shame-Based

Experience as a painful feeling of being exposed and flawed as a human being. Self is ruptured, self is split from self. Distrust of self and others.

"Otheration"

Experienced as over-reacting to things outside of self and under-reacting to things inside of self. Dependency problems. Impression management. External referencing. Relationship addiction. Excessive responsibility for meeting others' needs to the exclusion of your own. Belief that happiness lies outside of you. Hyper-vigilance.

Which lead to distress:

Unmanageability

1. Being perfect or being a slob.
2. Trying to control everyone or living out of control.
3. Hiding behind a false self. Pretending.
4. Being guarded lest you ever be caught offguard.
5. Feeling ashamed of feelings and needs.
6. Being a people-pleaser (nice guy or sweetheart) or raging and blaming.
7. Staying isolated and messed up because you feel you have no right to depend on anyone.

1. My self-worth comes from being approved of by someone outside of me.
2. Being a caretaker, martyr, rescuer or enabler in order to feel worthwhile.
3. Making yourself indispensable so that your partner can't leave you.
4. You are aware of others' feelings, needs and wants, but not your own.
5. You make decisions on the basis of what others think, want or expect.
6. Your self-worth comes from solving others' problems and relieving their pain.
7. You live an apathetic, passionless life or you get in a relationship with others, who are exciting and passionate, in order to experience aliveness through them.

GUIDELINE FOR WRITTEN 1ST STEP FOR CO-DEPENDENCE

Adult Symptoms of Abandonment

Which lead to distress:

Powerlessness
This happens automatically

Delusion, Denial, Defenses

Experience as denying and minimizing one's problems: the problem itself, its impact on you and the feelings about the problem (psychic numbness). The primary defenses of childhood (regression, dissociation, conversion, displacement) give way to more mature defenses (projection, rationalization, minimizing).

Extremes

Experienced as not knowing what normal is. Experienced as all or nothing. Grandiosity. You're unique or you're a worm. You're arrogant or you feel hopeless.

Unmangeability
Consequences or results of

1. You tell yourself it's not really so bad or it's not as bad as . . .
2. You overeat, get confused, get sick, become chronically depressed and pretend none of these are happening.
3. You tell yourself it's hopeless and there's nothing you can do about it.
4. You believe in spite of the **facts.**
5. You believe you can control what's happening if you really put your mind to it.
6. You feel numb all over. Don't know when you're tired or hungry or sick.
7. You feel a low-grade chronic depression, especially when you are alone.

1. You trust everyone or you trust no one.
2. You let everyone touch you or you won't let anyone touch you.
3. You can't initiate anything and once you do initiate something, you can't stop.
4. You're super-sweet or critical and abusive.
5. You're over-responsible or under-responsible.
6. You're totally involved or you're isolated and alone.
7. You have no opinion or you're rigid and judgmental and know it all.

GUIDELINE FOR WRITTEN 1ST STEP FOR CO-DEPENDENCE

Adult symptoms of Abandonment

Which lead to distress:

Powerlessness
Primary, Progressive, Pervasive

Experienced as tolerating more and more intolerable behavior. Violating moral values. Being dishonest and lying. Becoming more and more confused. Developing psychosomatic illnesses. While physical addictions are more primary, compulsivity itself cannot be cured until co-dependence is treated.

Unmanageability

1. You start doing things you said you'd never do — you have sex when you don't want to — you stay in a relationship where your partner is sleeping around.
2. You lie to please others and to make an impression.
3. You develop addictions to distract yourself from how bad you feel about yourself.
4. You stay in a relationship with an active substance abuser for two years without seeking help.
5. You stay in a physically or emotionally abusing relationship without seeking help.
6. You change your routines — change the structure of your life — become violent, suicidal.
7. You develop ulcers, heart disease, cancer, arthritis, hypertension.

Emotional Constraint
(with or without dramatic outbursts)

Experienced as being numb, having outbursts of feelings or distorting feelings (rackets). Anger covers up fear or self-righteousness covers up anger.

1. Feelings come out in short bombastic bursts and frighten those around us.
2. You don't know what you feel or you feel nothing.
3. Your fear of anger determines what you say and do.
4. You somatize your feelings: You're sick a lot.
5. You feel shame when you feel anything.
6. You feel only acceptable feelings.
7. You don't talk about or share feelings.

GUIDELINE FOR WRITTEN 1ST STEP FOR CO-DEPENDENCE

Adult symptoms of Abandonment

Powerlessness
Noetic Disorders

Experienced as being in your head. Detailing, generalizing, obsessing, ruminating, incompletion. The payoff in thinking and analyzing is that it cuts you off from your feelings. Life is a problem to be solved. You are always trying to solve things or figure them out.

Disabled Will

Experienced as willfulness; self will run riot and control madness. Also experienced as grandiosity — willing absolutes. The will is cut off from judgment reasoning and imagination through emotional blockage. The will then has no content but itself.

Which lead to distress:

Unmanageability

1. You worry about the most trivial and silly things,
2. You seem never to find clear answers and have a hard time with decisions.
3. You read about problems, rather than do anything about them.
4. You can't stop thinking about what someone said. You can't stop worrying about someone else's problem.
5. You worry a lot. You worry about things you have no control over — the past, the future, the communists, the church.
6. You abandon your needs because you are so worried about something.
7. You are perfectionistic to the point of driving others crazy.

1. You will what cannot be willed.
2. You try to control everything and everybody (known as taking hostages in relationships).
3. You are impulsive; act without thinking or you can't make a decision.
4. You will to will; want action and excitement.
5. You believe you can change another person.
6. You're self-centered and insensitive. You expect others to do it your way.
7. You play God — criticize and judge others.

GUIDELINE FOR WRITTEN 1ST STEP FOR CO-DEPENDENCE

Adult symptoms of Abandonment

Which lead to distress:

Powerlessness
Enmeshed Boundaries

Experienced as not having limits; not knowing where you end and another begins. A lack of individuality or differentiation. You have problems saying no.

Narcissistic Deprivation

Experienced as having a hole in your soul. An adult with an insatiable child living within who can never get enough. Neediness. Seeking praise, admiration and attention all the time.

Unmanageability

1. You don't know what your body is telling you.
   You sleep with people you don't like or know.
   You don't know when you're tired, horny, hungry or sick.
2. You're gullible; easily manipulated.
3. You expect others to know what you need, think or feel.
4. You value others' opinions more than your own.
5. You blame yourself for the reality of others and others for your reality.
6. You become like other people in order to be liked.
7. You feel embarrassed by the way your partner acts or dresses.

1. You find needy victims who adore you in order to be connected with someone.
2. You are egocentric. Always moving to center stage.
3. You put enormous energy into being righteous and good in everyone's eyes.
4. You are an addict and use your addiction to get narcissistic supplies.
5. You use your children for your narcissistic supplies.
6. You need money, possessions to feel worth.

GUIDELINE FOR WRITTEN 1ST STEP FOR CO-DEPENDENCE

Adult symptoms of Abandonment

Powerlessness
Communication Problems

Experienced as confusion about verbal and nonverbal interaction with others. Either being fused or in conflict. You don't understand others and misunderstand others. You have a no-talk rule about vulnerable things.

Emptiness

Experienced as having no inner reality and no clear identity. Really not knowing who you are. Spiritual bankruptcy. "My life feels like it has happened by chance, rather than by choice."

Which lead to distress:

Unmanageability

1. You talk too much or not at all.
2. You think that what you say is not important and apologize for bothering people.
3. Don't talk directly; "The car needs gas; there's no milk; it's cold in here." Don't ask for what you want.
4. Don't say what you mean or mean what you say, or know what you mean.
5. Blame, threaten, yell, coerce, beg, bribe and advise.
6. Use "you" messages (critical, judgmental, over-responsible statements) rather than "I" messages (self-responsible).
7. Take a long time getting to the point. Say things to please or provoke people.

1. You act as if you know who you are. But you really feel confused or frozen (i.e., in a rigid role.)
2. You don't believe compliments given to you and you don't admire yourself.
3. You feel unable to change your life the way you want it to be.
4. You don't like to be alone for very long.
5. You're in an act or performance a lot of the time.
6. You care for others in ways you don't care for yourself.
7. You fear getting too close to anyone for long.

Summary

The key points in this chapter can be summed up using the letters of the phrase **MOST COMMON ILLNESS.**

M. Major Family Problem — Co-dependence — The most common family problem is co-dependence. In a family system the whole is greater than the sum of the parts. Therefore if the family is dysfunctional, all the members share in that dysfunction. They are described as co-dependent.

O. Otheration — The world "otheration" is used to describe the core problem in co-dependence. All members of a dysfunctional family live in reaction to the major distressor. Since the distress is a threat to the members' existence, they must be alert and on guard all the time. They therefore have no time to go inward and care for their own feelings, needs or wants.

S. Survival Behaviors as Symptoms of Abandonment — Co-dependence is a set of normal reactive survival behaviors. Co-dependence is a symptom of the abandonment one has gone through.

T. Typical Structure in Any Dysfunctional Family — Any dysfunctional family will have common structure. The adult children of such families will embody similar behavioral traits.

C. Cultural Phenomenon — Co-dependence is looked upon as normal in our culture. The whole society is built on the poisonous pedagogy and operates like a dysfunctional family.

O. Outer-directed — Our society has been described as conformist and self-image actualizing rather than self-actualizing. Books like the *Lonely Crowd* and *The Organization Man* have described this with great thoroughness.

M. Marriage as Addiction — Our ideal of marriage in American society is actually an addiction (½ x ½ = ¼).

M. Manipulative Lifestyle — Manipulation, pretending (lying) playing the game are not only socially acceptable, they are positively encouraged.

O. Other Directed — People-pleasing and being *nice* are looked upon with the highest regard in our current social life. *Acting* selfless is more important than being selfless.

N. **Normal = Neurotic** — With the advent of *The Adjusted American* (normal neurosis in American society) by Snell and Gail Putney, it has become clearer and clearer just how life-denying and uncreative our accepted social norms are.

I. **Incest Families as Identified Patient** — The massive amount of incest and sexual abuse point to incest families as the identified patients of a sexually repressed and shame-ridden society.

L. **Logic (Reason) versus Emotions** — The rationalistic bias of reason and logic continues to influence our educational system. Right-brain thinking (felt thought), and good emotional integration are almost absent as part of our curricula. The prejudice against emotions and the belief that emotions are weak create our psychic numbness and compulsive addictive lifestyle.

L. **Loss of True Self** — It follows that if we are not allowed our own feelings and if we are to pretend and act out roles there is no way to be our genuine selves.

N. **Non-conflictual Relationships** — Our dominant relationship patterns are to maximize likenesses and minimize differences. These preclude the possibility of intimacy.

E. **Emotional Numbness** — This sets us up for our activism and addiction to excitement. Work and worry are ways to feel alive.

S. **Spiritual Bankruptcy** — The spiritual life is the inner life. Shame-based people become what Terry Kellog calls human doings rather than human beings. Performance and achievement are what count. There can be no inner life when one's inner life is ruptured and alienated.

S. **Step One** — An outline is offered to guide the reader in taking a written first step in identifying co-dependency.

9

Roadmap For Recovering Your Disabled Will

Stage I:
Willingness To Risk
A New Family Of Affiliation

*"In the midst of winter, I found within me an
invincible summer."*

Albert Camus

At some point in our life, we have to grow up if we want to be our own authentic self. "What I do is me — for that I came," the poet says. The natural place for this transition to begin is adolescence. Adolescence is characterized by what Erik Erikson calls the "Identity Crisis". Each of us needs to decide "who I really am". This identity question naturally emerges in adolescence. Each of us is called to find our own values and create our own destiny.

At best, adolescence is a time of awkwardness and aloneness. During adolescence we are flooded with new feelings, especially with the awakening of the sex drive. In adolescence the future becomes a problem for the first time. What am I going to do to provide for myself? Who am I going to love? These are our most crucial problems.

Our teen years are a time of monumental struggle to leave home and break away from our parents. Leaving home includes both physical and emotional leaving. Leaving home means becoming your own person. Even in the most functional family, leaving home is a painful and difficult task. Saying goodbye to parents and choosing our own values are parts of a long and arduous process, usually not completed until middle-age is resolved.

The human cycle is characterized by moving from environmental support to self-support. To become fully self-supporting involves becoming your own person — having your own physical, sexual, emotional, intellectual and spiritual boundaries. To do this we must leave our family of origin.

As adult children, many of us never really negotiated adolescence. Some may have never fully negotiated pre-adolescence.

The holes in the cup of our soul mark the places where our development was arrested. When a developmental need is not met at the proper time and in the proper sequence, the ego's energy gets frozen at the developmental level.

For most of us, our autonomy was not balanced by a healthy sense of shame. We internalized our shame and lost contact with it as an emotion that provided a good framework of limits. Once internalized, shame became a core identity and a state of being. We no longer had shame available to us to monitor *the limits* within which our will could healthily function. Without our shame, we became *shameless and grandiose*. We began willing what could not be willed. We believed we could stop our addiction any time we wanted to. We placed a premium on maintaining that our drinking, sexing, eating, working, relating, were voluntary. We believed we could change our own, our partner's, our children's and our parents' behavior. We became addicted to our own wills.

For us adult children to grow up and find our identity, we have to give up our delusions of grandeur. Our wills have gone astray. We have become functionally disabled. We are *full of will*. We've lost our true freedom of choice in our willfulness. We have to give up being absolutizing and willful children and become willing adults. A willing adult lives life within the "limits" of finitude and human possibility. An adult child lives life in grandiosity, either feeling hopeless (a symptom of grandiosity) or feeling godlike.

As a drinking alcoholic, I often felt unique, sometimes to the point of being extraordinary. I can remember believing that I was the most sensitive of all men. I drank because I experienced human suffering in a way few others knew. When I saw a poor man, I experienced his exact pain. (Later I found out that this was an outbreak of co-dependence.) Then after a drunken episode, I would experience myself as the most screwed-up person I knew. I felt degraded and wormlike. I was worthless. Someone has described addicts as "extraordinary worms". Both polarities — being extraordinary to the point of arrogance and being worthless to the point of being a worm are forms of grandiosity. For co-dependents hopelessness is almost always a manifestation of grandiosity. Hopelessness declares that I am so unique among humans *that there is no possibility of recovery for me.* A truly hopeless person sits in the back ward of some state hospital saying nothing and doing nothing.

Grandiosity accounts for the cycles of control and release that all addicts go through. I quit drinking every Lent for 12 years. I've been on a hundred diets and have lost 5,000 pounds. When I smoked, I'd cut down to six a day and do that for a month or two. The control phase is a part of every addiction. It is only an illusion and feeds the addict's grandiose belief that he can control his addiction.

Recovering Our Disabled Will

The first stage of recovery from co-dependence is recovering our disabled will. This involves letting go of any attempt to control the issues in our lives we've been trying to control. This is why I now ask you to write out a first step on co-dependence, and to pay attention to details. The concrete specific details help us to *feel* the powerlessness and unmanageability of our lives.

Without experiencing that I am powerless and my life is unmanageable, I stay in the grandiose delusion that *I can control* my husband's drinking, children's grades, parents' abuse, booze, work, eating, smoking, etc. The first action for adult children (anyone from a dysfunctional family) is to surrender.

Dr. Harry Tiebout, who was Bill W.'s (the founder of A.A.) therapist, made a great contribution by distinguishing between "compliance" and "surrender".

Compliance is motivated by guilt. In the last year of my seminary days, I asked to see a psychiatrist because of my sense of hopelessness. I told him I thought I was an alcoholic and that I needed help. He spent considerable time with me discussing my relationship with my mother. During this period he gave me prescriptions for sleeping pills and tranquilizers. I began to *feel* a whole lot better. I even *cut down* on my drinking! I enjoyed our visits and felt a sense of relief about my life. At the end of about three months, I terminated my treatment. Gradually my drinking got worse and worse. One year and a half later, I committed myself to Austin State Hospital for alcoholism. On December 11, 1965, I surrendered.

Surrender is motivated by the acceptance of shame. For an addict, surrender is the first true act of freedom since beginning the addiction. It certainly was for me.

Dr. Tiebout wisely understood that denial and delusion can continue in spite of the acknowledgment of guilt. Guilt can even be a way to distract one from the real problem. For example, it's not at all uncommon to hear a smoker or an overeater condemn themselves for creating a dangerous threat to their health with their addictions. *This is certainly preferable to stopping smoking or overeating.* As an alcoholic, I frequently accepted responsibility for the things I did when I drank. I felt guilt about them. It was a lot easier to admit to these harmful consequences than to admit my drinking was out of control. By being guilty I could deny that my life was unmanageable and out of control. Guilt was a useful way to continue my denial. Compliance and guilt are ways that many an unwary therapist has been hoodwinked by an addict.

Guilty people fear punishment and try to escape it. Shame-based people tend to seek and even embrace punishment. The two therapists I went to before joining a 12-step group praised my honesty and commitment. They said that by my acknowledging what drinking was doing to my life, I was being responsible. Both therapists were psychiatrists and both put me on chemical medication. Admitting my guilt and paying for it enhanced the denial of what I most deeply feared — quitting my drinking. To quit drinking would expose me as a flawed and defective human being. The only way out of the compulsive/addictive shame cycle is to embrace the shame. That is what it means to surrender.

The problem of the disabled will is the problem of dishonesty and the pain that dishonesty ultimately brings. By the time most of us are ready to do something about our lives, that pain has reached a point of great intensity. As my shame-based self went deeper and deeper into hiding, the intensity of my false self increased proportionately. My addiction to hiding my shame created the chronic pain of knowing that I was not the person I pretended to be (hiding in priestly robes) or was supposed to be. I literally was be-side myself. Tolstoy once said, "Men often act unlike themselves." Animals cannot become deanimalized. Tigers don't become detigered. But we humans can become dehumanized. The "otheration" of co-dependence is dehumanization.

For me the disease (co-dependence) had to wait until I dealt with its cover-up — my alcoholism. This point is crucial. For any acting-out substance abuser, the substance has to be stopped before one can treat the co-dependence (the disease of the disease). Alcoholism is caused by drinking alcohol. Alcoholism is a primary disease. That means it has to be treated first. The same is true for other drugs and chemicals.

Food, sex, work, and people addictions are somewhat different. You can't stop eating, drinking, sexing, working or peopling completely. Total abstinence would be death to self and the species. Each addiction has its own particular nuances for recovery but there are some commonalities. One commonality is surrendering the grandiose will.

Identity Formation

Whether you've identified with co-dependency or not, *everyone must go through a self-recovery, uncovery, discovery process.* What it is called for those of you graced by functional families is identity formation. In the natural life cycle, unencumbered by dysfunction, this process takes 40 years. The Delphic Oracle said, "The unexamined life is not worth living." Shakespeare wrote "To thine own self be true." The scripture tells us to become the image of God that we are. The spiritual masters and mystics of every tradition call us to a higher self and a state of at-one-ment and God-filled bliss.

For those of us who are adult children, the journey is not qualitatively any different from that of a person from a functional family. We just got started a whole lot later.

The journey to wholeness is a process made up of disenchantment and grieving. Our layers of defense must be collapsed one by one. The Buddhist Masters speak of enlightenment as progressive disillusionment.

Figure 9.1. Layers of Defense Hiding Shame Core

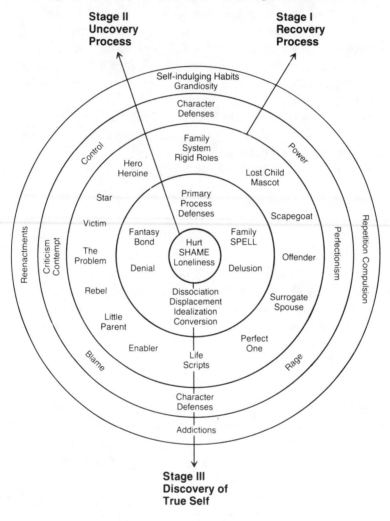

We must break through our delusions. Figure 9.1 gives you a way to visualize the layers of defense which must be collapsed.

Stage I Recovery deals with the outer layers. The outer layer defenses comprise our self-indulging habits and pain killers (our addictions) and our characterological strategies of defense against shame. Stage I deals with our compulsive/addictive behaviors and our control madness.

There are many ways one can begin the process. Most often it begins with new awareness. Shame keeps us so rigidly in hiding that we spend most of our energy on our defenses. Our mind is narrowed by emotional repression and our awareness is vastly limited.

Awareness can come from hearing a lecture or reading a book. It can come from a friend sharing his experience with us. I've received thousands of letters in response to the television series which prompted this book.

The first time I drew a five generation family map, I was comforted with a new awareness. For the first time I could see that there was something bigger than me or any one person in my family. I saw that I was carrying multigenerational illness. This is one of the positive aspects of family systems theory — it removes causality and blame. Everyone is responsible and accountable, but no one is to blame. Family systems theory also challenged me to do something about myself. It suggested that if I quit playing my role in the family system, the system would have to change. In fact, systems thinking puts the responsibility squarely on our individual shoulders.

Another way that the walls of defense are collapsed is through a confrontation process called intervention. We can literally intervene and confront another person's defenses. This form of confrontation needs careful planning and consideration.

The danger is twofold:

(1) we drive the person deeper into hiding and defensiveness;
(2) we actually shame the person more.

It is important to be aware of one's own motives when considering intervention. Am I doing this to help this person or as an interpersonal transfer of shame? Am I really willing to be there for them? Some of the pioneers working with addiction developed methods of intervention which have prove highly successful. I heartily recommend that if you are living in a dysfunctional family and you are thinking about confronting the primary addict in your system, that you seek some professional advice before you do it. This means going to someone who knows how to set up an intervention.

The most powerful way that our shame defenses crumble are through actual pain and suffering. Pain is a teacher that we cannot argue with. Our defenses are there to cover up the pain. Their purpose is to avoid suffering. When we start to experience suffering and pain that is greater than the pain we are trying to avoid, the walls start tumbling down. We can no longer control our defenses against our deep inner pain. What hurts moves us to change in a way that nothing else can.

There is an old slogan in 12-step programs that says, "No pain, No gain." And another therapeutic slogan says, "The way out of our pain is to go through our pain." Personally, I needed the pain before I was *willing* to risk doing something about my life. If you *really took* the first step for co-dependence, you will be willing to *take action.*

Talking about our problems, mapping out our family's dysfunction is not the same as taking action. Action means that I've let go of control and I'm willing to listen to someone else and *do it his way,* rather than my own way.

Unfortunately, I've always had to reach heights of pain before I was *willing* to do it someone else's way. I dabbled with my alcoholism for a year and a half before I surrendered. I tried to find an easier way, believing I didn't have to do what others had to do to get their alcoholism arrested. Finally, I reached an excruciating level of pain and voluntarily committed myself to Austin State Hospital. I didn't like it there and I thank God I'll never forget it. In six days I was released and headed for a 12-step program. I had dabbled with this group before, but I always intellectualized their program. I knew I needed help, but my denial was still very strong. I really didn't want to stop drinking. What would I do? Who would be my friends? Where would I go? My whole life centered around drinking. I was bonded to every friend I had on the basis of drinking. *Paradoxically most of them wanted me to quit.*

In my previous go round I felt the 12-step program was too simple for me. I had degrees in theology and philosophy and had taught both of these at the University level. I felt that my problems were more complex than with most of the people I met at the meetings. My drinking was a symptom of a deep and profound sensitive soul. I was one of William James' twice-born super-sensitive ones. This, of course, was all hogwash! Intellectuals create the most grandiose denials!

Thank God, there were some other intellectuals around. One man especially was important for me. His name was Fran and without him, I don't know what I would have done.

The group became the most important experience of my life. There were warmth, kindness, great patience tempered by firmness and rigorous honesty. My Hero and Superachiever roles continuously got in the way. I was used to being in control and distinguishing myself. I needed to be the best drunk seeking recovery. I needed to do the 12 steps perfectly.

My Surrender and Recovery

I quietly learned that control and perfectionism had reduced my life to shambles. I had to surrender and acknowledge my powerlessness. I had to feel as bad as I really felt. My use of alcohol and pills kept me from my feelings of deep shame and loneliness. My control and good guy act kept me away from my fear and sadness. Now I was losing both and the shame was starting to break through. For years I had been addicted to my shame. I had lived my life guarded so that I would never be caught off guard. During the years of studying to be a priest, I hid behind my Roman collar and black robe. I had been beside myself for so long, I didn't even know how lonely and empty I was. Coming out of hiding was terrifying, but the love and warmth of the group made it bearable. In fact, I couldn't believe it. The more I shared my truest feelings, the more acceptable I was. Being myself was acceptable and it was easy. Trying to control and doing my act — those are what took energy. This was the first step in recovery. I was accepting my limitations and gathering up my scattered self. I was experiencing being mirrored, and as the group accepted me, I was accepting myself.

My New Family

The group was my new family. It was my family of affiliation. We were a network of friends sharing our common problems. There were social equality and mutual respect. Each time I went to a meeting, I felt better. I couldn't understand it. Nothing was really happening. All we did was share our experiences or talk about one of the 12 steps.

I now see what was happening then. I had found a *new family. The rules were different in this family.* It was not only okay to make mistakes, it was a requirement for membership. Everyone was equal. There were no leaders. The group was based on mutual respect, social equality and rigorous honesty. People were talking about their feelings.

I was being accepted just for me — not because of my performance or achievements. I started recovering my self-respect. Each time I went to a meeting, I was coming out of hiding and *reducing my shame.* Each time I talked about me in an honest way (this was a gradual process), I was breaking old family rules. I was beginning to be real.

My own belief is that adult children *must* find a new family of affiliation. Our co-dependence was fostered by broken relationships. It is a product of social dysfunction. Therefore, we need a social context for healing.

The new family can be one of numerous 12-step groups. It could be an ACoA or co-dependency group. It could be a therapy group, an honest non-shaming church group, a therapist or a good friend that you can be honest with without being shamed. A group is crucial because of the shame. The only way out of the shame is to embrace the shame.

Finding My Self

Only through this honest truthful sharing and mirroring can one begin to recover his self-respect. My shame said that I was flawed, defective and unacceptable. The pain of my addiction finally forced me to show myself, and I was accepted and loved. I recovered my sense of self.

I was also recovering my own sense of values. As an alcoholic studying to be a priest, I lived a double life. One self was the young seminarian praying and meditating daily. The other self hid pills and whiskey in my room, using these chemicals late at night when the others were asleep. That double life caught up with me. I felt split. I was living a life unlike myself. I was doing things I did not really value. When a person gives up his compulsive/addictive behavior and begins a recovery program, he immediately starts embracing his own values.

The First Stages of Recovery

However, the early stages of recovery are painful. One has nothing to substitute for the pain. As one gets honest, there is often anger and hostility at oneself for messing up so badly and for so long. There is the actual physical withdrawal if it be a euphoric chemical substance one was addicted to. There is emotional withdrawal in other addictions. There is obsession and preoccupation with the addiction itself and a grieving over its loss. With sex, work, food and religious addictions, there is confusion as to how much is safe since one can't stop eating, working, worshipping or become celibate. These are hard questions and need time and trial and error. One needs lots of patience and it's imperative to get a sponsor. A sponsor is someone who has walked before you, who is working a successful program and who is *modeling* the quality of life that you desire.

All this takes time. I see the first stage of recovery as ranging anywhere from one to five years. One needs plenty of supportive interaction. Recovery is a process not an event. We didn't get messed up overnight and it will take energy to modify our addictive behavior. One needs to feel confident that he has the addiction under control. **One must learn to live one day at a time.**

This latter is a crucial part of any recovery and healthy living. Living one day at a time is a discipline that confronts one's willfulness. The new *willingness* to be in pain, to be confused and to accept the fact that recovery is a long process goes a long way in changing the grandiosity of the old willfulness. Living a day at a time means that one is willing to let go of trying to control things. It means that one has stopped looking for the grand experience — the visitation by God that heals everything.

The will is the most dis-eased part of any adult child's co-dependence. Our will is the executor of our life and the core of our freedom. Our will becomes disabled because it loses its eyes as it were. The blocked emotions from our abandonment build to the point of biasing our reasoning, judgments and perception. Our will has no source from which to make decisions so we turn to the will itself as the only object and resource available to us. We will to will. We become blindly willful. I believed for years I could stop drinking anytime I really wanted to. I pointed to my times of abstinence as proof of this. The fact was I could stop. But what I couldn't do was *stay stopped.*

All of us adult children have a distorted relationship to our will. We are willful and believe we can exercise control over all kinds of things — like other people's emotions, our relationships, our own emotions. My self-will ran riot.

When our will can only will itself, it loses all contact with reality. It is blind. When I was not able to resolve the problems of my life through sheer willpower, I became hopeless. It was all or nothing.

What I learned from my new family of affiliation was that there were many things in life that I have *no control over.*

Early on I was taught a prayer which said, "God grant me the serenity to accept the things I cannot change, give me the courage to change the things I can and the wisdom to know the difference." This prayer clearly made a distinction between being willing and being willful. The willing person accepts limited freedom and human finitude. In fact, willingness is rooted in healthy shame.

Willfulness is the belief that with strong willpower one can control massive areas of life. When one fails to control anything (even those things that obviously can't be controlled), one feels like a failure. Willfulness is rooted in internalized shame which is the legacy of abandonment. Once our shame is transformed from being a feeling to being a state of being, one has no access to the *feeling* of shame. Without the feeling of shame we become *shameless*.

So often during my drinking days I was asked, "Don't you have any shame?" The answer was that I was so defended against my shame that I not only guarded that I never be unguarded around other people, I was so guarded, I never had time to know what I felt.

Our disabled will has to be healed if we are to ever find our true and authentic self. By entering into a new family of affiliation, we can find new and trusting relationships. Out of those new relationships comes new mirroring.

As I saw myself in the eyes of my recovering brothers and sisters, I started to accept myself as they were accepting me. As I accepted myself, I accepted my feelings. As my trust grew, I came out of hiding more and more. I broke the no-talk rules, I shared my secrets, I was willing to be vulnerable, to be scared, awkward, embarrassed over the state of my life. As I felt and expressed those feelings, my three trillion circuited computer began to function better and better. My group called this "Getting your brains out of hock". It was true, after I expressed my emotions, I had clearer insight. I started trusting my own judgment and perceptions. Consequently, I started making decisions. I used the framework of living one day at a time.

Living one day at a time is a way to relativize the absolutizing and grandiose will. For 21 years I've only quit drinking one day at a time. I've never quit absolutely forever. Precisely because *one cannot* quit forever. Quitting forever is grandiosity. The paradox of all of this is as I became willing to accept my limitations, I actually began to have control over my life.

The 12-Step Programs

The 12-step programs have been unsurpassed in helping arrest compulsive/addictive behaviors. I'd like to briefly comment on the twelve steps:

The first three steps state:

1. We admitted we were powerless over *whatever the compulsive/ addictive behavior is* and our lives had become unmanageable.
2. We came to believe that a power greater than ourselves could restore us to sanity.
3. We made a decision to turn our wills and our lives over to the care of God as we understand Him.

These steps embody the unequivocal acceptance of limitation. They profess that the only way to deal with the addiction is to surrender. All attempts to *control* the addiction have led to the addict's life becoming unmanageable. The steps then address the spiritual bankruptcy created by the internalized shame.

Internalized shame has an absolutist quality. If I am a mistake, if I *am* flawed and defective as a human being, then *repair and reparation are not possible.* This hopelessness is grandiosity. This grandiosity is created by shame itself. Shame binds all feelings which then mar reason and judgment. All that is left is blind willpower. The will to will is playing God. So the steps immediately address this idolatry and spiritual emptiness by first calling on a power greater than ourselves and then calling that power God. The steps are clear about not trying to *control* anyone's conception of God (as if we could).

Winning By Losing

Steps 1 and 3 offer one the chance to embrace his shame and vulnerability. Only by embracing the shame can we come out of hiding and give up trying to control the shame. Paradoxically, the only way we can win is by losing. The steps also offer a restoration of the interpersonal bridge. Realizing that a shame-based person trusts no one (why would I trust any person when I couldn't trust my own father), the steps ask us to trust someone or something greater than anyone.

Steps 4, 5, 6 and 7 begin the process of moving us from shame to guilt. These steps say:

4. We made a searching and fearless moral inventory of ourselves.
5. We admitted to God, to ourselves and another human being the exact nature of our wrongs.
6. We were entirely ready to have God remove all these defects of character.

7. We humbly asked God to remove all our shortcomings.

By embracing our shame, we can look at our shame. We can take a fearless moral (not immoral) inventory of ourselves. We can honestly and squarely face our self.

It was here that I became aware of how my character defects were strategies I used to transfer my shame to others. My perfectionism, for example, was a great way not to feel shame. How could I be vulnerable if I never made a mistake. And since I was exceptional, those around me were usually one down.

My rage was another way I could keep people away from me. While in a rage, I was mood altered and didn't have to feel my shame. Below all the character defects was fear of exposure. And that flowed out of my shame.

The admission to self, others and God in Step 5 is a way to come out of hiding. Shame loves secrecy and darkness. To come out into the light is a way to overcome it. Steps 6 and 7 focus on becoming *willing*. I was entirely willing. I was vulnerable and asked for help and forgiveness. Asking for help is something no shame based person would do. *Shame believes that it doesn't have any right to depend on others and therefore ask for help.*

Steps 8 and 9 are action steps. They take us into guilt, conscience and reparation:

8. We made a list of all the people we have harmed and became willing to make amends.
9. We made direct amends to such people, whenever possible, except where to do so would injure them or others.

Internalized shame is irreparable. Therefore, it must be externalized. This means relativizing its grandiose claims.

Steps 1 through 7 have done precisely that. As shame is externalized and relativized, it becomes a feeling again. I can *feel shame* over some things I've done without concluding that I'm defective as a person. Shame as an emotion moves me to do something about what I've done. Shame triggers my guilt which triggers my conscience. I can then take action to repair the damage that I have done. With guilt I *made* a mistake and I can correct it wherever possible. Steps 8 and 9 restore me to respectability. I become a self-responsible person with a conscience.

Step 10 says "We continued to take personal inventory and when we were wrong, we promptly admitted it."

This is a maintenance step. It asks us to continue to be in touch with the healthy feeling of shame. Such a feeling tells us we are limited, finite and human. It tells us that *we will make mistakes* and that it is healthy to acknowledge them. With the restoration of healthy shame, we have accepted our humanness and our limitations. We can stop playing God. Our wills are restored.

I will discuss Steps 11 and 12 in chapter eleven. My own belief is that they are generally not a dominant part of this first stage of recovery.

I don't wish to impose my experience of the journey to wholeness on anyone else. No one can tell anyone else how to find his own most authentic self. Everyone's journey may look different from the outside. The stages I'm outlining are more in the order of logic. In actual experience things are not quite so neat and tidy. As you get the whole picture, I'm sure you'll know people who were doing Stage III stuff in Stage II or Stage II in Stage I. People may enter different stages at different times and by different doors.

Having said that, there is still some value in offering you ordered stages of recovery. I've seen several people jump to Stage III and do higher consciousness work without having gone through their ego work. I've seen people who have purported to have spiritual healings, who have never done any of the painful shame reduction work I spoke about in this chapter. I have seen them maintain this spirituality for a while only to go back to their compulsive/addictive lifestyle later on. And I've seen them become spiritually addicted.

I was in a monastery at 21 years of age. I meditated every morning. I prayed (sometimes six hours at a time) and fasted. I was celibate for nine and one half years. My own evaluation of that experience is that I was totally unprepared for the spiritual discipline that such spirituality demands (I hope God chalked up the nine and one half years of celibacy).

One needs strong ego boundaries before one is ready to let go of his boundaries (Stage III work). Adult children who have been abandoned through sexual, physical or emotional violence need to do repair work on their ego boundaries before they are ready to soar into higher consciousness. What I've described as Stage I work does not yet repair those ego boundaries. A lot more will have to be done for that.

Let me summarize Stage I using the phrase **Stage I Recovery**.

Summary

S   *Surrender to Pain*
T   *Trust and Telling Your Secrets*
A   *Affiliation Needs*
G   *Group Support — New Family Belonging*
E   *Experienced Powerlessness and Unmanageability*

I   *1st Order Change*

R   *Relativizing the Absolute Will*
E   *Experience Emotions*
C   *Collapsed Grandiosity — Give Up Denial*
O   *Oneness with Self — Self-acceptance*
V   *Values Restored*
E   *Externalization of Shame*
R   *Rigorous Honesty*
Y   *Yin/Yang Balance*

S. Surrender to Pain — Surrender means I give up trying to control my compulsive/addictive behavior. I am willing to let others help me and do it their way. I'm willing to go to any lengths to get well.

T. Trust and Telling Your Secrets — As you seek help, you are willing to *label* yourself an alcoholic, co-dependent, drug addict, sex addict, etc. You are willing to trust enough to ask for help. The labeling is crucial. You can't heal what has no name. An old 12-step program slogan is "We are as sick as our secrets."

A. Affiliation Needs — As you surrender to a recovery group, you come out of isolation. You are willing to let people care for you. You receive new mirroring, warmth and trust. You start believing that you can depend on the group.

G. Group Support — You now belong to a new family. There are good models here for your journey toward wholeness. You receive education on the nature of addiction and raise your awareness. You pick someone to be your sponsor — to model for you how to walk the walk.

E. **Experience Powerlessness and Unmanageability** — You experience this out of your pain. You come to see it more and more as you get your "brains out of hock".

I. **1st Order Change** — Stage I is a first order change because you have not done your work on your family system. First order change is a change of behavior within a given way of behaving. You are no longer acting out, but you are very *dependent* on the group. You are not yet your own person. You have to be careful that you do not become addicted to recovery. I've seen people embrace spiritual programs, make a god out of the religious guru. They stop drinking and drugging, etc., but they become addicted to the guru. One can be dry, and abstinent and still be compulsive. In A.A. this is known as a *dry drunk*. Recovering people frequently get addicted to recovery because they have not done the second order change work.

R. **Relativize the Absolutist Will** — You live one day at a time. You are learning to delay gratification. You accept the things you cannot change and change the things you can and you are learning the difference. You accept limitations.

E. **Experience Emotions** — You are no longer psychically numb. You are starting to experience your emotions. You feel awkward — like a teenager who is having emotions for the first time. You are angry over your past. You grieve the good times. You feel shame and embarrassment. You grieve over the loss of control and over a past which you wish had been different and often seems wasted. Healing demands the experiencing of the emotions. You can't heal what you don't feel.

C. **Collapse Grandiosity** — You have given up your denials about being able to control your compulsive/addictive behavior. You have given up the *Grand Expectation* and *The Big Fix*. You are more realistic and have more realistic expectations of yourself and others. You can laugh more at things. They are not so dramatic or serious.

O. **Oneness with Self** — You have seen yourself as acceptable in the eyes of your group. You are starting to accept yourself. You are accepting responsibility for your life and know that your happiness will depend on you. You're starting to trust your feelings, perceptions and wants.

V. Values Restored — Even amid confusion and painful feelings of shame, you have a sense of cleanness about yourself. For so long you've been split — living in opposition to your own values. Now you feel good about living according to *your* values.

E. Externalizing Shame — You have come out of hiding. You are working a program, asking for help and being vulnerable. As you embrace your shame, you see that you are not so bad. You're starting to grasp that 95% of your shame is about what happened to you, your abandonment. Shame is now a feeling and not a state of being.

R. Rigorous Honesty — You are being confronted by your sponsor or other group members on your character defects — such as perfectionism, judgment, rage, criticalness, manipulation and power-seeking. You are confronted when you are dishonest. You are becoming aware when you are being dishonest.

Y. Yin/Yang Balance — Your life is becoming balanced. It's not all or nothing. The peaks and valleys are not as dramatic.

10

Roadmap For Uncovering Your Lost Self

Stage II:
Breaking The Original Spell

*"I saw the angel in the marble and I just chiseled
'til I set him free."*

Michelangelo

Growing up means leaving home and becoming a self-supporting adult. I think this is the hardest task any human being has to face. It means breaking the fantasy bond and facing separation and aloneness.

Leaving home means giving up our family system roles and bringing our primary ego defenses into conscious focus so that we can let go of them. These layers of defense guard our hurt and lonely inner child. This child has ruled our adult life. These last layers of defense cover the most precious core of our self. To get this job done involves deep emotional pain. This is the legitimate suffering we have feared the most.

This child in us was abandoned. We've tried many ways to get his needs met and all have failed. Because of this inner child, our lives have been dominated by an unending restlessness. Great literary symbols have been used to represent this "homeless insatiability".

Wagner's symbol was the Flying Dutchman who was to roam the seas under a perpetual self-inflicted damnation. He was allowed on shore every seven years in search of a virgin maiden who alone could release him from his curse.

Goethe's Faust, Don Juan, Ahasuerus (the Wandering Jew) all have been used by 19th-century writers to symbolize these common themes of homelessness, perpetual craving and insatiability. The Flying Dutchman, Faust, Don Juan, Ahasuerus are the symbols of addiction, the selling of one's soul and the relinquishment of one's self to the outside.

Redemption is symbolized by the image of the Eternal Feminine — the woman who receives, nurtures and brings warmth in the silence of the night with her gentle embrace.

Many of the existentialist writers took up these themes of restlessness and perpetual craving. Each in his own way creatively intuited the ills that were to come as a product of the Age of Rationalism. Dostoyevsky's underground man decried the loss of emotion, spontaneity and vitality. He prophesied what Hegel's perfect logic would do to Russia. Marx turned that logic into dialectical materialism. Kafka offered vivid and intuitive prophesies of the Nazi S.S. Trooper's in his Penal Colony. Their quest for the woman who brings inner peace symbolizes our task in this second stage on the journey to wholeness.

Stage I was a *sine qua non* for survival. It's hard to imagine anyone doing Stage II work without the achievements of Stage I. In Stage I I found a new family with new models of maturity. I began to trust and share my vulnerable inner self. I experienced acceptance in the eyes of others and began to accept myself. I felt like I *truly belonged* in my new network of relationships. I gave up my alcohol addiction and began to give up my defensive character defects. I began to feel my emotions. I quit trying to control my feelings and my relationships. I gave up the grand adventure and settled into the "terrible dailiness", living one day at a time. I lost all conscious desire to drink or use chemicals. I recovered my disabled will and self respect.

I did this for some 10 years. As I said earlier, it was then that I began to become aware of my co-dependency issues. I had behavior modified my alcoholism. My disease was arrested.

The Compulsive Core of Co-dependence

What I hadn't dealt with was the *disease of my disease*. Vernon Johnson called it the *ism* of alcoholism. It's what I am calling co-dependence — the core and root of any and all compulsive/addictive behavior.

After 10 years of recovery, I found that I was still highly compulsive. Perhaps that's a good guideline for Stage II work. How compulsive are you still? Can you take a first step on co-dependence and honestly not identify with it? If you can, you can then proceed to Stage III.

Stage I allows us to see what Michelangelo called the angel in the marble. Once we've accepted that we are an angel, we still have the job of chiseling to set ourselves free. Stage I was a first-order change. We modified our behavior. We stopped using, eating, sexing, obsessing on relationships, buying, gambling, smoking, etc., and joined the human race. We accepted limitations. Two layers of our defensive shell were gone. But we still remained dependent. Many of us transferred our compulsivity to something else. Work addicts quit working and started drinking; smokers quit smoking and started eating; alcoholics quit drinking and started working addictively.

Often Stage I recovery becomes an addiction itself. We use the program to avoid dealing with the problems of what the Italians call "the terrible dailiness".

When I worked as counselor consultant for the Palmer Drug Abuse Program (PDAP) in Houston, person after person came to me who was using the program to avoid real honest responsibilities. Almost to a person they had money problems due to unrealistic buying addictions. In many cases, they were working a frantic program, but refused to go to work. The founder of that program is the best example I know of an addict who was dry but who desperately needed treatment for co-dependency. We have to treat co-dependence if we are to uncover the core problem. We have to start chiseling to get to the angel in the marble. We have to go deeper to mend the hole in our soul.

Dispelling the SPELL

This requires uncovering the delusions of the original family trance — the SPELL. Stage II is disenchantment. Children are magical and make gods out of their parents. Disenchantment is a natural process. Many primitive tribes construct situations of disenchantment to mark the entry into adulthood.

The invitation rite for Hopi children is a good example. The rite centers around Kachinas, masked gods who visit the village. During the rites of passage, the Kachinas tell the children secret stories and dance to entertain them. The Kachinas frighten them with ogre masks. As the ceremony reaches its climax, the children are taken to huts to await a Kachina dance. As they wait, they can hear the dancing gods calling as they approach the hut. But to the children's amazement, the Kachinas enter without their masks. The initiates learn, for the first time, that the Kachinas *are their parents impersonating the gods.*

The experience of disenchantment is the beginning of mature religious consciousness. We have to move from the delusions of childhood fantasy to the disenchantment of adult life.

I once heard the great psychologist-theologian, Sam Keen, say, "We have to move from the illusion of certainty to the certainty of illusion."

The family SPELL is powerful. My friend, Howard Trusch, compares it to instinct in animals. He writes:

"It is learned outside of one's awareness, it becomes just as much second nature to us as the spoken language."

Close Encounters of an Intimate Kind

Stage II involves breaking this SPELL. This is a second order change. First order change involves the change of one behavior to another within a given way of behaving. Second order change involves a change from one way of behaving to another. In second order change, one gives up his compulsivity. That certainly does not mean that one can go back to using chemicals at this stage. The ingestive addictions have their own inherent addictive properties. They are incurable.

Stage II is the process of going back and uncovering the original pain that occurred as a result of our being abandoned. We have to make the feelings about our abandonment real. This means giving up the primary process ego defenses — denial and delusion about our parents and family. Remember that abandonment includes narcissistic deprivation, neglect of our dependency needs, actual physical, emotional and sexual abuse, and our enmeshment in our family system needs.

Externalized Shame

By embracing this deep internalized shame, we can begin to externalize it. We began the externalization process in Stage I. It is a long process (will probably go on to death for some of us). The externalization process is a process by which we (a) transform the shame back into a feeling (internalization made our shame into a state of being); (b) reduce the shame; (c) give the shame back to those "shameless" significant others who interpersonally transferred it to us; (d) transform the energy of the shame into revolutionary action.

Giving the shame back to "shameless" caretakers involves dealing with what Pia Mellody has called "induced or carried shame". This was the shame our significant others dumped on us through their control, perfectionism, critical judgment, power trips, contempt and rage. This was the shame we had to carry whenever our caretakers acted "shameless" and played God. This was the shame resulting from the poisonous pedagogy.

Induced shame doesn't mean that it isn't our feeling of shame. It is *our feeling of shame*. But it resulted from our caretakers covering up their shame with one of their strategies of defense against shame.

For example, Mom feels shame over the state of her life, her children's suffering and her alcoholic non-intimate marriage. When the pain is too intense, she starts yelling at the kids to clean up their rooms or do the dishes. In her verbal shoulds, oughts and condemnation, she shames her children. Thus she shames her children as a way of defending against her shame. The children carry the shame. The transactional theorist call this "passing the hot potato".

Externalizing the shame is the process of owning the shame and then uncovering the sources from whence it came. Most of the internalized shame does *not belong to the person who carries it*. Therefore, it must be reduced and given back. Realizing how we were abandoned and expressing our feelings about it are the beginnings of Stage II. Alice Miller writes:

> "The greatest of all narcissistic wounds — not to have been loved just as one truly was — cannot heal without the work of mourning."
>
> *The Drama of the Gifted Child*

Mourning is the ultimate work of the externalization process. The mourning is the only way to heal the hole in the cup of our soul. Since we cannot go back in time and be children and get our needs met from our very own parents, we must grieve the loss of our childhood self and our childhood dependency needs. Grief, as Lindemann and Kiibler-Ross have shown us, is a process. According to these researchers, grieving is a complex process that involves a range of human emotions.

Grief work begins with shock and denial. It proceeds to a kind of bargaining, then to anger, guilt, remorse, sadness, hurt and finally acceptance. In truth, most of us have been stuck in the grief process all our life. We have been stuck at the levels of shock and denial. This is why most adult children have a low grade chronic depression.

Grieving for a loved one takes a long time. Emotional attachment is the criterion for the intensity and length of the grieving. When I say a long time, I mean years. The average grief span for widowed spouses who were highly attached and had achieved high levels of love is from two to four years. The loss of a child is usually longer. The loss of a parent shorter.

Stage II work can only happen because of the work begun in Stage I. It was there *you began to feel again*. You can't do the grief work if you can't feel. You can't feel if you are psychically numb.

The grief work is sometimes called the "original pain work". Alice Miller writes:

> "The achievment of freedom . . . is hardly possible without the felt mourning. This ability to mourn, i.e., to give up the illusion of a happy childhood, can restore vitality and creativity . . . If a person is able to experience that he was never loved as a child for what he was, but for his achievements, success and good qualities . . . and that he sacrificed his childhood for this love, this will shake him very deeply . . ."
>
> *Drama of the Gifted Child*

This work is painful and that's why we hold onto our denials and delusions. Why go back to the past? Why go through all that pain again? The fact is we really *never went through the pain*. We developed a fantasy bond and used our primary ego defenses to avoid the anger, hurt and pain of our abandonment. Then we avoided our avoidance with our rigid roles and characterological defenses. We missed expressing the feelings at the *crucial time*.

We missed it because our caretakers would not allow us to be angry or sad. They justified this with the poisonous pedagogy. We also missed it because it was so painful. Remember our drawings in Chapter 4 (figures

4.4, 4.5, 4.6). They give you a visual picture of the unexpressed feelings that keep you compulsively "acting out". Your emotions can only be your emotions by expressing them. Denying our emotions is a way that causes us to lose control over them. Once repressed and denied *you no longer have your emotions, they have you.*

Denying is lying. You no longer have the memories, but the repressed emotions form a frozen energy core that *unconsciously runs your life.* Compulsive/addictive behavior is by definition *outside one's control.* Emotional energy has to go somewhere. You either repress emotions (act them in); project them onto others (say others look needy when you feel shame over your own neediness) or "act them out".

My addiction was an acting out of my shame. Each drunken episode, which started as a way to feel better and overcome shame escalated into behavior of which I was ashamed. Hanging over the commode after a drinking bout (a fitting place to celebrate shame), I felt deep shame and remorse. What started as a way to cover up shame, ended with more shame. The vicious cycle (squirrel cage) was my repetition compulsion. It was the way I acted out "my unexpressed and unresolved internalized shame". Alice Miller calls this cycle "the logic of absurdity".

The only way out of this self-destructive deathstyle is to embrace the legitimate suffering. *You can only heal what you can feel.* Alice Miller writes:

> "Only the mourning for what he has missed, *missed at the crucial time* (italics mine) can lead to real healing."
>
> *Drama of the Gifted Child*

There are many ways to go about this work. None is the right way. Almost all major therapeutic schools offer some help along these lines. My only caution here would be to avoid a therapy that stayed only on the level of "cognitive insight". I agree with Alice Miller when she says:

> ". . . problems cannot be solved with *words,* but only through *experience,* not merely corrective experience as an adult but . . . through a reliving of early fear (sadness, anger) . . . Mere words, however skilled . . . will leave the split from which he suffers unchanged or even deepened."
>
> *Drama of the Gifted Child*

I don't wish to imply that cognitive therapy is not effective and useful. I just do not find it effective at this stage.

I covered my pain with cognitive insight. I was in my recovery for 10 years before I began any *feeling work*. I believed that because I no longer used any mind-changing chemical, I had arrested my addiction. The fact was that I was still enormously addicted. I was still controlling, out of touch with my feelings, grandiose and compulsive. My marriage was becoming progressively more non-intimate and I basically had no close friendships. When a marriage counselor confronted me with my "act", my grandiosity and my loneliness, I was shaken. Being a successful public speaker, TV personality and counselor was a great defense. I was receiving great adulation and praise. I was "helping" all kinds of people. *I was a professional co-dependent.* I had stopped my disease (the use of chemicals) but I had not dealt with the disease of my disease. The disease of my disease was the "hole in my soul", the insatiable child that was ruling my life. *I had to experience that child's pain.*

My belief is that every person who identifies himself as co-dependent will have to go through this process if he wants to be free of his compulsivity. When we are in touch with our true feelings, the energy to act them out is gone. Again, Alice Miller writes:

> "It is very striking to see how . . . acting out ceases when the patient begins to experience his *own feelings.*"

The Need for Therapy

As soon as one is in touch with his own feelings, this stage of recovery begins. One is usually not ready for the deep feeling work in Stage I.

The need for actual therapy is common at this stage. Had our families been healthier, therapy would not be necessary. Separation and self-formation would occur at the proper time and in the proper sequence. Healthy parents with healthy identities would model separation and want it for their children more than anything.

While I don't believe everyone needs to be in formal therapy, I believe that many people do. Therapy provides the kind of modeling and mirroring that most of us did not receive from our major caretakers. The kind of therapy is less important (as long as it's feeling work) than the therapist who is doing the work.

Martin Buber, the great Jewish Existentialist, studied all the available therapies and concluded that what heals is not so much the theory or the specific techniques of the therapist, but the *relationship between the therapist and client.* Our co-dependence resulted from, and ended in, pathological relationships. So a good relationship with a primary caregiver is a healing phenomenon. Actually a good loving relationship with anyone is healing. Eric Berne, the founder of transactional analysis, once said, "Love is nature's psychotherapy."

In choosing a therapist, you have every right to ask lots of questions before beginning. You can ask them who and what success they have had in treating co-dependency. You can ask if they consider themselves co-dependent and if so, what are they doing to deal with their problems. Ultimately, you can ask about their belief in group therapy.

Why this question? I believe that most effective therapists working with co-dependency will be moving their clients into groups. The groups may be 12-step groups, support groups, or interactive therapy groups (ideally a combination of all three). Co-dependent issues are basically about *relationship problems.*

Dr. Timmen Cermak writes:

> "The primary purpose of a long-term interactive group is to provide a setting in which the issues of co-dependency emerge spontaneously . . . Interactive group therapy works best when members discover themselves behaving inside the group much as they do in real life — being distrustful, controlling their feelings, sacrificing their own needs to ensure that others are taken care of, revealing only carefully chosen parts of themselves . . . when they finally understand that those behaviors reflect habitual and unconscious patterns, the group can become a laboratory for experimenting with alternative behaviors."
>
> *Diagnosing and Treating Co-Dependence*
> *(pp. 88, 89)*

In choosing a therapist or group, I recommend that you use simple criteria. Do you feel safe with this person or group? And can you reveal yourself *without being shamed?* I know many people who have been shamed by therapists and by groups.

Feeling work can also be done in workshop intensives. We offer such a workshop at our Center for Recovering Families in Houston. This workshop was designed in its current form by Terry Kellog. We call it The New Life Family Workshop.

Sharon Wegscheider-Cruse offers restoration workshops at her Onsite Center in Sioux Falls, South Dakota. She works with a powerful technique called family reconstruction.

Several therapist friends of mine have been involved in a process called Hakomi developed by Ron Kurtz. This process seems powerful and promising. The Hakomi Institute is located in Boulder, Colorado.

I offer a workshop with Kip Flock, my colleague in L.A. Kip Flock is the administrative director of LIFE PLUS Institute. We use life scripts and family roles as a way into the original pain. Our overall design uses techniques based on the work of Milton Erickson and Gestalt. We place *major emphasis on restoring the disabled will.* Our workshop is called "From Compulsivity to Choice".

Another group in San Francisco uses a process called the Quadrinity Process. This process was developed by Dr. Siegfried Fisher and Bob Hoffman. While I have not personally experienced the Quadrinity Process, it fits in with everything I believe about the original pain work.

I did my own feeling work using the techniques of Gestalt therapy and Bioenergetics. I would also recommend the work of Bob and Mary Goulding in Watsonville, California. The Gouldings combine Transactional Analysis with Gestalt. Their work has been widely acclaimed.

While it certainly is conceivable that one could do this feeling work without formal therapy, or without a confrontive group, it's highly improbable. The difficulty lies in the fact the the denial system that has to be broken is the primary ego defense system. The primary ego defenses *are activated in early life and function automatically and unconsciously.* We can't know what we don't know.

With these defenses we need confrontive mirrors. In Stage I, we needed echoing mirrors; in Stage II we need confronting mirrors. We need feedback pointing out and reflecting how we avoid or deny our feelings.

"Containment" is the therapeutic term for keeping a person in his feelings. Containment is done through confrontation. Confrontation is a form of mirroring. We show a person how he looks or sounds to us.

For example, a man in a share group I am in was describing how he had totally accepted his wife's recent affair. As he spoke *his fist was clenched* and *his voice tone was shaky.* I simply said to him, "Herkamer, when you said you had accepted your wife's affair, I saw that your hand was clenched and I heard your voice crack." This is confrontation. He can use what fits in that feedback or reject it. Two other men in our group gave him similar feedback. In this way, he has the opportunity to become aware of what he was not aware of.

I remember a time in my own uncovery process. I was sharing some details of my self-destructive behavior during my drinking days. I evidently had a smile on my face as I talked about some very painful stuff. (I now call this a *shame smile.*) One of the members of the group asked me to retell the experience, but to consciously avoid smiling. I started retelling the experience without the smile and within a few minutes, I was crying. My face muscles were part of the defense I had set up to avoid my sadness. Without mirroring eyes to see what I cannot see, I would have no way to confront my own unconscious defenses.

Corrective Experience

The work of Stage II needs to move past *re-experiencing* the early feelings. This step is necessary as part of the shame reduction work. But there is need for *corrective experience.* This involves uncovering the lost child that hides within us. As adults, many opportunities arise for us to embrace the child within us and do the work of reparenting ourselves. We can also learn, as adults, to let the nurturing we get from others be parenting.

The important phrase I want to emphasize here is "as an adult". The grief work was *not* a "corrective experience". *It was a reexperiencing of what I felt at the beginning and during my abandonment.* The solution to "acting out" behavior is to experience what one is "acting out". This is what the grief work accomplishes.

Once the "grief work" is done, it is possible to have "corrective experiences". All our experience is encoded and imprinted in our memory banks. Our developmental stages are like the circular layers of a tree. Each developmental stage is left intact. Figure 10.1 gives you a rough idea of what this looks like.

Hypnotic age regression work clearly suggests that each of these developmental stages remains intact. There are an infant, a toddler, a pre-school and a school-age child in each of us, who feel and experience just as we did when we were children. There is an adolescent in us who feels and thinks just like we did in adolescence.

The neurosurgeon, Wilder Penfield, corroborated some of this hypnotic work with experiments he made during open brain surgery. When he stimulated parts of the brain, the subject would experience the exact sensations and memories of a certain age level. This work formed the foundation of Eric Berne's famous model of personality as composing three distinct ego states.

Figure 10.1. Developmental Stages

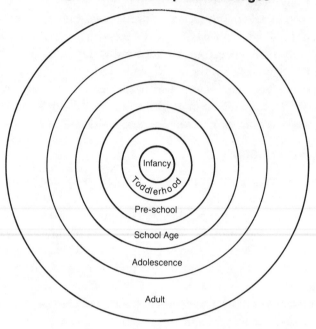

Berne theorized that we have an Adult Ego State (our current thought life); a Parent Ego (our recorded and unexamined life — an exact copy of our own parents); and a Child Ego State (our felt life, especially as we experienced it as a child).

There is strong agreement that the children we once were live in us as a complete energy state of feelings, thoughts and desires. If our developmental dependency needs were not met, the energy which would have accrued in the resolution of each developmental stage is blocked. This blocked energy is mostly composed of blocked emotions.

The basis of the "corrective experience" used in inner child work rests on the fact that, we can age regress and rework this blocked energy. Another presupposition of "inner child work" is that our developmental needs are recycled over and over again throughout our life.

In infancy, for example, the emotional need is basic trust. If that need is not met, one moves on to the next stage in a wounded manner. It will be much harder to experiment and separate from mother in toddlerhood if one does not have basic trust. Later in life, every time one goes into a brand new situation, the issues of infancy will come up.

I have developed a workshop which I'm now doing in several places in the country. My design is taken from several sources (most notably Pam Levin's soon to be published by Health Communications, *Cycles of Power*). The workshop allows participants to go through the developmental stages of childhood and offers them *corrective experiences* relating to each developmental stage. This is done by creating small groups which serve as nurturing mini-families. Each person receives from the group various kinds of mirroring and feedback appropriate to the age specific developmental need.

For example, in infancy, we all needed to be touched and nurtured. We needed to feel warmth and have the feeling that we could trust someone. We needed to hear words like: "Welcome to the world;" "I'm so glad you are here;" "You can count on me being here for *you*;" "You can take all the time you need to get your needs met, I will not rush you;" "I'm glad you're a boy;" "I'm glad you're a girl;" "I want to touch you, I want to hold you;" "I will accept you exactly like you are;" "Everything about you is okay with me."

When I facilitate the workshop, I ask one person at a time to move to the center of the group. The group then moves as close to that person as his boundaries permit. Each person in the group communicates one of the verbal affirmations while patting, stroking or just gently touching the subject. I have them go around the group several times amid lullaby music. The person in the center keeps his eyes closed and listens.

The first time I facilitated this exercise, I couldn't believe the intensity of feeling that emerged. Within seconds after beginning, some people in the center began sobbing deeply. As many of them were my clients, it suddenly dawned on me that almost all the ones sobbing so deeply were in the family system role of Lost Child. They were not wanted and never felt the primal trust an infant *needs to feel.*

When we touch the places in our souls that have holes, we feel it deeply. Watching Jack Nicklaus' son embrace him when he won his fifth Masters' title immediately brought tears to my eyes. Any time I see a father and son embrace, I feel a tinge of pain and sadness.

In my workshop we go through all the developmental stages of childhood, allowing each person to test whether he got those needs met or not. We offer *corrective experiences* in the workshop and we suggest other ways a person might work on getting those needs met.

For example, a Lost Child who is starting any new adventure needs to have a friend, a sponsor or a support group who will hug him, stand by him, or maybe take him out to eat (figuratively feed him). They can wrap up in a blanket, eat several snacks (nutritional, of course) the day before they start something new. Massages and bubble baths are also effective. These are ways, as an adult, they can take care of the child inside them. There are many other ways.

Later in the workshop we make contact with the child within through inner imagery and meditation. I have each person bring a picture of himself before age eight. By experiencing the child in internal imagery a contact is set up. I suggest that each one tells the child that he is from his future. And that he knows better than anyone what the child has been through. I further suggest a line from Jo Coudert's book *Advice From a Failure*. I suggest each one tell his inner child, "Of all the people you will ever know in your life, I'm the only one who you will never lose.". Then I ask each person if they are willing to add "and I will do my best never to leave you". The latter is important because out of our shame we have given up on our self and abandoned our inner child.

This experience is one of the most powerful I have ever witnessed. I began doing it with my clients about 12 years ago and have adapted it over the years.

I strongly suggest that each adult child sets aside a few minutes each day in order to meditate and make contact with his incomparable inner child. I recommend that each one keep a picture of his child in his wallet or on his desk. I have found this to be very healing. When I'm frustrated or in a hypervigilant stage, I like to look at my own four-year-old picture and talk to the little frightened boy within me. It's incredible how much it can help.

There is much more that can be said on inner child work. I'm in the process of writing a book called *Healing the Shame Which Binds You*. In that book, I will present this aspect of shame reduction work in great detail.

My work is not original. I have simply made a synthesis of many kinds of therapies that are going on in the field right now. I would especially recommend the work of Dr. Charles Whitfield called *Healing the Child Within*. Rokelle Lerner and Wayne Kritsberg are doing similar work. Pia Mellody has developed a workshop at *The Meadows* that helps a person make contact with his precious child. Inner child work is done regularly in T.A. groups. Thank God, it is going on.

Until we contact this vital spontaneous natural child who was abandoned by the rules of the poisonous pedagogy, we cannot begin to restore our inner life. Restoration of the inner life is the foundation for Stage III, the Discovery Process. We have to go back and contact our lost self if we are to discover our true self.

Leaving Home

We cannot find that lost self unless we *leave home*. We leave home by giving up our scripts and rigid roles. They denied us our authenticity. We played these rigid roles out of loyalty to our dysfunctional family systems. We got power and control from these roles, but they have cost us dearly.

Jo Courdet says, "You do not need to be loved, not at the cost of yourself." Each of us is an unrepeatable and incomparable precious child of God. We were born to be ourselves. This can only be done by separating from our family systems designations and from our parents' beliefs and opinions about us. Jesus Christ was strong in affirming the impossibility of finding God, much less ourselves, unless we left home. Matthew quotes Jesus as saying, "I have not come to bring peace, but a sword. For I have come to put sons against fathers and daughters against mothers . . . And a man's foes shall be those of his own household." (Mt. 10:34-36)

Leaving home means separating from our family system. It means giving up the idealizations and the fantasy of being bonded to our parents. Only by leaving and becoming separate can we have the choice of having *a relationship* with our parents. Relationship demands separation and detachment.

Once we've done the work, we may need a lot of distance from our family at first. For those who've been badly abused, you will have to make a prudent evaluation of how close you want to get to your original family. Some may find it too abusive to ever go back to their parents.

All in all, Stage II is a forgiveness stage. We are forgiving ourselves and we are forgiving our parents. Forgive means *to give as before*. It means that we give up the resentments and release the energy that has kept us in *bondage*. We can love our parents as the real wounded people they are, not as a magical child's absolutized and mythologized gods. Only by becoming separate can we have a relationship with *them*. Only breaking the SPELL with our family of origin can we have a life of our own choosing. Without breaking this SPELL our lives become multigenerational accidents.

Doing the work of Stage II often leaves us with what has come to be called "survivor's guilt". I can remember saying to a therapist during this stage of my work that I felt like a rat deserting a sinking ship.

My mother, brother, sister and I had been through a trauma and I was escaping from it. For a long time I put lots of energy into trying to get these members of my original family into therapy. I felt guilty for every good fortune that came my way. I felt I should split it four ways. It took me lots of therapeutic work to realize that I had a right to my own life. I came to see that I had a right to self-actualize and become my own unique individual self.

The guilt is a symptom of the family system dysfunction. Guilt in dysfunctional systems is a cover up for co-dependency. Guilt is the symptom of the family's enmeshment. As a frozen undifferentiated ego mass, no one in a dysfunctional family has a right to any autonomy and separateness. This lack of differentiation means that *no one has the right to be different*. Therefore, to be autonomous and different is to feel guilty. I still feel it from time to time.

There is nothing wrong with helping one's family as a care-giver providing it's a choice and not a family system duty. I love my mom. I held my father on his deathbed and told him I loved him. I had no unfinished business with him. I love my sister and brother and because of that, I refuse to play my Caretaker, Little Parent or Hero Role with them. I can't really love them if I don't love myself. To play these roles without any real relationship would continue the same old family dysfunction.

A client of mine reported to me that Renee Fredrickson, an authority on incest, was asked what gifts she would give her clients if she could give them any gift she wanted. Renee reportedly answered that she would give them the courage to stop trying to fix their family system and the courage, if necessary, to leave their parents to their fate.

This may not be an accurate quote, but it's a powerful way to focus Stage II recovery. Breaking the family SPELL means breaking the bonds of enmeshment. It means separating and focusing your energy on *your own life problems* (crucial for co-dependents). Some parents have never dealt with their neediness. They have never taken the responsibility for their own lives. After giving up one's childhood to take care of needy parents' emotions, one has a right (I would say a God-given duty) to focus on his own life. This may mean leaving your parents to their fate.

Re-experiencing the original pain and embracing one's lost child are the core of State II work. In order to secure and enhance the gains of this work, one must continue to do maintenance work.

Maintenance on Shame

This is especially crucial in regard to shame. Maintenance work on shame requires a continuous monitoring of the internal parental voices. These voices come in the form of drivers like Be Perfect, Be Strong, Please Me, Try Hard and Hurry Up. They also appear as Stoppers and Confusers. The Stoppers and Confusers are the introjected critical and contemptuous voices from our past shame experiences. We have to learn how to dramatize these voices and answer them. We also have to learn how to create new affirmations to confront our shame voices.

Shame is also maintained by internal imagery. The images of ourselves as flawed and the actual memories of being shamed are encoded in our neurological imprints.

There are powerful remapping techniques which can affect a healing of these memories. These techniques can also change our internal images. I plan to present these techniques in detail in my book *Healing the Shame Which Binds You.*

In conclusion, let me remind you again that recovery is a process and not an event. "It ain't over 'til it's over," Yogi Berra is quoted to have said. The grief work can be started in a therapy group or a workshop, but it may continue for many years. Once you've connected with your inner child and committed to be there for her or him, there's ongoing work to do. Love is the work of overcoming inertia and the courage to risk our time and attention. To embrace your lost child is the beginning of the work and courage of self-love. It's a life-long commitment. Remember, of all the people you will ever know, you are the only one you'll never lose!

I'd like to sum up Stage II Uncovery by using this phrase to organize the things we've been discussing. I've covered them sufficiently to eliminate commenting on each separate issue.

S   *Separation Process — Leaving Home*
T   *Trance Breaking — Breaking the SPELL*
A   *Anger and Resentment Work*
G   *Group Therapy*
E   *Embracing Your Incomparable Inner Child*

II *Second Order Change — Giving Up Your Primary Process Defenses and Rigid Roles — Stopping Compulsiveness*

U   *Uncovering Your Interpersonally Transferred "Carried Shame"*
N   *Normalcy and Averageness*
C   *Corrective Experiences Concerning Basic Needs*
O   *Original Pain — Grief Work for Abandonment*
V   *Values Formation*
E   *Ego Repair and Boundary Work*
R   *Recycling Childhood Needs as An Adult*
Y   *Yearning for Family Health — "Survivors Guilt"*

11

Roadmap For Discovering Your TRUE SELF

Stage III: Spiritual Awakening And Empowerment

*"if you can be, be. if not, cheer up and go on about other
people's business, doing and undoing unto others til you drop."*
                                                              e.e. cummings

The end of life brings wisdom, providing one has met and surmounted the various critical tasks along the way. Wisdom may be defined as knowing what is important and what isn't important. In wisdom we see the whole picture. This is why it takes a long time to truly become wise. It is only in the evening that we can evaluate the whole day. Wisdom is seeing the whole. Wisdom allows us to know the parts by knowing the whole.

As Sri Aurobini says, "You must know the highest before you can truly understand the lowest."

The third stage of our journey toward wholeness gives us a new perspective on all that has gone before. Stage III leads to wholeness itself. In becoming complete we can see more clearly what the core problem in our addictive lifestyle was.

The last of the 12 steps states:

12. *"Having had a spiritual awakening as a result of these steps, we tried to carry this message to other addicts and to practice these principles in all our affairs."*

This step makes it clear that the core of our addictive behavior is spiritual death. Co-dependence is a spiritual problem. Recovering from addiction leads to spiritual awakening. And not only is the end result a spiritual awakening, it is to be a permanent state kept alive by daily practice. Spiritual awakening involves a new way of seeing and a new way of being.

Stage III is **Spiritual Awakening.** In Stage III we begin a true journey of *discovery.* We enter into places we have never been before. Our past egoic meaning rests upon our doings and our accomplishments. In Stage III we move beyond ego and egoic-type meaning.

The new meaning is less about doing and more about being. We come to know our own beingness — our true self. This awareness is ahistorical. It is timeless and originates from within us.

In Chapter 3, I presented a chart of our basic human needs. That chart was based on the work of Dr. Abraham Maslow. Maslow spent his life studying the highest potentials of human nature. He wanted to know about human greatness. He spent much time studying what he called self-actualized people and peak human experiences. Out of these studies Maslow concluded that we human beings have a hierarchy of needs. Our most basic needs he called *deficiency* needs. I've called these *dependency* needs and I've been discussing the problems resulting from not getting those needs met.

Maslow believed that once the dependency needs are met, one can move on to a higher level of needs which he called *being needs.* The being needs have to do with identity, individuality, justice, truth, goodness, beauty, ultimate meaning and wisdom. The two sets of needs are connected. It's hard to imagine being a seeker of justice and truth if one is starving; or being concerned with issues of individuation and identity if one is starved for love and affection.

Maslow believed that each set of needs had a certain kind of consciousness or cognition which governed it. The lower order needs are the domain of ego. The higher order needs are the domain of higher or unity consciousness. Higher consciousness constitutes the realm of our *true self*. In the figures in Chapter 4, I visually presented this theory of human consciousness. From these drawings one can immediately see that the pathway to the *true self* rests upon the resolutions of one's ego issues. Many spiritual writers have said this before me.

Jacquelyn Small, in her book *Transformers*, states:

> "The ego will continually draw us backwards, toward the level where the unmet need exists, until the need is met."

The lack of fulfillment of childhood dependency needs, I've called the problem of the adult child. As an adult with unmet child dependency needs, one is continuously being drawn backwards in an attempt to get those needs met. Stage II uncovers these needs and provides a context to get these needs met as an adult. As the ego is reconstructed, one becomes free to move beyond ego.

On the path toward self-completion and wholeness, the ego must be transcended. The ego represents our limited or narrowed consciousness. Ego is to the *true self* what a flashlight is to a spotlight. The purpose of ego is adaptation, coping and survival. We cope with the world and get our basic dependency needs met by means of ego. To live life adequately we need strong ego boundaries. As hypervigilant co-dependent survivors, our life was dominated by distress and threat. We cannot even think of Stage III, whose task is discovering our *true self* as long as our boundaries are weak.

The Journey Within

We cannot start the journey inward until the family of origin SPELL is broken and the grief work is finished.

When our ego boundaries are strong, the world becomes less threatening. We know we can take care of ourselves. We know we have the inner resources to make it. We do not have to live in hypervigilance any longer. Our ego is now available for the work of expanding and moving beyond itself. Moving beyond myself is actually an inward journey.

Moving within is the journey toward spirituality. Without this journey, there is no way to know who I really am. My beingness, my ultimate selfness lies in a realm beyond the family roles and cultural sex roles. My true self cannot be discovered from the outside. My beingness can only be discovered in the silence of my inner life.

There are two points of major importance for the journey in Stage III. The first is the belief that we have a life beyond our ego. The second is that the ego cannot be bypassed if it has unfinished business from the past. Let me discuss each of these more thoroughly.

Life Beyond the Ego

Abraham Maslow believed he had empirical data to support the existence of a higher consciousness. As a psychologist, he believed spiritual life was the core of human life. He writes:

> "The spiritual life is . . . part of the human essence. It is a defining characteristic of human nature. Without which human nature is not full human nature."
>
> *The Farther Reaches of Human Nature*

Recently there have been a number of researchers looking into the phenomena of higher consciousness. Men like Ken Pelletier at the Langly Porter Neuropsychiatric Clinic in San Francisco, Elmer and Alice Green at Menninger's, Russel Targ, Gerald Putoff, Dr. Brugh Joy, Karl Pribrim and Fritz Capra have come to a surprising consensus about the powers available to us at the heights of consciousness. The Greens and Pelletier are research psychologists. Karl Pribrim is a brain physiologist. Targ, Putoff and Capra are physicists. Brugh Joy is a medical doctor.

Psychics like Olga Worrell and my friend Jack Schwarz have verified some of the great possibilities of higher power. Jack has eaten only three meals a week for the last 32 years. He sleeps only two hours a night. Jack can put twelve-inch knitting needles through his veins while maintaining alpha brain wave consciousness. He then heals the wounds. Jack has voluntary control over so-called involuntary processes.

Transcending the Ego

The central conclusion of all these scientists is that our full human consciousness is much more than our narrowed ego consciousness. All agree that there is a higher consciousness which transcends ego.

There is also evidence that this consciousness is connected to all created consciousness. The early work of J.B. Rhine at Duke in telepathy pointed clearly in this direction. The more recent work of Putoff and Targ at Stanford Research Institute (SRI) on Remote Viewing E.S.P., has offered powerful new data suggesting that once in higher consciousness, we have a higher power available to us. Their belief is that this power results from being connected to all other created consciousness.

There are also ancient traditions supporting a higher power through expanded consciousness. The Indian Medicine Healers believed there was a greater power available through the use of meditation and the fusion with power animals. Jesus told his followers that there were powers available to them that were greater than the powers he manifested. His human powers were clearly powers of psychokinesis, clairvoyance, telepathy and pre-cognition.

The remote viewing experiments at SRI have corroborated some of the conclusions of quantum physics. These experiments suggest that we are not limited by space and time. People in sealed rooms can see what someone else is seeing 30 miles away. Some especially gifted people can know what others are going to see before they have even been assigned a destination. This research is recorded in books like *The Silent Pause* by George Leonard and *Mind Reach* by Putoff and Targ.

What the bottom line conclusion states is that when we are in the highest moments of consciousness, we are one with the universe. We are a hologram of the world. The world is a system and we are partly a whole and wholly a part. *Each of us in his own way is the universe.* This is what all the great spiritual masters have been teaching us for centuries. The ego creates separation and illusion. Once beyond ego there is no separation. We are all one. Modern science is catching up with the perennial wisdom.

Modern science makes it clear that mind and body are not antagonists. Mind and body are two different forms of energy. Our consciousness is now being understood as high frequency energy. As forms of energy, mind and body influence each other.

We've spent considerable time talking about emotional energy and how it affects mind. It is clear that worry and mental agitation can greatly affect our bodies. Pelletier, in his book *Mind As Healer, Mind as Slayer*, states that some 60% of illnesses we bring to doctors are stress-related and could be controlled with stress-management techniques.

Letting Go

If mind and matter are the same stuff, we can learn to use matter in more powerful and profound ways. Learning to let go of ego control and to turn it over to higher consciousness is a powerful way to get results.

A slogan in A.A. says, "Let go and let God." People speak of powerful things happening in their life when they turn it over to their Higher Power. The findings I've been describing can be summarized as follows:

We are more than our ordinary ego consciousness. To find our true self we have to transcend our ordinary ego consciousness. This conclusion is:

1. Compatible with a growing amount of behavioral science data.
2. Is integral to almost all the world's religious traditions.
3. If fully believed at the personal level, would totally transform one's life.

*The propositions leading to this central conclusion are:

1. Much of our significant mental activity goes on outside of conscious awareness, e.g., biofeedback, dreams, intuitive knowing, family systems, roles and ego defenses.
2. The powers of suggestion and autosuggestion are far greater than we typically assume. We all operate in a post-hypnotic (borrowed existence) SPELL induced in early infancy. The major elements of this SPELL come from the family of origin and the culture we are born into. This SPELL operates unconsciously.
3. We will resist the knowledge which we most deeply desire. Language ego defenses, denials, delusions, family system and cultural roles keep us from higher consciousness.
4. Each of us has access to a supraconscious, creative, integrative, self-organizing, intuitive mind whose capabilities are apparently unlimited. This is the part of our consciousness that constitutes our God-likeness.
5. There is now extensive data to show that this higher consciousness is connected to all other forms of consciousness. (J.B. Rhine's experiments in telepathy at Duke the remote viewing experiments of Putoff and Targ at Stanford Research Institute.)
6. There is no reason to doubt that my creative/unconscious mind might have a *plan* in mind for me. As we look back over our lives,

*Adapted from the work of Willis Harman.

it often seems clear that there was such a plan. We are free to follow or disregard it.

7. Acting in accordance with my higher power's plan, I can expect my actions to be in harmony with the ultimate well-being of all of those around me.

8. There seems to be no reason to doubt that the necessary resources for actualizing the plan will be available whenever needed. Einstein has shown that mind and matter are both energy. There is copious evidence that proves the power of mind energy over matter energy, (psychokinesis, etc.).

9. It appears that a sober life is one in which *choosing* is given over to the creative/intuitive mind. This is accomplished through the conscious contact resulting from prayer and meditation.

10. One of the conditions for hearing an undistorted inner voice is the willingness to perceive differently. This involves a disciplined approach to prayer and meditation in which the ego is bypassed.

Unfinished Ego Needs

The second point of importance is that the ego cannot be bypassed in the journey toward wholeness if it is still involved in unfinished issues from the past. Each one of us needs a strong and healthy ego.

Jacquelyn Small writes:

> "On the path to self-creation, the ego must be transcended. But it can only be transcended by working through its needs at the personal and interpersonal levels — not by denial or by attempting to bypass them."
>
> *Transformers*

The jump into prayer, meditation, dream work, journaling and other spiritual disciplines is often done too quickly before the ego structures are secure enough to be a platform for expansion. I've seen many people espousing spiritually (some even teaching it) who are still extremely co-dependent. The spirituality thus becomes very deceptive forms of delusion and denial. One can easily become addicted to the highs of altered states of consciousness. Spirituality in these forms is downright dangerous and lends itself to compulsive/addictive behavior.

On the other hand, it is crucial to point out that there are those on the level of higher consciousness who often appear neurotic. Operating on the unity consciousness level often appears weird to ego consciousness.

For example, the ego cannot understand the language of dreams. People will often say, "I had this *weird* dream last night." The dream is weird to ego — not to unity consciousness, which thinks in symbols and holistic imagery. Jesus, Francis of Assisi, Gandhi, Joan of Arc, Schweitzer, Mother Teresa, may appear really weird to the materialistic ego. The spiritual person has often been symbolized as the clown or the fool. The "foolishness of God" is often hard to differentiate for addiction.

Most of us don't have to worry about heroic sanctity. So, generally speaking, we need to do our ego work before soaring into unity consciousness.

All of this is to say that Stage III work needs to be solidly based on Stages I and II. Stage III is a transformative journey. *Finding one's true self means seeing one's life quite differently.* One's addictive lifestyle was based on a *belief* that something outside of self could bring salvation. Unity consciousness makes it clear that there is nothing outside of self that can make one happy. Our happiness lies within the inner life, "The Kingdom is within".

As we encounter our true self we realize that this is our self made in the image of God. Our true self is our God Self (our Christ likeness, if you are Christian). The deep self consciousness that is connected to all other consciousness is the part of our life that participates in the life of God. This is truly a Higher Power. This is not just *becoming a better self, it is becoming a different self.* By changing our beliefs, we change our lives. This is crucial.

Belief Power

Our lives are limited by our beliefs. In my active addiction, I believed that my life and happiness depended upon external forces. I made decisions according to that belief. My false belief led me to wrong choosing. I ultimately created the kind of world I believed in.

I had a great example of how beliefs shape our worldview last Christmas. I went to the Galleria with a friend of mine and his uncle. The Galleria is the most crowded shopping center in Houston during the holidays. The traffic is terrible. It often takes 40 minutes to get there from my house which is only six miles away.

My friend is an up kind of person — very loving and warm. He has an infectious smile. He loves people and believes in the goodness of people. He was driving the car and got us to the Galleria in 20 minutes. His smile was captivating as he asked people to let us get through traffic lines. He created the kind of world he believed in.

His uncle asked to drive on the way back. His uncle is rather somber and believes people are "no damn good". It took us 20 minutes to get out of the Galleria parking lot! His uncle gave people dirty looks, yelling aggressively at other drivers. No one would let him in line. Finally, a sweet little old lady signaled for him to get ahead of her. He shot her the finger! Not only did he create the kind of world he believed in, when data emerged which could change his belief, he refused to look at the data.

Our beliefs create the kind of world we believe in. We always project our feelings, thoughts, and attitudes onto the world. I can create a different world by changing my belief about the world. Our inner state creates the outer and not vice versa. It took me 42 years to grasp this rather simple spiritual principle. Co-dependence is at bottom a spiritual disease because it believes exactly the opposite. The core belief of co-dependence is that my inner state is dependent upon what is outside me.

Stage III starts us on the journey to discover that inner kingdom. This involves the work of spiritual disciplines. Such disciplines demand the same attitude that the previous stages involved: resolve, commitment and working one day at a time. There are several approaches to dream work. Likewise with prayer and meditation.

Just as one needed a sponsor in Stage I; a support group or therapist in Stage II; so also one needs a spiritual director in Stage III. One may find such a person in his new family of affiliation. One may know of a spiritual master that he wishes to approach and ask to be his sponsor or guide. He may have a pastor, priest, rabbi, spiritual friend who appeals to him. Guidance is important in the beginning. Few people know anything about dream interpretation or dream integration. Almost no one has been taught how to meditate. Most people continue their childhood methods of prayer and have no idea about expanding their prayer life. Spiritual diaries and journal writing are not common practices for most people. A spiritual director is most useful in Stage III.

The 12-step programs lead directly to the inner kingdom. The 12-step programs grew from the six tenets of the Oxford movement. These six tenets were themselves the result of a spiritual experience given to a minister named Frank Buckner. The founders of A.A. were participants in the early Oxford movement in the United States. They built upon the tenets of the Oxford movement in forming their 12-step program.

One thing was clear from the beginning of the A.A. movement. And that is that true recovery only ensues when one has had a spiritual awakening. Bill W. and Dr. Bob were clear about the ultimate problem of alcoholism. For them it was "spiritual bankruptcy". The disease of the disease is spiritual barrenness. This is what I have described as a hole in the soul — the problem of co-dependency. This ism of alcoholism or any addiction is the inner self rupture called variously, internalized shame, self-will run riot or co-dependence. Each is a way to describe spiritual bankruptcy.

The 12th step spoke of a spiritual awakening. The 11th step speaks directly of prayer and meditation. It says:

"11. We sought through prayer and meditation to improve our conscious contact with God as we understand Him, praying only for knowledge of His will for us and the power to carry that out."

There are myriad approaches to both prayer and meditation. No way is the right way and no technique is the real thing. The real thing is the actual immediate experience of oneness with God. That is our destiny and without it, we are missing the mark. It's so important to emphasize that the spiritual quest is not some added benefit to our life, something you take if you have the time and inclination.

We are spiritual beings on an earthly journey. Our spirituality makes up our beingness. We are the kind of spiritual beings who, in order to adequately be spirits, need a body. We are not earthly beings trying to get spiritual. We are *essentially spiritual.* This is why the abandonment I have been describing is a spiritual problem.

If we humans are essentially spiritual, then to have our souls murdered is to be spiritually violated. Indeed when our caretakers acted shamelessly, they were playing God. Healthy shame tells us we are finite, limited and prone to mistakes. By our caretakers acting shamelessly, we were forced to carry their shame. Our souls were murdered by that shame. Co-dependence is the outcome of this abuse.

The False Gods of Addiction

As spiritual bankruptcy, co-dependence sets us up for false gods. Indeed co-dependence is a conflict of gods. The addictions which are the diseases of the co-dependency are little idolatries. They are the archaeological ruins of our quest for transcendence. They are aborted quests for God. Every addiction is spirituality gone awry. Every addict has a god, be it work, money, booze, cocaine, a lover, a spouse, a child, gambling, nicotine, sex, food, etc . . . No God ever had a more devoted follower. Addicts literally are ready and willing to give their life for their God.

Every addiction has its prayer, its mantras and its mental obsessive meditation. Every addiction has its rubric and its rituals. And every addiction has its professed moment of salvation, its at-one-ment. The mood alteration and adrenalin rush provide a moment when all self-rupture and alienation are overcome. We are high, ecstatic. We are one with ourselves. The weeping, the loneliness, the pain and the shame are momentarily overcome. We are enthused, (en-theos) one with our God. But unlike the permanent bliss taught by the spiritual masters, this high is a dud.

The Inner Life

Once we begin the journey inward, tremendous transformations take place. First a new kind of peace and calm comes over us. Our inner life belongs to us alone. It depends on us, not on something outside of us. We can depend on this inner world because we actually experience it. It will never go away. By having an inner life, we are no longer dependent on the outside for our good feelings, we can engender them from within.

As one advances in meditating, a new mental faculty emerges. The spiritual masters call it intuition or enlightenment. It's not like a perceptual intuition or intellectual intuition. It only emerges in silence and stillness.

Moving into the silence is what the spiritual disciplines are all about. Learning how to quieten the conscious mind (the ego's incessant chatter and self-talk) requires practice. The practice is done one day at a time. One needs to be very careful of grandiosity in pursuing skill in meditating. Grandiosity looks for the big experience, the visitation by God. Learning to meditate is more like the dripping of water on a rock. Over the course of time the rock will be eaten away. Co-dependents want to turn the water on full blast. That has little effect on the rock.

As one advances into the silence, the intuitive faculty becomes more and more available. The intuitive faculty is the power of immediately experiencing God. *"Be still and know that I am God,"* the Bible says.

To have immediate conscious contact is to experience bliss. Once experienced, bliss has no opposite. One wants more and more. One hungers and thirsts for such peace and oneness with all things. The desire and longing for bliss are signs that one is advancing in the inner kingdom.

The deep peace and calm that conscious contact brings transforms the vision of one's whole life. Since the new self is a new state of consciousness, one starts seeing their whole life from this new point of view.

On Getting Where I Am

In my own case, I'm beginning to see that everything that I have gone through had to be. From the perspective of my unity consciousness, I see that my parents were perfect. I needed to become a drunk so that I could have the experience for understanding the kind of suffering addiction causes. Coming out of a dysfunctional family, I could learn about the rules which create dysfunction in families. All of this is part of my self's purpose for being here.

Had my dad not been a drunk and my system not been dysfunctional, I could not have created a television series about families dysfunction and I wouldn't be writing a book. My life was just what it needed to be for me to be able to evolve and expand my consciousness through suffering. Leon Bloy once said, "There are places in the heart that do not yet exist: pain must be in order for them to be."

Without my suffering, I would not be able to bear witness to an addictive society and the pain it is causing its people. I could not be in the system enough to understand it and at the same time be in recovery enough to stand outside of it and confront the rules of the poisonous pedagogy which our society encourages and authorizes. From my true self point of view, my life has been perfect.

Once the contact was made with my lost child, I began the journey to discover my true self. The growth in self awareness comes from becoming more and more who I am. It is less and less a struggle with myself. And it has less and less to do with anything that I do. The only thing I do not have to struggle with is being myself. Transformation is effortless because as Jacquelyn Small says, "There is nothing that has to be done — there is only someone to be."

Spiritual growth comes through deepening insight into my being. This deepening insight is truly transformative. It is no longer a mosaic of beliefs about myself which come from *other peoples'* opinions and beliefs about me. My self-knowledge comes from the immediate conscious contact with God. In that conscious contact, I have an immediate awareness of my true being. It has nothing to do with sex roles, family system roles or any of my accomplishments. My true identity is beyond anything outside of me.

Years ago when I was in the monastery, I read and studied the things I'm writing about now. I felt very afraid. I remember reading Abe Maslow's description of how self-actualized people are no longer concerned about the impression they are making, how they love their solitude. He described self-actualized people as being interested in listening to other people's opinions of them, but being very little affected by those opinions. Maslow's self-actualized people transcended dichotomies. They no longer see anything in opposites.

Their consciousness was unified. Work and play merge for them. The more innocent and childlike they became, the more mature they became. The more individuated, the more they belonged to the group.

Being an ace *people-pleaser*, this all seemed terribly selfish and arrogant. I remember reading the great philosopher-mystic Krishnamurti and being terribly perplexed by his statement, "We must be extraordinarily capable of standing alone." Being alone triggered my abandonment issues. Co-dependents are terrified of being alone.

Today, I'm getting slow glimpses of what all this means. Today I belong to myself, and I'm willing to accept full responsibility for my life and my creations. What I do is me — for that I did come. And it's a long way to come — from being laid out on a stretcher in a state hospital to delving into higher consciousness. It's a long way to come, and yet *it was all there in my compulsions and addictions. I was seeking God, but I didn't know it.* I wanted ecstasy, oneness with self, oneness with the world and transformation. My control and willful exertion gave me the illusion of wholeness.

I'm happy that God writes straight with crooked lines. The fears of going inward and losing the familiar have completely left me. I have had real glimpses of the bliss so well described by Thomas Wolfe when he wrote:

"To lose the earth you know, for greater knowing; to lose the life you have, for greater life; to leave the friends you loved, for greater loving; to find a land more kind than home, more large than earth."

To which I add: To find a place where you are *never abandoned or alone; a place not measured by perfectionistic rules.*

Summary

S   *Spiritual Awakening — Zen Seeing*
T   *Transpersonal — Beyond Ego*
A   *Aloneness as Solitude*
G   *God Consciousness*
E   *Expanded Consciousness — See Life Differently*

III *Third Order of Change — Transformation*

D   *Differentiation — Individuation*
I   *Intuitive Vision — God — Self*
S   *Spiritual Disciplines — Prayer, Meditation*
C   *Creativity — Creative Love*
O   *Oneness — Unification of Polarity*
V   *Values Concerned with Being — Truth — Goodness — Beauty*
E   *Energized and Empowered*
R   *Reverence for Life — Peacemaking*
Y   *Yearning for Bliss*

   S. Spiritual Awakening — You see things from God's point of view. You're no longer a feverish clod of grievance and ailments. You want to be a force of nature and one with your creator.

   T. Transpersonal — Beyond Ego — You have let go of control. You trust your own resources and your network of friends to get your needs met.

   A. Aloneness as Solitude — You embrace and enjoy your time alone. The relationship with yourself is ongoing and enjoyable. You use your solitude for self-discovery.

   G. God Consciousness — You pray and/or meditate daily. You have conscious contact many times a day. You rarely feel lonely or frightened.

   E. Expanded Consciousness — You are beginning to see your whole life differently. You are connected with your purpose from God's point of view. You see your family system from the perspective of a higher purpose. You are evolving rather than revolving.

III. Third Order Change — You are becoming transformed. You are not getting better; you are a different person. You are *discovering yourself* from the inside. You have transcended all the rules.

D. Differentation — Individuation — You are coming to know the difference that makes a difference. You are realizing your true self. You know there has never been anyone like you and there never will be again. You love and affirm yourself.

I. Intuitive Vision — You are experiencing moments of powerful insight and enlightenment. At times you have an immediate knowledge of God's presence. You know yourself in contact with God.

S. Spiritual Disciplines — You are practicing meditation. You put aside time every day to make conscious contact with God. You pray to acknowlege God's glory. You spend time on your spiritual life. You study spirituality.

C. Creativity — Creative Love — You are more creative than ever before. You trust your sensations, feelings and thoughts. You go with your imagination. You are more creative in your love. You go beyond any kind of giving to get. You're committed to service. You do things no one will find out about.

O. Oneness — Unification of Polarity — You do not see the world in black and white. You see that there is no joy without sorrow; no pleasure without pain; no light without darkness; no life without death. The more individuated you become, the more intimate you are; the more mature, the more childlike.

V. Values Concerned with Being — You are most concerned about truth and honesty. You see beauty where you had never seen it before. You see goodness where you had never seen it before. You are less possessive and attached. Your life is less complex and more simple.

E. Energized and Empowered — You have more energy than ever before. You feel one with yourself and are not using energy for inner warfare. You are powerful in a personal way.

R. Reverence for Life — Peacemaking — You feel concerned about generating life. You want to leave the world better than when you came. You work for interpersonal and world peace.

Y. **Yearning for God — Bliss** — You have experienced high moments of oneness with God and all things. You've felt the unity and seen the illusion of separation. You have an urge for more peace, love, truth, goodness and beauty. You hunger for personal love and oneness with God.

References

The author gratefully wishes to acknowledge the following books, articles and tapes as sources for this book. I heartily recommend them to the reader.

Bach, J., Anderson, A., et al. "A Systems Model of Family Ordinal Position."

Berger, Peter, Thomas Luckmann. *The Social Construction of Reality.* (Doubleday Anchor).

Bowen, Murray. *Family Therapy in Clinical Practice.* (Jason Aronson).

Carnes, Patrick. *Out of the Shadows: Understanding Sexual Addiction.* (CompCare).

Cermak, Timmen. *Diagnosing and Treating Co-dependence.* (Johnson Institute).

Coudert, Jo. *Advice From A Failure.* (Scarborough).

Erikson, Erik. *Childhood and Society.* (W.W. Norton).

Erickson, Milton. *Hypnotic Realities.* (Irvington).

Farber, Leslie H. *The Ways of the Will.* (Colophon).

Frederickson, Renee. Tapes can be ordered from Frederickson & Associates, 821 Raymond Avenue, St. Paul, MN 55114.

Fossum & Mason. *Facing Shame.* (W.W. Norton).

Firestone, Robert. *The Fantasy Bond.* (Human Sciences).

Foley, Vincent. *An Introduction to Family Therapy.* (Grune & Stratton).

Forward, Susan. *Betrayal of Innocence.* (Penguin).

Hoffman. *No One Is To Blame.* (Science & Behavior).

Jackins, Harvey. *The Human Side of Human Beings.* (Rational Island).

Kellogg, Terry. Tapes can be ordered from 20300 Excelsior Boulevard, Minneapolis, MN 55331.

Kaufman, Gershen. *Shame: The Power of Caring.* (Schenkman).

Lynch, William. *Images of Hope.* (University of Notre Dame Press).

Miller, Alice. *The Drama of the Gifted Child.* (Basic Books).

Miller, Alice. *For Your Own Good.* (Farrar, Straus, Giroux).

Mellody, Pia. Tape series, *Permission To Be Precious,* can be obtained by writing: P.O. Box 1739, Wickenburg, Arizona 85358.

Peck, Scott. *The Road Less Traveled.* (Simon and Schuster).

Satir, Virginia. *Conjoint Family Therapy.* (Science and Behavior).

Schwarz, Jack. *Voluntary Controls.* (E.P. Dutton).

Seligman, M. "Falling Into Helplessness." *Psychology Today,* Vol. I:1.

Small, Jacquelyn. *Transformers.* (Devorss).

Trush, Howard. *Close Encounters of the Intimate Kind; or How to Stay a Couple by Really Trying.* (Vantage Press).

Targ, R. *The Mind Race.* (Villard).

Walker, Lenore. *The Battered Woman.* (Colophon).

Whitfield, Charles. *Healing The Child Within.* (Health Communications).

Wilber. *The Holographic Paradigm and Other Paradoxes.* (Shambhala).

Other Books By . . .

HEALTH COMMUNICATIONS, INC.

Enterprise Center
3201 Southwest 15th Street
Deerfield Beach, FL 33442
Phone: 800-851-9100

ADULT CHILDREN OF ALCOHOLICS
Janet Woititz
Over a year on The New York Times Best Seller list,this book is the primer
on Adult Children of Alcoholics.
ISBN 0-932194-15-X   **$6.95**

STRUGGLE FOR INTIMACY
Janet Woititz
Another best seller, this book gives insightful advice on learning to love
more fully.
ISBN 0-932194-25-7   **$6.95**

DAILY AFFIRMATIONS: For Adult Children of Alcoholics
Rokelle Lerner
These positive affirmations for every day of the year paint a mental picture
of your life as you choose it to be.
ISBN 0-932194-27-3   **$6.95**

*CHOICEMAKING: For Co-dependents, Adult Children and Spirituality
Seekers* — Sharon Wegscheider-Cruse
This useful book defines the problems and solves them in a positive way.
ISBN 0-932194-26-5   **$9.95**

LEARNING TO LOVE YOURSELF: Finding Your Self-Worth
Sharon Wegscheider-Cruse
"Self-worth is a choice, not a birthright", says the author as she shows us
how we can choose positive self-esteem.
ISBN 0-932194-39-7   **$7.95**

LET GO AND GROW: Recovery for Adult Children
Robert Ackerman
An in-depth study of the different characteristics of adult children of
alcoholics with guidelines for recovery.
ISBN 0-932194-51-6   **$8.95**

LOST IN THE SHUFFLE: The Co-dependent Reality
Robert Subby
A look at the unreal rules the co-dependent lives by and the way out of the
dis-eased reality.
ISBN 0-932194-45-1   **$8.95**

New Books . . .
from Health Communications

HEALING THE CHILD WITHIN: Discovery and recovery for Adult Children of Dysfunctional Families — Charles Whitfield
Dr. Whitfield defines, describes and discovers how we can reach our Child Within to heal and nurture our woundedness.
ISBN 0-932194-40-0 $8.95

WHISKY'S SONG: An Explicit Story of Surviving in an Alcoholic Home
Mitzi Chandler
A beautiful but brutal story of growing up where violence and neglect are everyday occurrences conveys a positive message of survival and love.
ISBN 0-932194-42-7 $6.95

New Books on Spiritual Recovery . . .
from Health Communications

THE JOURNEY WITHIN: A Spiritual Path to Recovery
Ruth Fishel
This book will lead you from your dysfunctional beginnings to the place within where renewal occurs.
ISBN 0-932194-41-9 $8.95

LEARNING TO LIVE IN THE NOW: 6-Week Personal Plan To Recovery
Ruth Fishel
The author gently introduces you to the valuable healing tools of meditation, positive creative visualization and affirmations.
ISBN 0-932194-62-1 $7.95

GENESIS: Spirituality in Recovery for Co-dependents
by Julie D. Bowden and Herbert L. Gravitz
A self-help spiritual program for adult children of trauma, an in-depth look at "turning it over" and "letting go".
ISBN 0-932194-56-7 $6.95

GIFTS FOR PERSONAL GROWTH AND RECOVERY
Wayne Kritsberg
Gifts for healing which include journal writing, breathing, positioning and meditation.
ISBN 0-932194-60-5 $6.95

Orders must be prepaid by check, money order, MasterCard or Visa. Purchase orders from agencies accepted (attach P.O. documentation) for billing. Net 30 days.

Minimum shipping/handling — $1.25 for orders less than $25. For orders over $25, add 5% of total for shipping and handling. Florida residents add 5% sales tax.

Coming this fall...

Healing The Shame That Binds You is a book about naming and healing an elusive and life-destroying monster called toxic shame. It is a major contribution to our understanding of how shame, which is a healthy human emotion, can be transformed into an autonomous and destructive state of being.

In an emotional and forceful way, Bradshaw shows how toxic shame is the core problem in the following psychological disorders:

- alcoholism and drug addiction
- eating disorders
- sexual addiction
- co-dependency
- personality disorders and criminality

Healing The Shame That Binds You presents a powerful and healing vision. Its beauty is its practicability as John Bradshaw offers a wide range of healing techniques, including:

- techniques for healing painful memories
- visualizations
- 'inner voice' work
- affirmations
- 'inner child' healing meditations

Bradshaw's new work on shame promises to mark a decisive turning point in the prevention and treatment of co-dependency and addiction.
